DE ARCHITECTURA

TEN BOOKS ON ARCHITECTURE

MARCUS VITRUVIUS POLLIO

ILLUSTRATIONS BY ANDREA PALLADIO & SÉBASTIEN LECLERC

CONTENT

BOOK I..5
BOOK II..40
BOOK III...85
BOOK IV..111
BOOK V..145
BOOK VI..189
BOOK VII...227
BOOK VIII..269
BOOK IX..301
BOOK X...339

DE ARCHITECTURA

BOOK I

*Town planning, architecture,
and the qualifications required of an architect*

INTRODUCTION

Whilst, O Caesar, your god-like mind and genius were engaged in acquiring the dominion of the world, your enemies having been all subdued by your unconquerable valour ; whilst the citizens were extolling your victories, and the conquered nations were awaiting your nod; whilst the Roman senate and people, freed from alarm, were enjoying the benefit of your opinions and counsel for their governance; I did not presume, at so unfit a period, to trouble you, thus engaged, with my writings on Architecture, lest I should have incurred your displeasure. When, however, I found that your attention, not exclusively devoted to state affairs, was bestowed on the state of the public buildings, so that the republic was not more indebted to you for its extended empire, in the addition of so many provinces, than for your numerous public buildings by which its grandeur is Damply manifested, I considered it right that no time should be lost in laying these precepts before you. My reverence for the memory of your virtuous father, to whom I was well known, and from whom, now a participator in council with the gods, the empire descended to you, has been the cause of your good will towards me. Hence, together with M. Aurelius, P. Numisius, and Cn. Cornelius, I have been appointed to, and receive the emoluments arising from the care of, the various engines of war which you assigned to me on the recommendation of your sister. As, through your kindness, I have been thus placed beyond the reach of poverty, I think it right to address this treatise to you ; and I feel the more induced to do so from your having built, and being still engaged in the erection of, many edifices. It is proper to deliver down to posterity, as a memorial, some account of these your magnificent works. I have therefore given such definite directions for the conduct of works, that those already exe-

cuted, as well as those hereafter to be constructed, may be by you well known and understood.
In the following pages I have developed all the principles of the art.

CHAPTER I.

WHAT ARCHITECTURE IS: AND OF THE EDUCATION OF AN ARCHITECT.

Architecture is a science arising out of many other sciences, and adorned with much and varied learning; by the help of which a judgment is formed of those works which are the result of other arts. Practice and theory are its parents. Practice is the frequent and continued contemplation of the mode of executing any given work, or of the mere operation of the hands, for the conversion of the material in the best and readiest way. Theory is the result of that reasoning which demonstrates and explains that the material wrought has been so converted as to answer the end proposed. Wherefore the mere practical architect is not able to assign sufficient reasons for the forms he adopts ; and the theoretic architect also fails, grasping the shadow instead of the substance. He who is theoretic as well as practical, is therefore doubly armed ; able not only to prove The propriety of his design, but equally so to carry it into execution. In architecture, as in other arts, two considerations must be constantly kept in view ; namely, the intention, and the matter used to express that intention : but the intention is founded on a conviction that the matter wrought will fully suit the purpose; he therefore, who is not familiar with both branches of the art, has no pretension to the title of architect. An architect should be ingenious, and apt in the acquisition of knowledge. Deficient in either of these qualities, he cannot be a perfect master. He should be a good writer, a skilful draftsman, versed in geometry and optics, expert at figures, acquainted with history, informed on the principles of natural and moral philosophy, somewhat of a musician, not ignorant of the sciences both of law and physic, nor of the motions, laws, and relations to each other, of the heavenly bodies. By means of the first named acquirement, he is to commit to writing his observations and experience, in order to assist his memory.

Drawing, is employed in representing the forms of his designs. Geometry affords much aid to the architect : to it he owes the use of the right line and circle, the level and the square ; whereby his delineations of buildings on plane surfaces are greatly facilitated. The science of optics enables him to introduce with judgment the requisite quantity of light, according to the aspect. Arithmetic estimates the cost, and aids in the measurement of the works ; this, assisted by the laws of geometry, determines those abstruse questions, wherein the different proportions of some parts to others are involved. Unless acquainted with history, he will be unable to account for the use of many ornaments which he may have occasion to introduce.

For instance; should anyone wish for information on the origin of those draped matronal figures crowned with a mutulus and cornice, called Caryatides, he will explain it by the following history. Carya, a city of Peloponnesus, joined the Persians in their war against the Greeks. These in return for the treachery, after having freed themselves by a most glorious victory from the intended Persian yoke, unanimously resolved to levy war against the Caryans. Carya was, in consequence, taken and destroyed, its male population extinguished, and its matrons carried into slavery. That these circumstances might be better remembered, and the nature of the triumph perpetuated, the victors represented them draped, and apparently suffering under the burthen with which they were loaded, to expiate the crime of their native city. Thus, in their edifices, did the ancient architects, by the use of these statues, hand down to posterity a memorial of the crime of the Caryans.

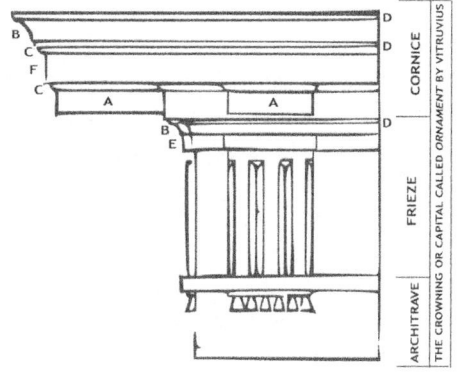

A. Mutulus or mutules of the Doric order.

B. This moulding in the superior part of the Doric Order cornice as well as I, en the superior part of the Corinthian, is generally called Cyma or Sima by Vitruvius.

C. This part alone is called Ogee, jointed with D. it is called Cymaise & Cymation by Vitruvius.

D.   Fillet, orlet, or Petit quarré, called Sercilium by Vitruvius.

E.   Jack-arch, or straight arch placement in the Doric frieze. Called the "Triglyph's Capital" by Vitruvius.

F.   Hood mould or Mouchette, sometimes called Corona by Vitruvius, even though Corona often means the whole Cornice, which is called for better distinction Coronix.

G.   The Modillions of the Corinthian Order, invented since Vitruvius by imitating the Doric Order Mutulus.

H.   Doucine, or big cyma.

I.   Echinus, or Ovolo.

J.   Astragal.

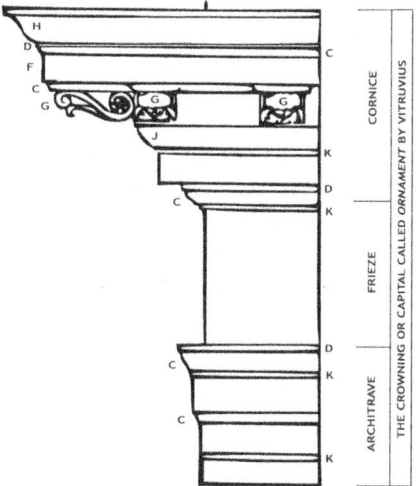

Again; a small number of Lacedaemonians, under the command of Pausanias, the son of Cleombrotus, overthrew the prodigious army of the Persians at the battle of Platea. After a triumphal exhibition of the spoil and booty, the proceeds of the valour and devotion of the victors were applied by the government in the erection of the Persian portico; and, as an appropriate monument of the victory, and a trophy for the admiration of posterity, its roof was supported by statues of the barbarians, in their magnificent costume; indicating, at the same time, the merited contempt due to their haughty projects, intimidating their enemies by fear of their courage, and acting as a stimulus to their fellow countrymen to be always in readiness for the defence of the nation. This is the origin of the Persian order for the support of an entablature ; an invention which has enriched many a design with the singular variety it exhibits. Many other matters of history have a connexion with architecture, and prove the necessity of its professors being well versed in it. Moral philosophy will teach the architect to be above meanness in his dealings, and to avoid arrogance: it will make him just, compliant and faithful to his employer ; and what is of the highest importance, it will prevent avarice gaining an ascendancy over him : for he should not be occupied with the thoughts of filling his coffers, nor with the desire of grasping every thing in the shape of gain, but, by the gravity of his manners, and a good character, should be careful to preserve his dignity. In these respects we see the importance of moral philosophy ; for such are her precepts. That branch of philosophy which the Greeks call φυσιολογία, or the doctrine of physics, is necessary to him in the solution of various problems ; as for instance, in the conduct of water, whose natural force, in its meandering and expansion over flat countries, is often such as to require restraints, which none know how to apply, but those who are acquainted with the laws of nature : nor, indeed, unless grounded in the first principles of physic, can he study with profit the works of Ctesibius, Archimedes, and many other authors who have written on the subject. Music assists him in the use of harmonic and mathematical proportion. It is, moreover, absolutely necessary in adjusting the force of the balistae, catapultae, and scorpions, in whose frames are holes for the passage of the homotona, which are strained by gut-ropes attached to windlasses worked by hand-spikes. Unless these ropes are equally extended, which only a nice ear can discover by their sound when struck, the bent arms of the engine do not give an equal impetus when disengaged, and the strings, therefore, not being in equal states of tension, prevent the direct flight of the weapon. So the vessels called ἠχεῖα, by the Greeks, which are placed in certain recesses under the seats of theatres, are fixed and arranged with a due regard to the laws of harmony and physics, their tones being fourths, fifths, and octaves ; so that when the voice of the actor is in unison with the pitch of these instruments, its power is increased and mellowed by impinging there-on. He would, moreover, be at a loss in constructing hydraulic and other engines, if ignorant of music. Skill in physic enables him to ascertain the salubrity of different tracts of country, and to determine the variation of climates, which the Greeks call κλίματα : for the air and water of different situations, being matters of the highest importance, no building will be healthy without attention to those points. Law should be an object of his study, especially those parts of it which relate to party-walls, to the free course and discharge of the eaves' waters, the regulations of sesspools and sewage, and those relating to window lights. The laws of sewage require his particular attention, that he may prevent his employers being involved in law-suits when the building is finished. Contracts, also, for the execution of the works, should be drawn with care and precision : because, when without legal flaws, neither party will be able to take advantage of

the other. Astronomy instructs him in the points of the heavens, the laws of the celestial bodies, the equinoxes, solstices, and courses of the stars; all of which should be well understood, in the construction and proportions of clocks. Since, therefore, this art is founded upon and adorned with so many different sciences, I am of opinion that those who have not, from their early youth, gradually climbed up to the summit, cannot, without presumption, call themselves masters of it. Perhaps, to the uninformed, it may appear unaccountable that a man should be able to retain in his memory such a variety of learning; but the close alliance with each other, of the different branches of science, will explain the difficulty. For as a body is composed of various concordant members, so does the whole circle of learning consist in one harmonious system. Wherefore those, who from an early age are initiated in the different branches of learning, have a facility in acquiring some knowledge of all, from their common connexion with each other. On this account Pythius, one of the ancients, architect of the noble temple of Minerva at Priene, says, in his commentaries, that an architect should have that perfect knowledge of each art and science
which is not even acquired by the professors of any one in particular, who have had every opportunity of improving themselves in it. This, however, cannot be necessary; for how can it be expected that an architect should equal Aristarchus as a grammarian, yet should he not be ignorant of grammar. In music, though it be evident he need not equal Aristoxenus, yet he should know something of it. Though he need not excel, as Apelles, in painting, nor as Myron or Polycletus, in sculpture yet he should have attained some proficiency in these arts.

So, in the science of medicine, it is not required that he should equal Hippocrates. Thus also, in other sciences, it is not important that pre-eminence in each be gained, but he must not, however, be ignorant of the general principles of each. For in such a variety of matters, it cannot be supposed that the same person can arrive at excellence in each, since to be aware of their several niceties and bearings, cannot fall within his power. We see how few of those who profess a particular art arrive at perfection in it, so as to distinguish themselves : hence, if but few of those practising an individual art, obtain lasting fame, how should the architect, who is required to have a knowledge of so many, be deficient in none of them, and even excel those who have professed any one exclusively. Wherefore Pythius seems to have been in error, forgetting that art consists in practice and theory. Theory is common to, and maybe known by all, but the result of practice occurs to the artist in his own art only. The physician and musician are each obliged to have some regard to the beating of the pulse, and the motion of the feet, but who would apply to the latter to heal a wound or cure a malady? so, without the aid of the former, the musician affects the ears of his audience by modulations upon his instrument. The astronomer and musician delight in similar proportions, for the positions of the stars, which are quartile and trine, answer to a fourth and fifth in harmony. The same analogy holds in that branch of geometry which the Greeks call λόγος ὀπτικός: indeed, throughout the whole range of art, there are many incidents common to all. Practice alone can lead to excellence in any one : that architect, therefore, is sufficiently educated, whose general knowledge enables him to give his opinion on any branch when required to do so. Those unto whom nature has been so bountiful that they are at once geometricians, astronomers, musicians, and skilled in many other arts, go beyond what is required of the architect, and may be properly called mathematicians, in the extended sense of that word. Men so gifted, discriminate acutely, and are rarely met with. Such, however, was Aristarchus of Samos, Philolaus and Archytas of Tarentum, Apollonius of Perga, Eratosthenes of Gyrene, Archimedes and Scopinas of

Syracuse : each of whom wrote on all the sciences. Since, therefore, few men are thus gifted, and yet it is required of the architect to be generally well informed, and it is manifest he cannot hope to excel in each art, I beseech you, O Caesar, and those who read this my work, to pardon and overlook grammatical errors ; for I write neither as an accomplished philosopher, an eloquent rhetorician, nor an expert grammarian, but as an architect : in respect, however, of my art and its principles, I will lay down rules which may serve as an authority to those who build, as well as to those who are already somewhat acquainted with the science.

CHAPTER II.

OF THOSE THNGS ON WHICH ARCHITECTURE DEPENDS.

Architecture depends on fitness (ordinatio) and arrangement (dispositio), the former being called τάξις, in Greek, and the latter διάθεσις; it also depends on proportion, uniformity, consistency, and economy, which the Greeks call οἰκονομία. Fitness is the adjustment of size of the several parts to their several uses, and requires due regard to the general proportions of the fabric : it arises out of dimension (quantitas), which the Greeks call ποσότης Dimension regulates the general scale of the work, so that the parts may all tell and be effective.

Arrangement is the disposition in their just and proper places of all the parts of the building, and the pleasing effect of the same ; keeping in view its appropriate character. It is divisible into three heads, which, considered together, constitute design : these, by the Greeks, are named ἰδέαι : they are called ichnography, orthography, and scenography. The first is the representation on a plane of the ground-plan of the work, drawn by rule and compasses. The second is the elevation of the front, slightly shadowed, and shewing the forms of the intended building. The last exhibits the front and a receding side properly shadowed, the lines being drawn to their proper vanishing points. These three are the result of thought and invention. Thought is an effort of the mind, ever incited by the pleasure attendant on success in compassing an object. Invention is the effect of this effort; which throws a new light on things the most recondite, and produces them to answer the intended purpose. These are the ends of arrangement. Proportion is that agreeable harmony between the several parts of a building, which is the result of a just and regular agreement of them with each

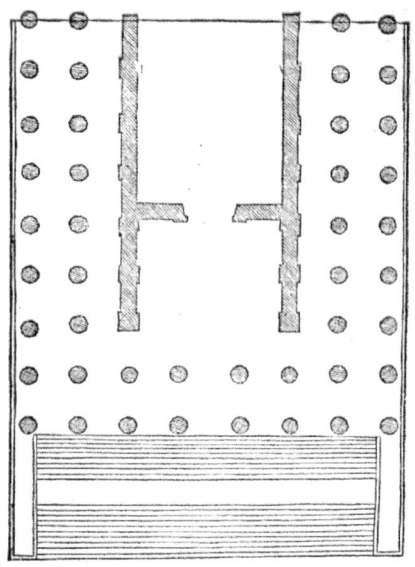

ICHNOGRAPHY
FROM FRANCISCUS FRANCISCIUS AND JOANNES CRUGHER,
1567 EDITION

other ; the height to the width, this to the length, and each of these to the whole. Uniformity is the parity of the parts to one another ; each corresponding with its opposite, as in the human figure. The arms, feet, hands, fingers, are similar to, and symmetrical with, one another; so should the respective parts of a building correspond. In sacred buildings, for instance, the diameter of the columns and the width of the triglyphs must be similar. In the ballista, by the size of the hole which the Greeks call περίτρητον, in ships, by the space between the thowls, which space in Greek is called διπηχαικὴ, we have a measure, by the knowledge of which the whole of the construction of a vessel may be developed. Consistency is found in that work whose whole and detail are suitable to the occasion. It arises from circumstance, custom, and nature. From circumstance, which the Greeks call
θεματισμὸς, when temples are built, hypaethral and uninclosed, to Jupiter, Thunderer, Coelus, the Sun and Moon; because these divinities are continually known to us by their presence night and day, and throughout all space. For a similar reason, temples of the Doric order are erected to Minerva, Mars, and Hercules; on account of whose valour, their temples should be of masculine proportions, and without

I. Orthography
O. Scenography

delicate ornament. The character of the Corinthian order seems more appropriate to Venus, Flora, Proserpine, and Nymphs of Fountains ; because its slenderness, elegance and richness, and its ornamental leaves surmounted by volutes, seem to bear an analogy to their dispositions. A medium between these two is chosen for temples to Juno, Diana, Bacchus, and other similar deities, which should be of the Ionic order, tempered between the severity of the Doric and the slenderness and delicacy of the Corinthian order. In respect of custom, consistency is preserved when the vestibules of magnificent edifices are conveniently contrived and richly finished : for those buildings cannot be said to be consistent, to whose splendid interiors you pass through poor and mean entrances. So also, if dentilled cornices are used in the Doric order, or triglyphs applied above the voluted Ionic, thus transferring parts to one order which properly belong to another, the eye will be offended, because custom otherwise applies these peculiarities. Natural consistency arises from the choice of such situations for temples as possess the advantages of salubrious air and water; more especially in the case of temples erected to Aesculapius, to the Goddess of Health, and such other divinities as possess the power of curing diseases. For thus the sick, changing the unwholesome air and water to which they have been accustomed for those that are healthy, sooner convalesce ; and a reliance upon the divinity will be therefore increased by proper choice of situation. Natural consistency also requires that chambers should be lighted from the east; baths and winter apartments from the south-west ; picture and other galleries which require a steady light, from the north, because from that quarter the light is not sometimes brilliant and at other tunes obscured, but is nearly the same throughout the day. Economy consists in a due and proper application of the means afforded according to the ability of the employer and the situation chosen; care being taken that the expenditure is prudently conducted. In this respect the architect is to avoid the use of materials which are not easily procured and prepared on the spot. For it cannot be expected that good pit-sand, stone, fir of either sort, or marble, can be procured every where in plenty, but they must, in some instances, be brought from a distance, with much trouble and at great expense. In such cases, river or sea-sand may be substituted for pit-sand ; cypress, poplar, elm, and pine, for the different sorts of fir ; and the like of the rest, according to circumstances. The other branch of economy consists in suiting the building to the use which is to be made of it, the money to be expended, and the elegance appropriate thereto; because, as one or other of these circumstances prevails, the design should be varied. That which would answer very well as a town house, would ill suit as a country house, in which store-rooms must be provided for the produce of the farm. So the houses of men of business must be differently designed from those which are built for men of taste. Mansions for men of consequence in the government must be adapted to their particular habits. In short, economy must ever depend on the circumstances of the case.

CHAPTER III.

OF THE DIFFERENT BRANCHES OF ARCHITECTURE.

Architecture consists of three branches; namely, building, dialling, and mechanics. Building is divided into two parts. The first regulates the general plan of the walls of a city and its public buildings; the other relates to private buildings. Public buildings are for three purposes ; defence, religion, and the security of the public. Buildings for defence are those walls, towers, and gates of a town, necessary for the continual shelter of its inhabitants against the attacks of an enemy. Those for the purposes of religion are the fanes and temples of the immortal gods. Those for public convenience are gates, fora or squares for market-places, baths, theatres, walks, and the like ; which, being for public use, are placed in public situations, and should be arranged so as best to meet the convenience of the public. All these should possess strength, utility and beauty. Strength arises from carrying down the foundations to a good solid bottom, and from making a proper choice of materials without parsimony. Utility arises from a judicious distribution of the parts, so that their purposes be duly answered, and that each have its proper situation. Beauty is produced by the pleasing appearance and good taste of the whole, and by the dimensions of all the parts being duly proportioned to each other.

CHAPTER IV.

OF THE CHOICE OF HEALTHY SITUATIONS.

In setting out the walls of a city the choice of a healthy situation is of the first importance : it should be on high ground, neither subject to fogs nor rains; its aspects should be neither violently hot nor intensely cold, but temperate in both respects. The neighbourhood of a marshy place must be avoided ; for in such a site the morning air, uniting with the fogs that rise in the neighbourhood, will reach the city with the rising sun ; and these fogs and mists, charged with the exhalation of the fenny animals, will diffuse an unwholesome effluvia over the bodies of the inhabitants, and render the place pestilent. A city on the sea side, exposed to the south or west, will be insalubrious ; for in summer mornings, a city thus placed would be hot, at noon it would be scorched. A city, also, with a western aspect, would even at sunrise be warm, at noon hot, and in the evening of a burning temperature. Hence the constitutions of the inhabitants of such places, from such continual and excessive changes of the air, would be much vitiated. This effect is likewise produced on inanimate bodies : nobody would think of lighting his wine-cellar from the south or the west, but from the north, an aspect not liable to these violent changes. In granaries whose aspects are south of the east or west, the stores are soon ruined; and provisions, as well as fruits, cannot be long preserved unless kept in apartments whose aspects are north of the east or west. For heat, which acts as an alterative, by drying up the natural moisture of any body, destroys and rots those substances on which it acts. Iron, for instance, naturally of a hard texture, becomes so soft when heated in a forge as to be easily wrought into any form ; but if, when heated, it is suddenly immersed in cold water, it immediately regains its original quality. Thus, not only in unwholesome, but also in salubrious districts, the summer heats produce languor and relaxation of body ; and in winter, even the most pestilential situations become wholesome, inasmuch as the cold strengthens and restores the constitution of the inhabitants.

Hence, those who change a cold for a hot climate, rarely escape sickness, but are soon carried off; whereas, on the other hand, those who pass from a hot to a cold climate, far from being injured by the change, are thereby generally strengthened.

Much care, then, should be taken so to set out the walls of a city, that it may not be obnoxious to the pestilential blasts of the hot winds. For as, according to those principles which the Greeks call στοιχεια all bodies are compounded of fire, water, earth, and air, by whose union and varying proportions the different qualities of animals are engendered ; so, in those bodies wherein fire predominates, their temperament is destroyed, and their strength dissipated. Such is the case in exposure to certain aspects of the heavens whence the heat insinuates itself through the pores in a greater degree than the temperature of the system will bear. Bodies which contain a greater proportion of water than is necessary to balance the other elements, are speedily corrupted, and lose their virtues and properties. Hence bodies are much injured by damp winds and atmosphere. Lastly, the elements of earth and air being increased or diminished more than is consistent with the temperature of any given body, will have a tendency to destroy its equilibrium ; the earthy elements by repletion, the aerial by the weight of the atmosphere. If anyone doubt this, let him study the different natures of birds, fishes, and animals of the land, and he will easily perceive the truth of these principles, from the variety existing among them. For there is one flesh of birds, another of fishes, and another, very different, of land animals. Birds have a small proportion of earth and water in their nature, a moderate quantity of heat, and a considerable portion of air; whence, being light by nature, from their component elements, they more easily raise themselves in the air. Fishes, by nature adapted to the watery element, are compounded of but a moderate degree of heat, a considerable proportion of air and earth, and a very small portion of water, the element in which they live; and hence, easier exist in it. Wherefore, when removed from it, they soon die. Terrestrial animals, being constituted with much air, heat, and water, and but little earth, cannot live in the water, on account of the quantity of that element naturally preponderating in their composition. Since, then, we are thus constantly reminded, by our senses, that the bodies of animals are so constituted, and we have mentioned that they suffer and die from the want or superabundance of any one element not suitable to their temperament, surely much circumspection should be used in the choice of a temperate and healthy site for a city. The precepts of the ancients, in this respect, should be ever observed. They always, after sacrifice, carefully inspected the livers of those animals fed on that spot whereon the city was to be built, or whereon a stative encampment was intended. If the livers were diseased and livid, they tried others, in order to ascertain whether accident or disease was the cause of the imperfection ; but if the greater part of the experiments proved, by the sound and healthy appearance of the livers, that the water and food of the spot were wholesome, they selected it for the garrison. If the reverse, they inferred, as in the case of cattle, so in that of the human body, the water and food of such a place would become pestiferous ; and they therefore abandoned it, in search of another, valuing health above all other considerations. That the salubrity of a tract of land is discovered by the pastures or food which it furnishes, is sufficiently clear, from certain qualities of the lands in Crete, situate in the vicinity of the river Pothereus, which lie between the two states of Gnosus and Gortyna. There are pasturages on each side of this river: the cattle, however, pastured on the Gnossian side, when opened, are found with their spleens perfect ; whilst those on the opposite side, nearer to Gortyna, retain no appearance of a spleen. Physicians, in their endeavours to account for this singular circumstance, discovered a species of herb eaten by the cattle, whose property was that of diminishing the spleen. Hence arose the use of the herb which the Cretans call ἄσπληνος, as a cure for those affected with enlarged spleen. When, therefore, a city is built in a marshy situation near the sea-coast, with a northern, north-eastern, or eastern aspect, on a marsh whose level is higher than the shore of the sea, the site is not altogether improper ; for by means of sewers the waters may be discharged into the sea : and at those times, when violently agitated by storms, the sea swells and runs up the sewers, it mixes with the water of the marsh, and prevents the generation of marshy insects ; it also soon destroys such as are passing from the higher level, by the saltness of its water to which they are unaccustomed. An instance of this kind occurs in the Gallic marshes about Altinum, Ravenna, and Aquileia, and other places in Cisalpine Gaul, near marshes which, for the reasons above named, are remarkably healthy. When the marshes are stagnant, and have no drainage by means of rivers or drains, as is the case with the Pontine marshes, they become putrid, and emit vapours of a heavy and pestilent nature. Thus the old city of Salapia, in Apulia, built, as some say, by Diomedes on his return from Troy, or, as others write, by Elphias the Rhodian, was so placed that the inhabitants were continually out of health. At length they applied to Marcus Hostilius, and publicly petitioned him, and obtained his consent, to be allowed to seek and select a more wholesome spot to which the city might be removed. Without delay, and with much judgment, he bought an estate on a healthy spot close to the sea, and requested the Roman senate and people to permit the removal of the city. He then set out the walls, and assigned a portion of the soil to each citizen at a moderate valuation. After which, opening a communication between the lake and the sea, he converted the former into an excellent harbour for the city. Thus the Salapians now inhabit a healthy situation, four miles from their ancient city.

CHAPTER V.

OF THE FOUNDATIONS OF WALLS AND TOWERS.

When we are satisfied with the spot fixed on for the site of the city, as well in respect of the goodness of the air as of the abundant supply of provisions for the support of the population, the communications by good roads, and river or sea navigation for the transport of merchandise, we should take into consideration the method of constructing the walls and towers of the city. Their foundations should be carried down to a solid bottom, if such can be found, and should be built thereon of such thickness as may be necessary for the proper support of that part of the wall which stands above the natural level of the ground. They should be of the soundest workmanship and materials, and of greater thickness than the walls above. From the exterior face of the wall towers must be projected, from which an approaching enemy may be annoyed by weapons, from the embrasures of those towers, right and left. An easy approach to the walls must be provided against: indeed they should be surrounded by uneven ground, and the roads leading to the gates should be winding and turn to the left from the gates. By this arrangement, the right sides of the attacking troops, which are not covered by their shields, will be open to the weapons of the besieged. The plan of a city should not be square, nor formed with acute angles, but polygonal ; so that the motions of the enemy may be open to observation. A city whose plan is acute-angled, is with difficulty defended ; for such a form protects the attacker more than the attacked. The thickness of the walls should be sufficient for two armed men to pass each other with ease.

The walls ought to be tied, from font to rear, with many pieces of charred olive wood; by which means the two faces thus connected, will endure for ages. The advantage of the use of olive is, that it is neither affected by weather, by rot, or by age. Buried in the earth, or immersed in water it lasts unimpaired : and for this reason, not only walls, but foundations, and such walls as are of extraordinary thickness, tied together therewith, are exceedingly lasting. The distance between each tower should not exceed an arrow's flight ; so that if, at any point between them, an attack be made, the besiegers may be repulsed by the scorpions and other missile engines stationed on the towers right and left of the point in question. The walls will be intercepted by the lower parts of the towers where they occur, leaving an interval equal to the width of the tower; which space the tower will consequently occupy: but the communication across the void inside the tower, must be of wood, not at all fastened with iron : so that, if the enemy obtain possession of any part of the walls, the wooden communication may be promptly cut away by the defenders, and thus prevent the enemy from penetrating to the other parts of the walls without the danger of precipitating themselves into the vacant hollows of the towers. The towers should be made either round or polygonal. A square is a bad form, on account of its being easily fractured at the quoins by the battering-ram ; whereas the circular tower has this advantage, that when battered, the pieces of masonry whereof it is composed being cuneiform, they cannot be driven in towards their centre without displacing the whole mass. Nothing tends more to the security of walls and towers, than backing them with walls or terraces : it counteracts the effects of rams as well as of undermining. It is not, however, always necessary to construct them in this manner, except in places where the besiegers might gain high ground very near the walls, from which, over level ground, an assault could be made. In the construction of ramparts, very wide and deep trenches are to be first excavated ; the bottom of which must be still further dug out, for receiving the foun-

dation of the wall. This must be of sufficient thickness to resist the pressure of the earth against it. Then, according to the space requisite for drawing up the cohorts in military order on the rampart, another wall is to be built within the former, towards the city.

The outer and inner walls are then to be connected by cross walls, disposed on the plan after the manner of the teeth of a comb or of a saw, so as to divide the pressure of the filling in earth into many and less forces, and thus prevent the walls from being thrust out. I do not think it requisite to dilate on the materials whereof the wall should be composed ; because those which are most desirable, cannot, from the situation of a place, be always procured. We must, therefore, use what are found on the spot; such as square stones, flint, rubble stones, burnt or unburnt bricks; for every place is not provided, as is Babylon, with such a substitute for lime and sand as burnt bricks and liquid bitumen; yet there is scarcely any spot which does not furnish materials whereof a durable wall may not be built.

CHAPTER VI.

OF THE DISTRIBUTION AND SITUATION OF BUILDINGS WITHIN THE WALLS.

Their circuit being completed, it behoves us to consider the manner of disposing of the area of the space enclosed within the walls, and the proper directions and aspects of the streets and lanes. They should be so planned as to exclude the winds : these, if cold, are unpleasant ; if hot, are hurtful ; if damp, destructive. A fault in this respect
must be therefore avoided, and care taken to prevent
that which occurs in so many cities. For instance ; in
the island of Lesbos, the town of Mytilene is magnificently and elegantly designed, and well built, but imprudently placed. When the south wind prevails in it the inhabitants fall sick; the north-west wind affects them with coughs; and the north wind restores them to health: but the intensity of the cold therein is so great, that no one can stand about in the streets and lanes. Wind is a floating wave of air, whose undulation continually varies.
It is generated by the action of heat upon moisture, the rarefaction thereby produced creating a continued rush of wind. That such is the case, may be satisfactorily proved by observations on brazen aeolipylae, which clearly shew that an attentive examination of human inventions often leads to a knowledge of the general laws of nature. .Aeolipylae are hollow brazen vessels, which have an opening or mouth of small size, by means of which they can be filled with water. Previous to the water being heated over the fire, but little wind is emitted, as soon, however, as the water begins to boil, a violent wind issues forth. Thus a simple experiment enables us to ascertain and determine the causes and effects of the great operations of the heavens and the winds. In a place sheltered from the winds, those who are in health pre-

serve it, those who are ill soon convalesce, though in other, even healthy places, they would require different treatment, and this entirely on account of their shelter from the winds. The disorders difficult to cure in exposed situations are colds, the gout, coughs, phthisis, pleurisy, spitting of blood, and those diseases which are treated by replenishment instead of exhaustion of the natural forces. Such disorders are cured with difficulty. First, because they are the effect of cold; secondly, because the strength of the patient being greatly diminished by the disorder, the air agitated by the action of the winds becomes poor and exhausts the body's moisture, tending to make it low and feeble; whereas, that air which from its soft and thick nature is not liable to great agitation, nourishes and refreshes its strength. According to some, there are but four winds, namely, Solanus, the east wind, Auster, the south wind, Favonius, the west wind, and Septentrio, the north wind. But those who are more curious in these matters reckon eight winds; among such was Andronicus Cyrrhestes, who, to exemplify the theory, built at Athens an octagonal marble tower, on each side of which was sculptured a figure representing the wind blowing from the quarter opposite thereto. On the top of the roof of this tower a brazen Triton with a rod in his right hand moved on a pivot, and pointed to the figure of the quarter in which the wind lay. The other winds not above named are Eurus, the south-east wind, Africus, the south-west wind, Caurus, by many called Corus, the north-west wind, and Aquilo the north-east wind. Thus are expressed the number and names of the winds and the points whence they blow. To find and lay down their situation we proceed as follows : let a marble slab be fixed level in the centre of the space enclosed by the walls, or let the ground be smoothed and levelled, so that the slab may not be necessary. In the centre of this plane, for the purpose of marking the shadow correctly, a brazen gnomon must be erected. The Greeks call this gnomon σκιαθήρας. The shadow cast by the gnomon is to be marked about the fifth ante-meridianal hour, and the extreme point of the shadow accurately determined. From the central point of the space whereon the gnomon stands, as a centre, with a distance equal to the length of shadow just observed, describe a circle. After the sun has passed the meridian, watch the shadow which the gnomon continues to cast till the moment when its extremity again touches the circle which has been described. From the two points thus obtained in the circumference of the circle describe two arcs intersecting each other, and through their intersection and the centre of the circle first described draw a line to its extremity: this line will indicate the north and south points. One-sixteenth part of the circumference of the whole circle is to be set out to the right and left of the north and south points, and drawing lines from the points thus obtained to the centre of the circle, we have one-eighth part of the circumference for the region of the north, and another eighth part for the region of the south. Divide the remainders of the circumference on each side into three equal parts, and the divisions or regions of the eight winds will be then obtained: then let the directions of the streets and lanes be determined by the tendency of the lines which separate the different regions of the winds. Thus will their force be broken and turned away from the houses and public ways ; for if the directions of the streets be parallel to those of the winds, the latter will rush through them with greater violence, since from occupying the whole space of the surrounding country they will be forced up through a narrow pass. Streets or public ways ought therefore to be so set out, that when the winds blow hard their violence may be broken against the angles of the different divisions of the city, and thus dissipated. Those who are accustomed to the names of so many winds, will perhaps be surprised at our division of them into eight only; but if they reflect that the circuit of the earth was ascertained by Eratosthenes of Cyrene, from mathematical calculations, founded on the sun's course, the shadow of an equinoctial gnomon, and the obliquity of the heavens, and was discovered to be equal to two hundred and fifty-two thousand stadia or thirty-one millions and five hundred thousand paces, an eighth part whereof, as occupied by each wind, being three millions nine hundred and thirty-seven thousand five hundred paces, their surprise will cease, because of the number of impediments and reverberations it must naturally be subject to in travelling such distance through such varied space. To the right and left of the south wind blow respectively Euronotus and Altanus. On the sides of Africus, the south-west wind, Libonotus southward and Subvesperus northward. On the southern side of Favonius, the west wind, Argestes, and on its northern side Etesiae. On the western side of Caurus, the north-west wind, Circius, on its northern side Corus. On the western and eastern sides respectively of Septentrio, the north wind, Thrascias and Gallicus. From the northern side of Aquilo, the north-east wind, blows Supernas, from its southern side Boreas. Solanus, the east wind, has Carbas on its northern side, and Ornithiæ on its southern side. Eurus, the south-east wind, has Cæcias and Vulturnus on its eastern and southern sides respectively. Many other names, deduced from particular places, rivers, or mountain storms, are given to the winds.

There are also the morning breezes, which the sun rising from his subterranean regions, and acting violently on the humidity of the air collected during the night, extracts from the morning vapours. These remain after sunrise, and are classed among the east winds, and hence receive the name of εὖρος given by the Greeks to that wind, so also from the morning breezes they called the morrow αὔριον. Some deny that Eratosthenes was correct in his measure of the earth, whether with propriety or otherwise, is of no consequence in tracing the regions whence the winds blow: for it is clear there is a great difference between the forces with which the several winds act. Inasmuch as the brevity with which the foregoing rules are laid down may prevent their being clearly understood, I have thought it right to add for the clearer understanding thereof two figures, or as the Greeks call them σχήματα, at end of this book. The first shews the precise regions whence the different winds blow. The second, the method of disposing the streets in such a manner as to dissipate the violence of the winds and render them innoxious. Let A be the centre of a perfectly level and plane tablet whereon a gnomon is erected. The ante-meridianal shadow of the gnomon being marked at B, from A, as a centre with the distance AB, describe a complete circle. Then replacing the gnomon correctly, watch its increasing shadow, which after the sun has passed his meridian, will gradually lengthen till it become exactly equal to the shadow made in the forenoon, then again touching the circle at the point C. From the points B and C, as centres, describe two arcs cutting each other in D. From the point D, through the centre of the circle, draw the line EF, which will give the north and south points.

Divide the whole circle into sixteen parts. From the point E, at which the southern end of the meridian line touches the circle, set off at G and H to the right and left a distance equal to one of the said sixteen parts, and in the same manner on the north side, placing one foot of the compasses on the point F, mark on each side the points I and K, and with lines drawn through the centre of the circle join the points GK and HI, so that the space from G to H will be given to the south wind and its region; that from I to K to the north wind. The remaining spaces on the right and left are each to be divided into three equal parts ; the extreme points of the dividing lines on the east sides, to be designated by the letters L and M ; those on the west by the letters NO; from M to O and from L to N draw lines crossing each other : and thus the whole circumference will be divided into eight equal spaces for the winds. The figure thus described will be furnished with a letter at each angle of the octagon. Thus, beginning at the south, between the regions of Eurus and Auster, will be the letter G; between those of Auster and Africus, H; between Africus and Favonius, N; between that and Caurus, O; K between Caurus and Septentrio ; between Septentrio and Aquilo, I; between Aquilo and Solanus, L ; and between that and Eurus, M. Thus adjusted, let a bevel gauge be applied to the different angles of the octagon, to determine the directions of the different streets and lanes.

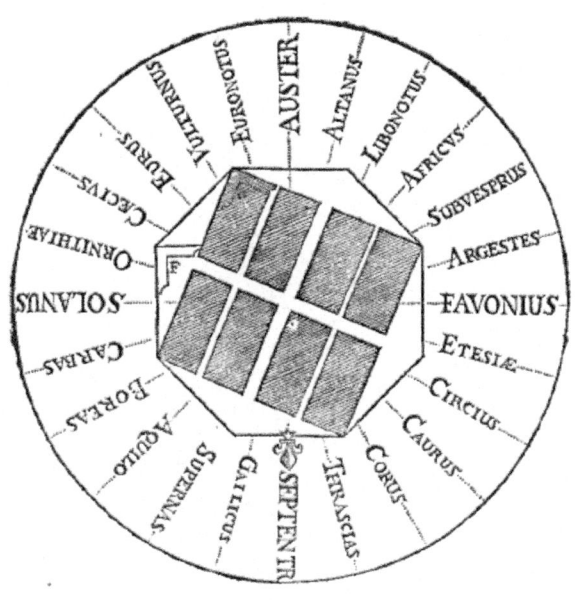

CHAPTER VII.

OF THE CHOICE OF SITUATIONS FOR PUBLIC BUILDINGS.

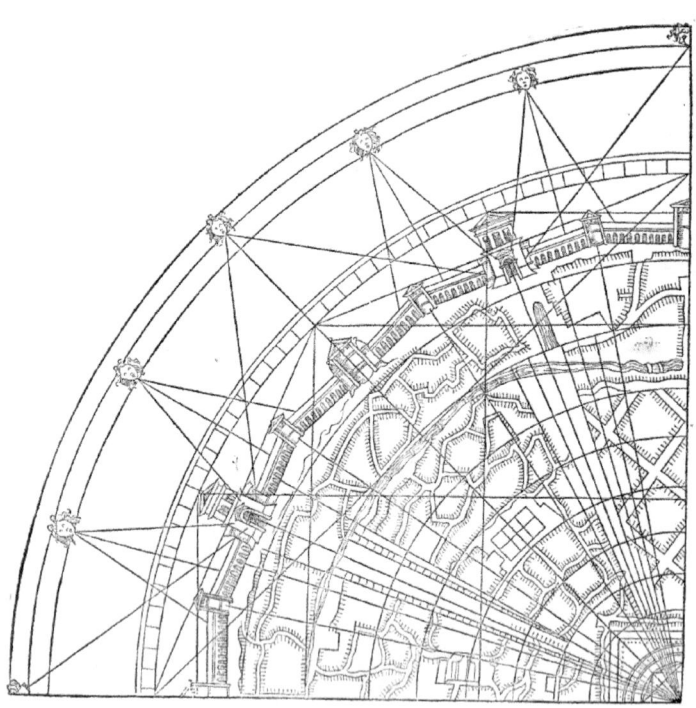

The lanes and streets of the city being set out, the choice, of sites for the convenience and use of the state remains to be decided on ; for sacred edifices, for the forum, and for other public buildings. If the place adjoin the sea, the forum should be placed close to the harbour : if inland, it should be in the centre of the town. The temples of the gods, protectors of the city, also those of Jupiter, Juno, and Minerva, should be on some eminence which commands a view of the greater part of the city. The temple of Mercury should be either in the forum, or, as also the temple of Isis and Serapis, in the great public square. Those of Apollo and Father Bacchus near the theatre. If there be neither amphitheatre nor gymnasium, the temple of Hercules should be near the circus The temple of Mars should be out of the city, in the neighbouring country. That of Venus near to the gate. According to the regulations of the Hetrurian Haruspices, the temples of Venus, Vulcan, and Mars should be so placed that those of the first be not in the way of contaminating the matrons and youth with the influence of lust ; that those of Vulcan be away from the city, which would consequently be freed from the danger of fire ; the divinity presiding over that element being drawn away by the rites and sacrifices performing in his temple. The temple of Mars should be also out of the city, that no armed frays may disturb the peace of citizens, and that this divinity may, moreover, be ready to preserve them from their enemies and the perils of war. The temple of Ceres should be in a solitary spot out of the city, to which the public are not necessarily led but for the purpose of sacrificing to her. This spot is to be reverenced with religious awe and solemnity of demeanour, by those whose affairs lead them to visit it. Appropriate situations must also be chosen for the temples and places of sacrifice to the other divinities. For the construction and proportions of the edifices themselves, I shall give rules in the third and fourth books ; because it appears to me, that in the second book I ought to explain the nature of the different materials employed in building, their qualities and use ; and then, in the other books, to give rules for the dimensions of buildings, the orders, and their proportions.

DE ARCHITECTURA

BOOK II

Building materials

INTRODUCTION

Dinocrates the architect, relying on the powers of his skill and ingenuity, whilst Alexander was in the midst of his conquests, set out from Macedonia to the army, desirous of gaining the commendation of his sovereign. That his introduction to the royal presence might be facilitated, he obtained letters from his countrymen and relations to men of the first rank and nobility about the king's person ; by whom being kindly received, he besought them to take the earliest opportunity of accomplishing his wish. They promised fairly, but were slow in performing ; waiting, as they alleged, for a proper occasion. Thinking, however, they deferred this without just grounds, he took his own course for the object he had in view. He was, I should state, a man of tall stature, pleasing countenance, and altogether of dignified appearance. Trusting to the gifts with which nature had thus endowed him, he put off his ordinary clothing, and having anointed himself with oil, crowned his head with a wreath of poplar, slung a lion's skin across his left shoulder, and carrying a large club in his right hand, he sallied forth to the royal tribunal, at a period when the king was dispensing justice. The novelty of his appearance excited the attention of the people; and Alexander soon discovering, with astonishment, the object of their curiosity, ordered the crowd to make way for him, and demanded to know who he was. "A Macedonian architect," replied Dinocrates, "who suggests schemes and designs worthy your royal renown. I propose to form Mount Athos into the statue of a man holding a spacious city in his left hand, and in his right a huge cup, into which shall be collected all the streams of the mountain, which shall thence be poured into the sea." Alexander, delighted at the proposition, made immediate inquiry if the soil of the neighbourhood were of a quality capable of yielding sufficient produce for such a state.

When, however, he found that all its supplies must be furnished by sea, he thus addressed Dinocrates : "I admire the grand outline of your scheme, and am well pleased with it : but I am of opinion he would be much to blame who planted a colony on such a spot. For as an infant is nourished by the milk of its mother, depending thereon for its progress to maturity, so a city depends on the fertility of the country surrounding it for its riches, its strength in population, and not less for its defence against an enemy. Though your plan might be carried into execution, yet I think it impolitic. I nevertheless request your attendance on me, that I may otherwise avail myself of your ingenuity." From that time Dinocrates was in constant attendance on the king, and followed him into Egypt ; where Alexander having perceived a spot, at the same time naturally strong, the centre of the commerce of the country, a land abounding with corn, and having those facilities of transport which the Nile afforded, ordered Dinocrates to build a city whose name should be Alexandria. Dinocrates obtained this honour through his comely person and dignified deportment. But tome, Emperor, nature hath denied an ample stature; my face is wrinkled with age, and sickness has impaired my constitution. Deprived of these natural accomplishments, I hope, however, to gain some commendation through the aid of my scientific acquirements, and the precepts I shall deliver. In the first book I have treated of architecture, and the parts into which it is divided ; of the walls of a city, and the division of the space within the walls. The directions for the construction of sacred buildings, their proportions and symmetry, will follow and be explained : but I think they will be out of place, unless I previously give an account of the materials and workmanship used in their erection, together with an investigation of their several properties and application in different cases. Even this I must preface with an inquiry into the origin and various species of the earliest buildings, and their gradual advance to perfection. In this I shall follow the steps of Nature herself, and those who have written on the progress from savage to civilized life, and the inventions consequent on the latter state of society. Thus guided, I will proceed.

CHAPTER I.

OF THE ORIGIN OF BUILDING

Mankind originally brought forth like the beasts of the field, in woods, dens, and groves, passed their lives in a savage manner, eating the simple food which nature afforded. A tempest, on a certain occasion, having exceedingly agitated the trees in a particular spot, the friction between some of the branches caused them to take fire; this so alarmed those in the neighbourhood of the accident, that they betook themselves to flight. Returning to the spot after the tempest had subsided, and finding the warmth which had thus been created extremely comfortable, they added fuel to the fire excited, in order to preserve the heat, and then went forth to invite others, by signs and gestures, to come and witness the discovery. In the concourse that thus took place, they testified their different opinions and expressions by different inflexions of the voice. From daily association words succeeded to these indefinite modes of speech; and these becoming by degrees the signs of certain objects, they began to join them together, and conversation became general. Thus the discovery of fire gave rise to the first assembly of mankind, to their first deliberations, and to their union in a state of society. For association with each other they were more fitted by nature than other animals, from their erect posture, which also gave them the advantage of continually viewing the stars and firmament, no less than from their being able to grasp and lift an object, and turn it about with their hands and fingers. In the assembly, therefore, which thus brought them first together, they were led to the consideration of sheltering themselves from the seasons, some by making arbours with the boughs of trees, some by excavating caves in the mountains, and others in imitation of the nests and habitations of swallows, by making dwellings of twigs interwoven and covered with mud or clay. From observation of and improvement on each others' expedients for sheltering themselves, they soon began to provide a better species of huts. It was thus that men, who are by nature of an imitative and docile turn of mind, and proud of their own inventions, gaining daily experience also by what had been previously executed, vied with each other in their progress towards perfection in building. The first attempt was the mere erection of a few spars united together with twigs and covered with mud. Others built their walls of dried lumps of turf, connected these walls together by means of timbers laid across horizontally, and covered the erections with reeds and boughs, for the purpose of sheltering themselves from the inclemency of the seasons. Finding, however, that flat coverings of this sort would not effectually shelter them in the winter season, they made their roofs of two inclined planes meeting each other in a ridge at the summit, the whole of which they covered with clay, and thus carried off the rain. We are certain that buildings were thus originally constructed, from the present practice of uncivilized nations, whose buildings are of spars and thatch, as may be seen in Gaul, in Spain, in Portugal, and in Aquitaine. The woods of the Colchi, in Pontus, furnish such abundance of timber, that they build in the following manner.

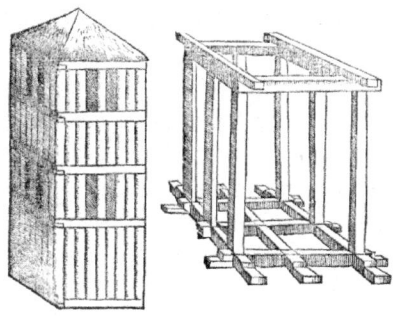

Two trees are laid level on the earth, right and left, at such distance from each other as will suit the length of the trees which are to cross and connect them. On the extreme ends of these two trees are laid two other trees transversely: the space which the house will inclose is thus marked out. The four sides being thus set out, towers are raised, whose walls consist of trees laid horizontally but kept perpendicularly over each other, the alternate layers yoking the angles. The level interstices which the thickness of the trees alternately leave, is filled in with chips and mud. On a similar principle they form their roofs, except that gradually reducing the length of the trees which traverse from angle to angle, they assume a pyramidal form. They are covered with boughs and smeared over with clay ; and thus after a rude fashion of vaulting, their quadrilateral roofs are formed. The Phrygians, who inhabit a champain country destitute of timber, choose natural hillocks, which they pierce and hollow out for their accommodation, as well as the nature of the soil will permit. These dwellings they cover with roofs constructed of logs bound together, covered with reeds and straw, and coated with a large quantity of earth. This species of covering protects the hut from the extreme heat of the summer, as well as from the piercing cold of the winter. The weeds which grow in the vicinity of pools are used in other parts of the covering of huts. Each nation, in short, has its own way of building, according to the materials afforded and the habits of the country. At Marseilles the roofs are covered with straw and earth mixed up together, instead of tiles. At Athens, even to this day, the Areopagus, an example of remote antiquity, is covered with clay; and the house of Romulus in the capitol, by its thatched roof, clearly manifests the simple manners and habits of the ancients. It is from such specimens we are enabled to form just ideas of the early method of building. Daily practice made the original builders more skilful, and experience increased their confidence ; those who took more delight in the science making it their exclusive profession. Thus man, who, in addition to the senses which other animals enjoy in common with him, is gifted by nature with such powers of thought and understanding, that no subject is too difficult for his apprehension, and the brute creation are subject to him from his superiority of intellect, proceeded by degrees to a knowledge of the other arts and sciences, and passed from a savage state of life

to one of civilization. From the courage which his gradual success naturally excited, and his engagement in those various speculations with which the arts are connected, his ideas expanded ; and from building huts he soon proceeded to the erection of houses constructed with brick walls or with stones, whose roofs were of timber covered with tiles. Thus by experience and observation the knowledge of certain proportions was attained, which in the beginning were fluctuating and uncertain ; and advantage being taken of the bounty of nature, in her supply of timber and other building materials, the rising art was so cultivated that by the help of other arts mere necessity was lost sight of; and by attending to the comforts and luxuries of civilized society, it was carried to the highest degree of perfection. I shall now, to the best of my ability, proceed to treat of those materials which are used in building, their quality, and use. Lest any one object that the order of my treatise on the matters in question be not well arranged, and that this book should have had precedence of the last, I think it proper to state, that in writing a Dissertation on Architecture I considered myself bound, in the first place, to set forth those branches of learning and science with which it is connected, to explain its origin and different species, and to enumerate the qualifications which an architect should possess.

Hence, having first adverted to those principles on which the art depends, I shall now proceed to an explanation of the nature and use of the different materials employed in the practice of it. This work not being intended for a treatise on the origin of architecture; that origin, and the degrees by which it passed to its present state of perfection, is only incidentally mentioned. This book is consequently in its proper place. I shall now proceed to treat, in an intelligible manner, of the materials which are appropriate for building, how they are formed by nature, and of the analysis of their component parts. For there is no material nor body of any sort whatever which is not composed of various elementary particles; and if their primary composition be not duly understood, no law of physics will explain their nature to our satisfaction.

CHAPTER II.

OF THE ORIGIN OF ALL THINGS ACCORDING TO THE OPINIONS OF PHILOSOPHERS.

Thales thought that water was the first principle of all things. Heraclitus, the Ephesian, who, on account of the obscurity of his writings, was called σκοτεινὸς by the Greeks, maintained a similar doctrine in respect of fire. Democritus, and his follower Epicurus, held similar opinions with regard to atoms; by which term is understood such bodies as are incapable of being cut asunder, or, as some say, of further division. To water and fire the philosophy of the Pythagoreans added air and earth. Hence Democritus, though loosely expressing himself, seems to have meant the same thing, when he calls the elements indivisible bodies; for when he considers them incapable of corruption or alteration, and of eternal duration and infinite solidity, his hypothesis makes the particles not yet so connected as to form a body.
Since, therefore, all bodies consist of and spring from these elements, and in the great variety of bodies the quantity of each element entering into their composition is different, I think it right to investigate the nature of their variety, and explain how it affects the quality of each in the materials used for building, so that those about to build may avoid mistakes, and be, moreover, enabled to make a proper choice of such materials as they may want.

CHAPTER III.

OF BRICKS.

I shall first treat of bricks, and the earth of which they ought to be made. Gravelly, pebbly, and sandy clay are unfit for that purpose; for if made of either of these sorts of earth, they are not only too ponderous, but walls built of them, when exposed to the rain, moulder away, and are soon decomposed, and the straw, also, with which they are mixed, will not sufficiently bind the earth together, because of its rough quality. They should be made of earth of a red or white chalky, or a strong sandy nature. These sorts of earth are ductile and cohesive, and not being heavy, bricks made of them are more easily handled in carrying up the work.

The proper seasons for brick-making are the spring and autumn, because they then dry more equably. Those made in the summer solstice are defective, because the heat of the sun soon imparts to their external surfaces an appearance of sufficient dryness, whilst the internal parts of them are in a very different state; hence, when thoroughly dry, they shrink and break those parts which were dry in the first instance; and thus broken, their strength is gone. Those are best that have been made at least two years; for in a period less than that they will not dry thoroughly. When plastering is laid and set hard on bricks which are not perfectly dry, the bricks, which will naturally shrink, and consequently occupy a less space than the plastering, will thus leave the latter to stand of itself. From its being extremely thin, and not capable of supporting itself, it soon breaks to pieces; and in its failure sometimes involves even that of the wall. It is not, therefore, without reason that the inhabitants of Utica allow no bricks to be used in their buildings which are not at least five years old, and also approved by a magistrate.

There are three sorts of bricks; the first is that which the Greeks call Didoron (διδῶρον), being the sort we use; that is, one foot long, and half a foot wide. The two other sorts are used in Grecian buildings; one is called Pentadoron, the other Tetradoron. By the word Doron the Greeks mean a palm, because the word δῶρον signifies a gift which can be borne in the palm of the hand. That sort, therefore, which is five palms each way is called Pentadoron; that of four palms, Tetradoron. The former of these two sorts is used in public buildings, the latter in private.

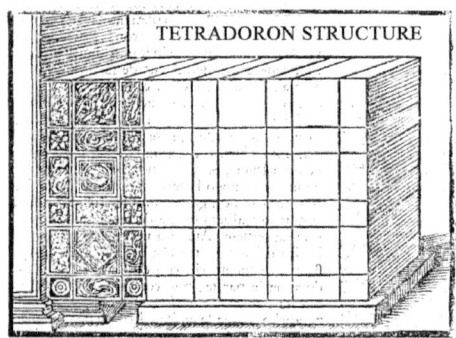

Each sort has half bricks made to suit it; so that when a wall is executed, the course on one of the faces of the wall shews sides of whole bricks, the other face of half bricks; and being worked to the line on each

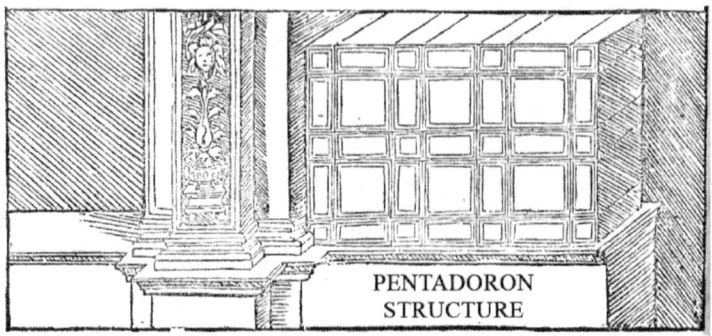

face, the bricks on each bed bond alternately over the course below. Besides the pleasant varied appearance which this method gives, it affords additional strength, by the middle of a brick, on a rising course, falling over the vertical joints of the course thereunder. The bricks of Calentum in Spain, Marseilles in France, and Pitane in Asia, are, when wrought and dried, specifically lighter than water, and hence swim thereon. This must arise from the porosity of the earth whereof they are made; the air contained in the pores, to which the water cannot penetrate, giving them a buoyant property. Earth of this sort being, therefore, of such a light and thin quality, and impervious to water, be a lump thereof of whatever size, it swims naturally like pumice-stone. Bricks of this sort are of great use for building purposes; for they are neither heavy nor liable to be injured by the rain.

CHAPTER IV.

OF SAND.

In buildings of rubble work it is of the first importance that the sand be fit for mixing with the lime, and unalloyed with earth. The different sorts are these; black, white, deep red, and bright red. The best of each of these sorts is that which, when rubbed between the fingers, yields a grating sound. That, also, which is earthy, and does not possess the roughness above named, is fit for the purpose, if it merely leave a stain or any particles of earth on a white garment, which can easily be brushed away.

If there be no sand-pits where it can be dug, river sand or sifted gravel must be used. Even sea sand may be had recourse to, but it dries very slowly; and walls wherein it is used must not be much loaded, unless carried up in small portions at a time. It is not, however, fit for those walls that are to receive vaulting. In plastered walls, built with sea sand, the salt which exudes destroys the plaster; but plaster readily adheres to and dries on walls built with new pit sand, and vaulting may safely spring from them. If sand have been dug a long time, and exposed to the sun, the moon, and the rain, it loses its binding quality, and becomes earthy; neither when used does it bind the rubble stones together so as to prevent them sliding on their beds and falling out: nor is it fit to be used in walls where great weights are to be supported. Though pit sand is excellent for mortar, it is unfit for plastering; for being of a rich quality, when added to the lime and straw, its great strength does not suffer it to dry without cracks. The poorness of the river sand, when tempered with beaters, makes the plastering as hard as cement.

CHAPTER V.

OF LIME.

Having treated of the different sorts of sand, we proceed to an explanation of the nature of lime, which is burnt either from white stone or flint. That which is of a close and hard texture is better for building walls; as that which is more porous is better for plastering. When slaked for making mortar, if pit sand be used, three parts of sand are mixed with one of lime. If river or sea sand be made use of, two parts of sand are given to one of lime, which will be found a proper proportion. If to river or sea sand, potsherds ground and passed through a sieve, in the proportion of one third part, be added, the mortar will be better for use.

The cause of the mass becoming solid when sand and water are added to the lime, appears to be, that stones, like other bodies, are a compound of elements: those which contain large quantities of air being soft, those which have a great proportion of water being tough, of earth, hard, of fire, brittle. For stones which, when burnt, would make excellent lime, if pounded and mixed with sand, without burning, would neither bind the work together, nor set hard; but having passed through the kiln, and having lost the property of their former tenacity by the action of intense heat, their adhesiveness being exhausted, the pores are left open and inactive. The moisture and air which were in the body of the stone, having, therefore, been extracted and exhausted, the heat being partially retained, when the substance is immersed in water before the heat can be dissipated, it acquires strength by the water rushing into all its pores, effervesces, and at last the heat is excluded.

Hence, limestone, previous to its burning, is much heavier than it is after having passed through the kiln: for, though equal in bulk, it is known, by the abstraction of the moisture it previously contained, to lose one-third of its weight by the process. The pores of limestone, being thus opened, it more easily takes up the sand mixed with it, and adheres thereto; and hence, in drying, binds the stones together, by which sound work is obtained.

CHAPTER VI.

OF POZZOLANA.

There is a species of sand which, naturally, possesses extraordinary qualities. It is found about Baiæ and the territory in the neighbourhood of Mount Vesuvius; if mixed with lime and rubble, it hardens as well under water as in ordinary buildings. This seems to arise from the hotness of the earth under these mountains, and the abundance of springs under their bases, which are heated either with sulphur, bitumen, or alum, and indicate very intense fire. The inward fire and heat of the flame which escapes and burns through the chinks, makes this earth light; the sand-stone (tophus), therefore, which is gathered in the neighbourhood, is dry and free from moisture. Since, then, three circumstances of a similar nature, arising from the intensity of the fire, combine in one mixture, as soon as moisture supervenes, they cohere and quickly harden through dampness; so that neither the waves nor the force of the water can disunite them.

That these lands are affected with heat, as surmised, is evident, because in the mountains of Cumæ and at Baiæ, sweating places are excavated, in which the hot vapour rising upwards from the intensity of the fire, strikes through the earth, and so escapes in these places that they are singularly beneficial for the purpose. It is moreover said that in former times fires under Vesuvius existed in abundance, and thence evolved flames about the fields. Thus that which we call sponge-stone, or Pompeian pumice-stone, burnt from another species of stone, appears to be acted on by fire so as to possess a quality of this sort.

The species of sponge-stone, however, thence obtained, is not found except in the neighbourhood of Ætna and the hills of Mysia, which the Greeks call κατακεκαυμένοι, and places of such description. If, therefore, in these places hot springs and heated vapours are found in the cavities of the mountains, and the spots are recorded by the ancients to have been subject to fires issuing out of the lands, it seems certain that the moisture is extracted from the sand-stone and earth in their neighbourhood, by the strength of the fire, as from lime-stone in a kiln.

Dissimilar and unequal actions being thus concentrated towards the same end, the great want of moisture quickly supplied by water binds and strongly cements them, and also imparts a rapid solidity, by means of the heat common to both the bodies. It is needless to enquire why, as there are many hot springs in Tuscany, we do not there find a powder, which, for the same reason, would harden under water: should I be thereon questioned, I would thus explain the circumstance.

All lands do not possess similar qualities; nor is stone universally found. Some lands are earthy, others gravelly, others gritty, others sandy: in short, the quality of land, in different parts of the earth, varies as much as even the climate itself. For instance; on the side of the Apennines towards Tuscany, sand-pits are found in abundance; whereas, on the other side of the Apennines, facing the Adriatic, none are discoverable: so also in Achaia, Asia, and universally on the other side of the sea, such things are not known. It does not therefore follow, that in all places abounding with hot springs all other circumstances should be similar. Nature has not made all things to suit the convenience of man, but differently and fortuitously.

Hence, in places where the mountains are not earthy, but of stone, the force of the fire escaping through the chinks burns that which is soft and tender, whilst that which is hard is left. Thus the earth of Campania, when burnt, becomes a powder; that of Tuscany a coal. Both of these are of great use in building, one species being very serviceable in land works, the other in works under water. In Tuscany, however, the quality of the material is softer than sandstone, but harder than earth; and from its entire subjection to the action of the sub-existing fire, it becomes that sort of sand which is called carbunculus.

CHAPTER VII.

OF STONE QUARRIES.

I have described the different species of lime and sand, and their qualities. Stone quarries, from which square and rubble stones are procured and prepared for the purposes of building, will now be considered. The qualities of these differ very much. Some stone is soft; the red, for instance, found in the neighbourhood of Rome, in the countries of the Pallienses, Fidenates, and Albanæ. Some moderately so, as the Tiburtine, Amiternine, Soractine, and those of that sort. Others are hard, even as flints. There are many other species, as the red and black sandstone (tophus) of Campania, and the white sort of Umbria, Picenum, and Venice, which is cut with a saw like wood.

The soft species have this advantage, that when recently taken from the quarry they are easily worked, and answer well under cover; but when used in open and exposed situations, and subjected to the action of the frost and rain, they soon become friable, and moulder away. They are also much affected by the salt near the sea-shore, and are not capable of preserving their strength when exposed to great heat. The Tiburtine stones, and those of a similar nature, resist great weights no less than the action of the weather, but are easily injured by fire. The instant they are exposed to that they are ruined, from their possessing so small a quantity of moisture; their earthy particles, also, are few, and the quantity of air and fire in them considerable. Hence, from the small portion of earth and water which they contain, the fire easily acts upon them, and, occupying the interstices, drives out the air with accumulated violence, and communicates its own hot quality to them.

There are many quarries on the borders of the Tarquinienses, called the Anician quarries, in colour much resembling the

Alban stone. They are worked in most abundance in the neighbourhood of the Volscinian lake, and in the prefecture of Statonia. This stone has numberless good qualities; neither frost nor fire affects it. It is hard and durable, from its containing but little air and fire, but a moderate quantity of moisture, and much earth. Close in texture, it is not injured by the weather nor by heat.

The monuments about Ferentinum, which are built of this stone, prove its durability; among these may be observed large statues well executed, bas-reliefs on a smaller scale, and acanthus leaves and flowers elegantly carved, which, though long since wrought, appear as fresh as though they were but recently finished. From the stones of the above quarries the metal founders make their casting moulds, for which they are well calculated. If this stone were to be had near Rome, it would be used in all works about the city, to which it is indeed worthy to be applied.

But as necessity, on account of proximity to the quarries, obliges us to use the red sort of stone, that of the Pallienses and other species in the immediate vicinity of the city, in order to find that which is least defective, let it be selected as follows. Two years before the commencement of the building, the stones should be extracted from the quarries in the summer season; by no means in the winter; and they should then be exposed to the vicissitudes and action of the weather. Those which, after two years' exposure, are injured by the weather, may be used in the foundations; but those which continue sound after this ordeal, will endure in the parts above ground. These rules apply equally to squared as to rubble or unsquared stone work.

CHAPTER VIII.

OF THE DIFFERENT KINDS OF WALLS.

The different species of walls are, the RETICULATUM (net-like), a method now in general use, and the INCERTUM (uncertain), which is the ancient mode. The reticulatum is the most beautiful, but is very liable to split, from the beds of the stones being unstable, and its deficiency in respect of bond. The incertum, on the contrary, course over course, and the whole bonded together, does not present so beautiful an appearance, though stronger than the reticulatum.

Both species should be built of the smallest sized stones, that the walls, by sucking up, and attaching themselves to, the mortar, may last the longer. For as the stones are of a soft and porous nature, they absorb, in drying, the moisture of the mortar, and this, if used plentifully, will consequently exercise a greater cementing power; because from their containing a larger portion of moisture, the wall will not, of course, dry so soon as otherwise; and as soon as the moisture is absorbed by the pores of the stone from the mortar, the lime, losing its power, leaves the sand, so that the stones no longer adhere to it, and in a short time the work becomes unsound.

We may see this in several monuments about the city, which have been built of marble or of stones squared externally; that is, on the face, but filled up with rubble run with mortar. Time, in these, has taken up the moisture of the mortar, and destroyed its efficacy, by the porosity of the surface on which it acted. All cohesion is thus ruined, and the walls fall to decay.

He who is desirous that this may not happen to his work, should build his two face walls two feet thick either of red stone or of brick or common flint, binding them together with iron cramps run with lead, and duly preserving the middle space or cavity. The materials, in this case, not being thrown in at random, but the work well brought up on the beds, the upright joints properly arranged, and the face walls, moreover, regularly tied together, they are not liable to bulge, nor be otherwise disfigured.

In these respects one cannot refrain from admiring the walls of the Greeks. They make no use of soft stone in their buildings: when, however, they do not employ squared stone, they use either flint or hard stone; and, as though building with brick, they cross or break the upright joints, and thus produce the most durable work. There are two sorts of this species of work; one called ISODOMUM, the other PSEUDISODOMUM.

The first is so called, because in it all the courses are of an equal height; the latter received its name from the unequal heights of the courses. Both these methods make sound work: first, because the stones are hard and solid, and therefore unable to absorb the moisture of the mortar, which is thus preserved to the longest period; secondly, because the beds being smooth and level, the mortar does not escape; and the wall moreover, bonded throughout its whole thickness, becomes eternal.

There is still another method, which is called ἔμπλεκτον (EMPLECTUM), in use even among our country workmen. In this species the faces are wrought. The other stones are, without working, deposited in the cavity between the two faces, and bedded in mortar as the wall is carried up. But the workmen, for the sake of despatch, carry up these casing walls, and then tumble in the rubble between them; so that there are thus three distinct thicknesses; namely, the two sides or facings, and the filling in. The Greeks, however, pursue a different course, laying the stones flat, and breaking the vertical joints; neither do they fill in the middle at random, but, by means of bond stones, make the wall solid, and of one thickness or piece. They moreover cross the wall, from one face to the other, with bond stones of a single piece, which they call διατόνοι, (DIATONI) tending greatly to strengthen the work.

He, therefore, who is desirous of producing a lasting structure, is enabled, by what I have laid down, to choose the sort of wall that will suit his purpose. Those walls which are built of soft and smooth-looking stone, will not last long. Hence, when valuations are made of external walls, we must not put them at their original cost; but having found, from the register, the number of lettings they have gone through, we must deduct for every year of their age an eightieth part of such cost, and set down the remainder or balance as their value, inasmuch as they are not calculated to last more than eighty years.

This is not the practice in the case of brick walls, which, whilst they stand upright, are always valued at their first cost. Hence, in some states, not only public and private buildings, but even royal structures, are built of brick. We may instance that part of the wall at Athens towards Mounts Hymettus and Pentelicus, the temples of Jupiter and Hercules, in which the cells are of brick, whilst the columns and their entablatures are of stone, in Italy the antient and exquisitely wrought wall of Arezzo, and at Tralles a palace for the Attalic kings, which is the official residence of the priest. Some pictures painted on brick walls at Sparta, after being cut out, were packed up in wooden cases and transported to the Comitium to grace the Ædileship of Varro and Murena.

In the house of Croesus, which the Sardians call Gerusia, established for the repose and comfort of the citizens in their old age, as also in the house of Mausolus, a very powerful king of Halicarnassus, though all the ornaments are of Proconnesian marble, the walls are of brick, are remarkably sound at the present day, and the plastering with which they are covered is so polished that they sparkle like glass. The prince who caused them to be thus built was not, however, restrained by economy; for, as king of Caria, he must have been exceedingly rich.

Neither could it be urged that it was from want of skill and taste in architecture, that he did so. Born at Mylasa, and perceiving that Halicarnassus was a situation fortified by nature, and a place well adapted for commerce, with a commodious harbour, he fixed his residence there. The site of the city bears a resemblance to a theatre, as to general form. In the lowest part of it, near the harbour, a forum was built: up the hill, about the middle of the curve, was a large square in the centre of which stood the mausoleum, a work of such grandeur that it was accounted one of the seven wonders of the world. In the centre, on the summit of the hill, was the temple of Mars, with its colossal statue, which is called ἀκρόλιθος, sculptured by the eminent hand of Leocharis. Some, however, attribute this statue to Leocharis; others to Timotheus. On the right, at the extreme point of the curve, was the temple of Venus and Mercury, close to the fountain of Salmacis.

It is a vulgar error, that those who happen to drink thereat are affected with love-sickness. As, however, this error is general, it will not be amiss to correct the impression. It is not only impossible that the water should have the effect of rendering men effeminate and unchaste; but, on the contrary, that alluded to is clear as crystal, and of the finest flavour. The origin of the story, by which it gained the reputation of the above quality, is as follows. When Melas and Arevanias brought to the place a colony from Argos and Trœzene, they drove out the barbarous Carians and Lelegæ. These, betaking themselves to the mountains in bodies, committed great depredations, and laid waste the neighbourhood. Some time afterwards, one of the colonists, for the sake of the profit likely to arise from it, established close to the fountain, on account of the excellence of its water, a store where he kept all sorts of merchandize; and thus it became a place of great resort of the barbarians who were drawn thither. Coming, at first, in small, and at last in large, numbers, the barbarians by degrees shook off their savage and uncivilized habits, and changed them, without coercion for those of the Greeks. The fame, therefore, of this fountain, was acquired, not by the effeminacy which it is reputed to impart, but by its being the means through which the minds of the barbarians were civilized.

I must now, however, proceed to finish my description of the city. On the right summit we have described the temple of Venus and the above named fountain to have been placed: on the left stood the royal palace, which was planned by Mausolus himself. This commanded, on the right, a view of the forum and harbour, and of the whole circuit of the walls: on the left, it overlooked a secret harbour, hidden by the mountains, into which no one could pry, so as to be aware of what was transacting therein. In short, from his palace, the king, without any person being aware of it, could give the necessary orders to his soldiers and sailors.

After the death of Mausolus, the Rhodians, indignant at his wife, who succeeded to the government, governing the whole of Caria, fitted out a fleet, for the purpose of seizing the kingdom. When the news reached Artemisia, she commanded her fleet to lie still in the secret harbour; and having concealed the sailors and mustered the marines, ordered the rest of the citizens to the walls. When the well appointed squadron of the Rhodians should enter the large harbour, she gave orders that those stationed on the walls should greet them, and promise to deliver up the town. The Rhodians, leaving their ships, penetrated into the town; at which period Artemisia, by the sudden opening of a canal, brought her fleet round, through the open sea, into the large harbour; whence the Rhodian fleet, abandoned by its sailors and marines, was easily carried out to sea. The Rhodians, having now no place of shelter, were surrounded in the forum and slain.

Artemisia then embarking her own sailors and marines on board of the Rhodian fleet, set sail for Rhodes. The inhabitants of that city seeing their vessels return decorated with laurels, thought their fellow citizens were returning victorious, and received their enemies. Artemisia having thus taken Rhodes, and slain the principal persons of the city, raised therein a trophy of her victory. It consisted of two brazen statues, one of which represented the state of Rhodes, the other was a statue of herself imposing a mark of infamy on the city. As it was contrary to the precepts of the religion of the Rhodians to remove a trophy, they encircled the latter with a building, and covered it after the custom of the Greeks, giving it the name ἄβατον.

If therefore, kings of such great power did not despise brick buildings, those who, from their great revenue and spoils in war, can afford the expense not only of squared and rough stone, but even of marble buildings, must not despise brick structures when well executed. I shall now explain why this species of walls is not permitted in the city of Rome, and also why such walls ought not to be permitted.

The public laws forbid a greater thickness than one foot and a half to be given to walls that abut on a public way, and the other walls, to prevent loss of room, are not built thicker. Now brick walls, unless of the thickness of two or three bricks, at all events of at least one foot and a half, are not fit to carry more than one floor, so that from the great population of the city innumerable houses would be required. Since, therefore, the area it occupies would not in such case contain the number to be accommodated, it became absolutely necessary to gain in height that which could not be obtained on the plan. Thus by means of stone piers or walls of burnt bricks or unsquared stones, which were tied together by the timbers of the several floors, they obtained in the upper story excellent dining rooms. The Roman people by thus multiplying the number of stories in their houses are commodiously lodged.

Having explained why, on account of the narrowness of the streets in Rome, walls of brick are not allowed in the city, I shall now give instructions for their use out of the city when required, to the end that they may be durable. On the top of a wall immediately under the roof, there should be a course of burnt bricks, about one foot and a half in height, and projecting over the walls like the corona of a cornice; thus the injury to be guarded against in such a wall, will be prevented; for if any tiles should be accidentally broken or dislodged by the wind, so as to afford a passage for the rain, the burnt brick, a protection to it, will secure the wall itself from damage, and the projection will cause the dropping of the water to fall beyond the face of the wall and thus preserve it. To judge of such burnt bricks as are fit for the purpose is not at first an easy matter; the only way of ascertaining their goodness is to try them through a summer and winter, and, if they bear out through these undamaged, they may be used. Those which are not made of good clay are soon injured by the frost and rain; hence if unfit to be used in roofs they will be more unfit in walls. Walls built of old tiles are consequently very lasting.

As to wattled walls, would they had never been invented, for though convenient and expeditiously made, they are conducive to great calamity from their acting almost like torches in case of fire. It is much better, therefore, in the first instance, to be at the expense of burnt bricks, than from parsimony to be in perpetual risk. Walls moreover, of this sort, that are covered with plaster are always full of cracks, arising from the crossing of the laths; for when the plastering is laid on wet, it swells the wood, which contracts as the work dries, breaking the plastering. But if expedition, or want of funds, drives us to the use of this sort of work, or as an expedient to bring work to a square form, let it be executed as follows. The surface of the foundation whereon it is to stand must be somewhat raised from the ground or pavement. Should it ever be placed below them it will rot, settle, and bend forward, whereby the face of the plastering will be injured. I have already treated on walls, and generally on the mode of preparing and selecting the materials for them. I shall now proceed to the use of timber in framing, and to a description of its several sorts, as also of the mode of fitting timbers together, so that they may be as durable as their nature will permit.

FIGURE EXPLANATION

A = Reticulatum structure
B= Incertum structure
C= Diatoni structure
D= Isodumum structure
E= Pseudisodomum structure
FGHI= Emplectum structure
KLM= Unnamed "cramp" structure

75

CHAPTER IX.

OF TIMBER.

Timber should be felled from the beginning of the Autumn up to that time when the west wind begins to blow; never in the Spring, because at that period the trees are as it were pregnant, and communicate their natural strength to the yearly leaves and fruits they shoot forth. Being empty and swelled out, they become, by their great porosity, useless and feeble, just as we see females after conception in indifferent health till the period of their bringing forth. Hence slaves about to be sold are not warranted sound if they be pregnant; for the foetus which goes on increasing in size within the body, derives nourishment from all the food which the parent consumes, and as the time of delivery approaches, the more unwell is the party by whom it is borne: as soon as the foetus is brought forth, that which was before allotted for the nourishment of another being, once more free by the separation of the foetus, returns to reinvigorate the body by the juices flowing to the large and empty vessels, and to enable it to regain its former natural strength and solidity.

So, in the Autumn, the fruits being ripened and the leaves dry, the roots draw the moisture from the earth, and the trees are by those means recovered and restored to their pristine solidity. Up to the time above-mentioned the force of the wintry air compresses and consolidates the timber, and if it be then felled the period will be seasonable.

In felling, the proper way is to cut through at once to the middle of the trunk of the tree, and then leave it for some time, that the juices may drain off; thus the useless liquor contained in the tree, running away through its external rings, all tendency to decay is removed, and it is preserved sound. After the tree has dried and the draining has ceased, it may be cut down and considered quite fit for use.

That this should be the method pursued, will appear from the nature of shrubs. These, at the proper season, when pierced at the bottom, discharge from the heart through the holes made in them all the redundant and pernicious juices, and thus drying acquire strength and durability. On the contrary, when those juices do not escape, they congeal and render the tree defective and good for nothing. If, therefore, this process of draining them whilst in their growing state does not destroy their vigour, so much the more if the same rules are observed when they are about to be felled, will they last for a longer period when converted into timber for buildings.

The qualities of trees vary exceedingly, and are very dissimilar, as those of the oak, the elm, the poplar, the cypress, the fir, and others chiefly used in buildings. The oak, for instance, is useful where the fir would be improper; and so with respect to the cypress and the elm. Nor do the others differ less widely, each, from the different nature of its elements, being differently suited to similar applications in building.

First, the fir, containing a considerable quantity of air and fire, and very little water and earth, being constituted of such light elements, is not heavy: hence bound together by its natural hardness it does not easily bend, but keeps its shape in framing. The objection to fir is, that it contains so much heat as to generate and nourish the worm which is very destructive to it. It is moreover very inflammable, because its open pores are so quickly penetrated by fire, that it yields a great flame.

The lower part of the fir which is close to the earth, receiving by its proximity to the roots, a large portion of moisture, is previous to felling straight and free from knots; the upper part, throwing out by the strength of the fire it contains, a great many branches through the knots, when cut off at the height of twenty feet and rough squared, is, from its hardness, called Fusterna. The lower part, when cut down, is sawed into four quarters, and after the outer rings of the tree are rejected, is well adapted to joinery works, and is called Sapinea.

The oak, however, containing among its other elements a great portion of earth, and but a small quantity of water, air, and fire, when used under ground is of great durability, for its pores being close and compact, the wet does not penetrate it; in short its antipathy to water is so great that it twists and splits very much the work in which it is used.

The holm oak (esculus), whose elements are in very equal proportions, is of great use in buildings; it will not however stand the damp which quickly penetrates its pores, and its air and fire being driven off, it soon rots. The green oak (cerrus), the cork tree, and the beech soon rot, because they contain equal quantities of water, fire, and earth, which are by no means capable of balancing the great quantity of air they contain. The white and black poplar, the willow, the lime tree (tilia), the withy (vitex), are of great service in particular works on account of their hardness. They contain but a small portion of earth, a moderate proportion of water, but abound with fire and air. Though not hard on account of the earth in them, they are very white, and excellently adapted for carving.

The alder, which grows on the banks of rivers, and is to appearance an almost useless wood, possesses nevertheless most excellent qualities, inasmuch as it contains much air and fire, not a great deal of earth, and less water. Its freeness from water makes it almost eternal in marshy foundations used for piling under buildings, because, in these situations, it receives that moisture which it does not possess naturally. It bears immense weights and does not decay. Thus we see that timber which above ground soon decays, lasts an amazing time in a damp soil.

This is most evident at Ravenna, a city, the foundations of whose buildings, both public and private, are all built upon piles. The elm tree and the ash contain much water and but little air and fire, with a moderate portion of earth. They are therefore pliant, and being so full of water, and from want of stiffness, soon bend under a superincumbent weight. When, however, from proper keeping after being felled, or from being well dried while standing to discharge their natural moisture, they become much harder, and in framings are, from their pliability, capable of forming sound work.

The maple tree, which contains but little fire and earth, and a considerable portion of air and water, is not easily broken, and is, moreover, easily wrought. The Greeks, therefore, who made yokes for oxen (called by them ζυγὰ) of this timber, call the tree ζυγεία. The cypress and pine are also singular in their nature; for though they contain equal portions of the other elements, yet, from their large proportion of water, they are apt to bend in use; they last, however, a long time, free from decay; the reason whereof is, that they contain a bitter juice, whose acrid properties prevent the rot, and are not less efficacious in destroying the worm. Buildings, in which these sorts of timber are used, last an amazing number of years.

The cedar and juniper trees possess the same qualities as the two last named; but as the cypress and pine yield a resin, so the cedar tree yields an oil called cedrium, with which, whatsoever is rubbed, as books, for instance, will be preserved from the worm as well as the rot. The leaves of this tree resemble those of the cypress, and its fibres are very straight. The statue of the goddess, as also the ceiled roof in the temple of Diana at Ephesus, are made of it; and it is used in many other celebrated temples, on account of its great durability. These trees grow chiefly in the island of Crete, in Africa, and in some parts of Syria.

The larch, which is only known in the districts on the banks of the Po and the shores of the Adriatic, on account of the extreme bitterness of its juices, is not subject to rot and attack of the worm, neither will it take fire or burn of itself, but can only be consumed with other wood, as stone is burnt for lime in a furnace; nor even then does it emit flame nor yield charcoal, but, after a long time, gradually consumes away, from the circumstance of its containing very little fire and air. It is, on the contrary, full of water and earth; and being free from pores, by which the fire could penetrate, it repels its power, so that it is not quickly hurt thereby. Its weight is so great, that it will not float in water, when transported to any place, and is either conveyed in vessels, or floated on fir rafts.

This property of the wood was discovered under the following circumstances. Julius Cæsar, being with his army near the Alps, ordered the towns to supply him with provisions. Among them was a fortress called Larignum, whose inhabitants, trusting to their fortifications, refused to obey the mandate. Cæsar ordered his forces to the spot immediately. In front of the gate of this fortress stood a tower built of this species of timber, of considerable height, and constructed after the manner of a funeral pile, with beams alternately crossing each other at their extremities, so that the besieged might, from its top, annoy the besiegers with darts and stones. It appearing that the persons on the tower had no other arms than darts, which, from their weight, could not be hurled any great distance from the walls, orders were given to convey bundles of fire-wood and torches to the tower, which were quickly executed by the soldiers.

As soon as the flames, reaching almost to the heavens, began to encompass the tower, every one expected to see its demolition. But as soon as the fire was extinct, the tower appeared still unhurt; and Cæsar, wondering at the cause of it, ordered it to be blockaded out of arrow's flight, and thus carried the town, which was delivered up to him by its trembling inhabitants. They were then asked where they obtained this sort of wood, which would not burn. They shewed him the trees, which are in great abundance in those parts. Thus, as the fortress was called Larignum, so the wood, whereof the tower was built, is called larigna (larch). It is brought down the Po to Ravenna, for the use of the municipalities of Fano, Pesaro, Ancona, and the other cities in that district. If there were a possibility of transporting it to Rome, it would be very useful in the buildings there; if not generally, at least it would be excellent for the plates under the eaves of those houses in Rome which are insulated, as they would be thus secured from catching fire, since they would neither ignite nor consume, nor burn into charcoal.

The leaves of these trees are similar to those of the pine-tree; the fibres of them straight, and not harder to work in joinery than the pine-tree. The wood contains a liquid resin, of the colour of Attic honey, which is a good remedy in cases of phthisis. I have now treated of the different sorts of timber, and of their natural properties, as well as of the proportion of the elements in each. It only remains to enquire, why that species of fir, which is known in Rome by the name of Supernas, is not so good as that which is called Infernas, whose durability in buildings is so great. I shall therefore explain how their good and bad qualities arise from the situations in which they grow, that they may be clearly understood.

CHAPTER X.

OF THE FIRS CALLED SUPERNAS AND INFERNAS, AND OF THE APENINES.

The Apennines begin from the Tyrrhene Sea, extending to the Alps on one side, and the borders of Tuscany on the other; and their summits spreading in the shape of a bow, almost touch the shores of the Adriatic in the centre of their range, which ends near the Straits of Sicily. The hither side of them towards Tuscany and Campania, is in point of climate extremely mild, being continually warmed by the sun's rays. The further side, which lies towards the upper sea, is exposed to the north, and is enclosed by thick and gloomy shadow. The trees, therefore, which grow in that part being nourished by continual moisture, not only grow to a great size, but their fibres being too much saturated with it, swell out considerably. When hewn, therefore, and squared, and deprived of their natural vegetation, they change in drying the hardness of the grain, and become weak and apt to decay, on account of the openness of their pores. They are, therefore, of little durability in buildings.

On the contrary, those which grow on the side opposite to the sun, not being so porous, harden in drying, because the sun draws the moisture from trees no less than from the earth. Hence, those which grow in open sunny places, are more solid, on account of the closeness of their pores, and when squared for use, are exceedingly lasting. The fir, which goes by the name of Infernas, brought from the warm open parts, is therefore preferable to the sort called Supernas, which comes from a closely and thickly wooded country.

To the best of my ability I have treated on the materials necessary for building, and their natural temperaments in respect of the different proportions of the elements which they contain, as well as on their good and bad qualities, in order that those who build may be well informed thereon. Those who follow my directions, and choose a proper material for the purpose whereto it is applied, will do right. Having thus considered the preparations to be made, we shall proceed, in the following books, to the consideration of buildings themselves, and first, to that of the temples of the immortal gods, and their symmetry and proportions as the importance of the subject requires, which will form the subject of the following book.

DE ARCHITECTURA

BOOK III
Temples and the Orders of Architecture

INTRODUCTION

The Delphic Apollo, by the answer of his priestess, declared Socrates the wisest of men. Of him it is said he sagaciously observed that it had been well if men's breasts were open, and, as it were, with windows in them, so that every one might be acquainted with their sentiments. Would to God they had been so formed. We might then not only find out the virtues and vices of persons with facility, but, being also enabled to obtain ocular knowledge of the science they profess, we might judge of their skill with certainty; whereby those who are really clever and learned would be held in proper esteem. But as nature has not formed us after this fashion, the talents of many men lie concealed within them, and this renders it so difficult to lay down an accurate theory of any art. However an artist may promise to exert his talents, if he have not either plenty of money, or a good connexion from his situation in life; or if he be not gifted with a good address or considerable eloquence, his study and application will go but little way to persuade persons that he is a competent artist.

We find a corroboration of this by reference to the ancient Sculptors and Painters, among whom, those who obtained the greatest fame and applause are still living in the remembrance of posterity; such, for instance, as Myron, Polycletus, Phidias, Lysippus, and others who obtained celebrity in their art. This arose from their being employed by great cities, by kings, or by wealthy citizens. Now others, who, not less studious of their art, nor less endued with great genius and skill, did not enjoy equal fame, because employed by persons of lower rank and of slenderer means, and not from their unskilfulness, seem to have been deserted by fortune; such were Hellas the Athenian, Chion of Corinth, Myagrus the Phocæan, Pharax the Ephesian, Bedas of Byzantium, and many more; among the Painters, Aristomenes of Thasos, Polycles of Adramyttium, Nicomachus and others, who were wanting neither in industry, study of their art, nor talent. But their poverty, the waywardness of fortune, or their ill success in competition with others, prevented their advancement.

Nor can we wonder that from the ignorance of the public in respect of art many skilful artists remain in obscurity; but it is scandalous that friendship and connexion should lead men, for their sake, to give partial and untrue opinions. If, as Socrates would have had it, every one's feelings, opinions, and information in science could be open to view, neither favor nor ambition would prevail, but those, who by study and great learning acquire the greatest knowledge, would be eagerly sought after. Matters are not however in this state as they ought to be, the ignorant rather than the learned being successful, and as it is never worth while to dispute with an ignorant man, I propose to shew in these precepts the excellence of the science I profess.

In the first book, O Emperor, I laid before you an explanation of the art, its requisites, and the learning an architect should possess, and I added the reasons why he should possess them. I also divided it into different branches and defined them: then, because chiefest and most necessary, I have explained the proper method of setting out the walls of a city, and obtaining a healthy site for it, and have exhibited in diagrams, the winds, and quarters whence they blow. I have shewn the best methods of laying out the streets and lanes, and thus completed the first book. In the second book I have analysed the nature and qualities of the materials used in building, and adverted to the purposes to which they are best adapted. In this third book I shall speak of the sacred temples of the immortal gods, and explain them particularly.

CHAPTER I.

OF THE DESIGN AND SYMMETRY OF TEMPLES.

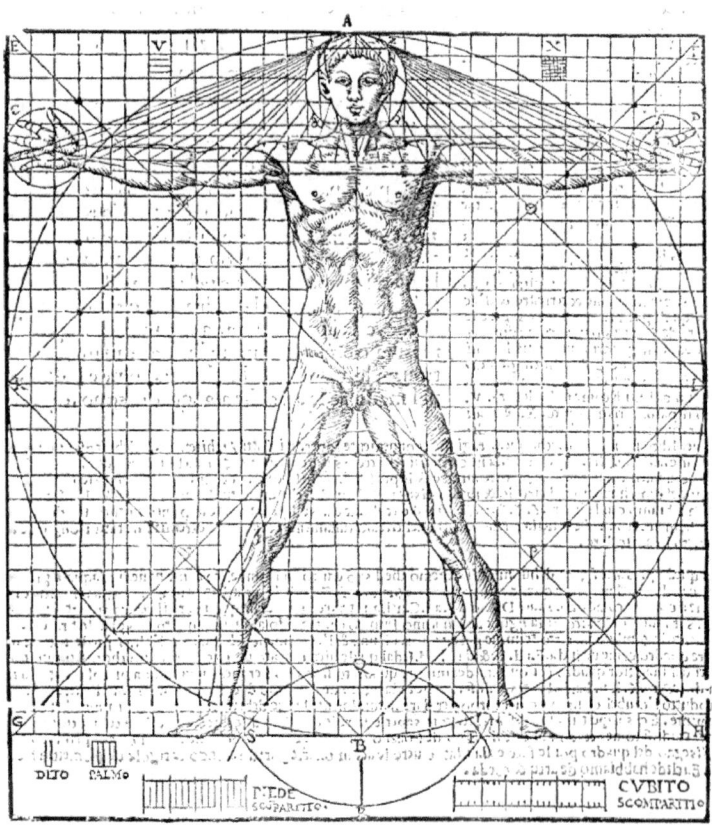

The design of Temples depends on symmetry, the rules of which Architects should be most careful to observe. Symmetry arises from proportion, which the Greeks call ἀναλογία. Proportion is a due adjustment of the size of the different parts to each other and to the whole; on this proper adjustment symmetry depends. Hence no building can be said to be well designed which wants symmetry and proportion. In truth they are as necessary to the beauty of a building as to that of a well formed human figure, which nature has so fashioned, that in the face, from the chin to the top of the forehead, or to the roots of the hair, is a tenth part of the height of the whole body. From the chin to the crown of the head is an eighth part of the whole height, and from the nape of the neck to the crown of the head the same. From the upper part of the breast to the roots of the hair a sixth; to the crown of the head a fourth. A third part of the height of the face is equal to that from the chin to the under side of the nostrils, and thence to the middle of the eyebrows the same; from the last to the roots of the hair, where the forehead ends, the remaining third part. The length of the foot is a sixth part of the height of the body. The fore-arm a fourth part. The width of the breast a fourth part. Similarly have the other members their due proportions, by attention to which the ancient Painters and Sculptors obtained so much reputation.

Just so the parts of Temples should correspond with each other, and with the whole. The navel is naturally placed in the centre of the human body, and, if in a man lying with his face upward, and his hands and feet extended, from his navel as the centre, a circle be described, it will touch his fingers and toes. It is not alone by a circle, that the human body is thus circumscribed, as may be seen by placing it within a square. For measuring from the feet to the crown of the head, and then across the arms fully extended, we find the latter measure equal to the former; so that lines at right angles to each other, enclosing the figure, will form a square.

If Nature, therefore, has made the human body so that the different members of it are measures of the whole, so the ancients have, with great propriety, determined that in all perfect works, each part should be some aliquot part of the whole; and since they direct, that this be observed in all works, it must be most strictly attended to in temples of the gods, wherein the faults as well as the beauties remain to the end of time.

It is worthy of remark, that the measures necessarily used in all buildings and other works, are derived from the members of the human body, as the digit, the palm, the foot, the cubit, and that these form a perfect number, called by the Greeks τέλειος. The ancients considered ten a perfect number, because the fingers are ten in number, and the palm is derived from them, and from the palm is derived the foot. Plato, therefore, called ten a perfect number, Nature having formed the hands with ten fingers, and also because it is composed of units called μονάδες in Greek, which also advancing beyond ten, as to eleven, twelve, &c. cannot be perfect until another ten are included, units being the parts whereof such numbers are composed.

The mathematicians, on the other hand, contend for the perfection of the number six, because, according to their reasoning, its divisors equal its number: for a sixth part is one, a third two, a half three, two-thirds four, which they call δίμοιρος; the fifth in order, which they call πεντάμοιρος, five, and then the perfect number six. When it advances beyond that, a sixth being added, which is called ἔφεκτος, we have the number seven. Eight are formed by adding a third, called triens, and by the Greeks, ἐπίτριτος. Nine are formed by the addition of a half, and thence called sesquialteral; by the Greeks ἡμιόλιος; if we add the two aliquot parts of it, which form ten, it is called bes alterus, or in Greek ἐπιδίμοιρος. The number eleven, being compounded of the original number, and the fifth in order is called ἐπιπεντάμοιρος. The number twelve, being the sum of the two simple numbers, is called διπλασίων.

Moreover, as the foot is the sixth part of a man's height, they contend, that this number, namely six, the number of feet in height, is perfect: the cubit, also, being six palms, consequently consists of twenty-four digits. Hence the states of Greece appear to have divided the drachma, like the cubit, that is into six parts, which were small equal sized pieces of brass, similar to the asses, which they called oboli; and, in imitation of the twenty-four digits, they divided the obolus into four parts, which some call dichalca, others trichalca.

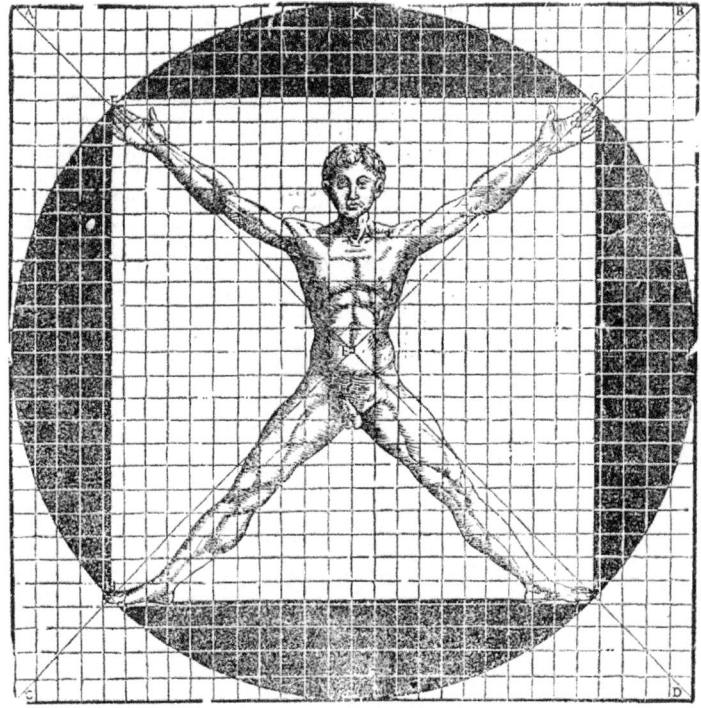

Our ancestors, however, were better pleased with the number ten, and hence made the denarius to consist of ten brass asses, and the money to this day retains the name of denarius. The sestertius, a fourth part of a denarius, was so called, because composed of two asses, and the half of another. Thus finding the numbers six and ten perfect, they added them together, and formed sixteen, a still more perfect number. The foot measure gave rise to this, for subtracting two palms from the cubit, four remain, which is the length of a foot; and as each palm contains four digits, the foot will consequently contain sixteen, so the denarius was made to contain an equal number of asses.

If it therefore appear, that numbers had their origin from the human body, and proportion is the result of a due adjustment of the different parts to each other, and to the whole, they are especially to be commended, who, in designing temples to the gods, so arrange the parts that the whole may harmonize in their proportions and symmetry.

The principles of temples are distinguished by their different forms. First, that known by the appellation IN ANTIS, which the Greeks call ναὸς ἐν παραστάσι; then the PROSTYLOS, PERIPTEROS, PSEUDODIPTEROS, DIPTEROS, HYPÆTHROS. Their difference is as follows.

A temple is called IN ANTIS, when it has antæ or pilasters in front of the walls which enclose the cell, with two columns between the antæ, and crowned with a pediment, proportioned as we shall hereafter direct. There is an example of this species of temple, in that of the three dedicated to Fortune, near the Porta Collina.

The PROSTYLOS temple is similar, except that it has columns instead of antæ in front, which are placed opposite to antæ at the angles of the cell, and support the entablature, which returns on each side as in those in antis. An example of the prostylos exists in the temple of Jupiter and Faunus, in the island of the Tyber.

The AMPHIPROSTYLOS is similar to the prostylos, but with this addition, that the columns and pediment in the front are repeated in the rear of the temple.

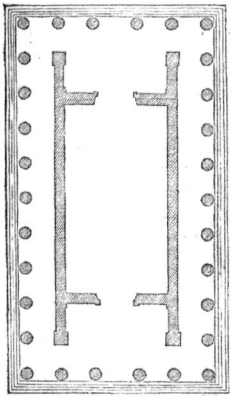
The PERIPTEROS has six columns in the front and rear, and eleven on the flanks, counting in the two columns at the angles, and these eleven are so placed that their distance from the wall is equal to an intercolumniation, or space between the columns all round, and thus is formed a walk around the cell of the temple, such as may be seen in the portico of the theatre of Metellus, in that of Jupiter Stator, by Her-

modus, and in the temple of Honour and Virtue without a POSTICUM designed by Mutius, near the trophy of Marius.

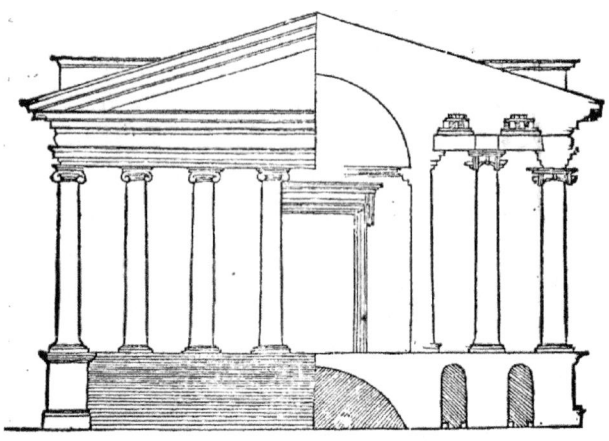

The PSEUDODIPTEROS is constructed with eight columns in front and rear, and with fifteen on the sides, including those at the angles. The walls of the cell are opposite to the four middle columns of the front and of the rear. Hence from the walls to the front of the lower part of the columns, there will be an interval equal to two intercolumniations and the thickness of a column all round. No example of such a temple is to be found in Rome, but of this sort was the temple of Diana, in Magnesia, built by Hermogenes of Alabanda, and that of Apollo, by Menesthes.

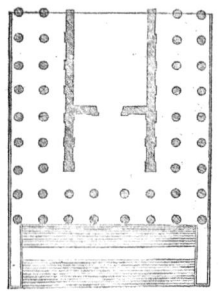

The DIPTEROS is octastylos like the former, and with a pronaos and posticum, but all round the cell are two ranks of columns. Such are the Doric temple of Quirinus, and the temple of Diana at Ephesus, built by Ctesiphon.

The HYPÆTHROS is decastylos, in the pronaos and posticum. In other respects it is similar to the dipteros, except that in the inside it has two stories of columns all round, at some distance from the walls, after the manner of the peristylia of porticos. The middle of the interior part of the temple is open to the sky, and it is entered by two doors, one in front and the other in the rear. Of this sort there is no example at Rome, there is, however, an octastyle specimen of it at Athens, the temple of Jupiter Olympius.

CHAPTER II.

OF THE FIVE SPECIES OF TEMPLES.

There are five species of temples, whose names are, PYCNOSTYLOS, that is, thick set with columns: SYSTYLOS, in which the columns are not so close: DIASTYLOS, where they are still wider apart: ARÆOSTYLOS, when placed more distant from each other than in fact they ought to be: EUSTYLOS, when the intercolumniation, or space between the columns, is of the best proportion.

PYCNOSTYLOS, is that arrangement wherein the columns are only once and a half their thickness apart, as in the temple of the god Julius, in that of Venus in the forum of Cæsar, and in other similar buildings. SYSTYLOS, is the distribution of columns with an intercolumniation of two diameters: the distance between their plinths is then equal to their front faces. Examples of it are to be seen in the temple of

Fortuna Equestris, near the stone theatre, and in other places.

This, no less than the former arrangement, is faulty; because matrons, ascending the steps to supplicate the deity, cannot pass the intercolumniations arm in arm, but are obliged to enter after each other; the doors are also hidden, by the closeness of the columns, and the statues are too much in shadow. The passages moreover round the temple are inconvenient for walking.

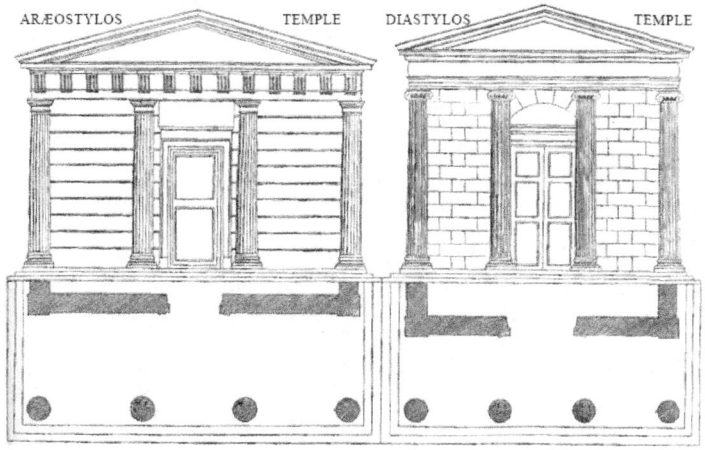

DIASTYLOS has intercolumniations of three diameters, as in the temple of Apollo and Diana. The inconvenience of this species is, that the epistylia or architraves over the columns frequently fail, from their bearings being too long.

In the ARÆOSTYLOS the architraves are of wood, and not of stone or marble; the different species of temples of this sort are clumsy, heavy roofed, low and wide, and their pediments are usually ornamented with statues of clay or brass, gilt in the Tuscan fashion. Of this species is the temple of Ceres, near the Circus Maximus, that of Hercules, erected by Pompey, and that of Jupiter Capitolinus.

We now proceed to the EUSTYLOS, which is preferable, as well in respect of convenience, as of beauty and strength. Its intercolumniations are of two diameters and a quarter. The centre intercolumniation, in front and in the posticum, is three diameters. It has not only a beautiful effect, but is convenient, from the unobstructed passage it affords to the door of the temple, and the great room allowed for walking round the cell.

The rule for designing it is as follows. The extent of the front being given, it is, if tetrastylos, to be divided into eleven parts and a half, not including the projections of the base and plinth at each end: if hexastylos, into eighteen parts: if octastylos, into twenty-four parts and a half. One of either of these parts, according to the case, whether tetrastylos, hexastylos, or octastylos, will be a measure equal to the diameter of one of the columns. Each intercolumniation, except the middle one, front and rear, will be equal to two of these measures and one quarter, and the middle intercolumniation three. The heights of the columns will be eight parts and a half. Thus the intercolumniations and the heights of the columns will have proper proportions. There is no example of eustylos in Rome; but there is one at Teos in Asia, which is octastylos, and dedicated to Bacchus. Its proportions were discovered by Hermogenes, who was also the inventor of the octastylos or pseudodipteral formation. It was he who first omitted the inner ranges of columns in the dipteros, which, being in number thirty-eight, afforded the opportunity of avoiding considerable expense. By it a great space was obtained for walking all round the cell, and the effect of the temple was not injured because the omission of the columns was not perceptible; neither was the grandeur of the work destroyed.

The pteromata, or wings, and the disposition of columns about a temple, were contrived for the purpose of increasing the effect, by the varied appearance of the returning columns, as seen through the front intercolumniations, and also for providing plenty of room for the numbers frequently detained by rain, so that they might walk about, under shelter, round the cell. I have been thus particular on the pseudodipteros, because it displays the skill and ingenuity with which Hermogenes designed those his works; which cannot but be acknowledged as the sources whence his successors have derived their best principles.

In aræostyle temples the diameter of the columns must be an eighth part of their height. In diastylos, the height of the columns is to be divided into eight parts and a half; one of which is to be taken for the diameter of the column. In systylos, let the height be divided into nine parts and a half; one of those parts will be the diameter of a column. In pycnostylos, one-tenth part of the height is the diameter of the columns. In the eustylos, as well as in the diastylos, the height of the columns is divided into eight parts and a half; one of which is to be taken for the thickness of the column. These, then, are the rules for the several intercolumniations.

For, as the distances between the columns increase, so must the shafts of the columns increase in thickness. If, for instance, in the aræostylos, they were a ninth or a tenth part of the height, they would appear too delicate and slender; because the air interposed between the columns destroys and apparently diminishes, their thickness. On the other hand, if, in the pycnostylos, their thickness or diameter were an eighth part of the height, the effect would be heavy and unpleasant, on account of the frequent repetition of the columns, and the smallness of the intercolumniations. The arrangement is therefore indicated by the species adopted.

Columns at the angles, on account of the unobstructed play of air round them, should be one-fiftieth part of a diameter thicker than the rest, that they may have a more graceful effect. The deception which the eye undergoes should be allowed for in execution.

The diminution of columns taken at the hypotrachelium, is to be so ordered, that for columns of fifteen feet and under, it should be one-sixth of the lower diameter. From fifteen to twenty feet in height, the lower diameter is to be divided into six parts and a half; and five parts and a half are to be assigned for the upper thickness of the column. When columns are from twenty to thirty feet high, the lower diameter of the shaft must be divided into seven parts, six of which are given to the upper diameter. From thirty to forty feet high, the lower diameter is divided into seven parts and a half, and six and a half given to the top. From forty to fifty feet, the lower diameter of the shaft is to be divided into eight parts, seven of which must be given to the thickness under the hypotrachelium. If the proportion for greater heights be required, the thickness at top must be found after the preceding method; always remembering, that as the upper parts of columns are more distant from the eye, they deceive it when viewed from below, and that we must, therefore, actually add what they apparently lose. The eye is constantly seeking after beauty; and if we do not endeavour to gratify it by proper proportions and an increase of size, where necessary, and thus remedy the defect of vision, a work will always be clumsy and disagreeable. Of the swelling which is made in the middle of columns, which the Greeks call ἔντασις, so that it may be pleasing and appropriate, I shall speak at the end of the book.

CHAPTER III.

OF FOUNDATIONS;
AND OF COLUMNS AND THEIR ORNAMENTS

If solid ground can be come to, the foundations should go down to it and into it, according to the magnitude of the work, and the substruction should be built up as solid as possible. Above the ground of the foundation, the wall should be one-half thicker than the columns it is to receive, so that the lower parts which carry the greatest weight, may be stronger than the upper part, which is called the stereobata: nor must the mouldings of the bases of the columns project beyond the solid. Thus, also, should be regulated the thickness of all walls above ground. The intervals between the foundations brought up under the columns, should be either rammed down hard, or arched, so as to prevent the foundation piers from swerving.

If solid ground cannot be come to, and the ground be loose or marshy, the place must be excavated, cleared, and either alder, olive, or oak piles, previously charred, must be driven with a machine, as close to each other as possible, and the intervals, between the piles, filled with ashes. The heaviest foundations may be laid on such a base.

When they are brought up level, the stylobatæ (plinths) are placed thereon, according to the arrangement used, and above described for the pycnostylos, systylos, diastylos or eustylos, as the case may be. In the aræostylos it is only necessary to preserve, in a peripteral building, twice the number of intercolumniations on the flanks that there are in front, so that the length may be twice the breadth. Those who use twice the number of columns for the length, appear to err, because they thus make one intercolumniation more than should be used.

The number of steps in front should always be odd, since, in that case, the right foot, which begins the ascent, will be that which first alights on the landing of the temple. The thickness of the steps should not, I think, be more than ten inches, nor less than nine, which will give an easy ascent. The treads not less than one foot and a half, nor more than two feet; and if the steps are to go all round the temple, they are to be formed in the same manner.

A. PLINTHS   B. TORUS   C. SCOTIA   E: APOPHYGE SLAB
F. APOPHYGE   t. COLLUMN DIAMETER

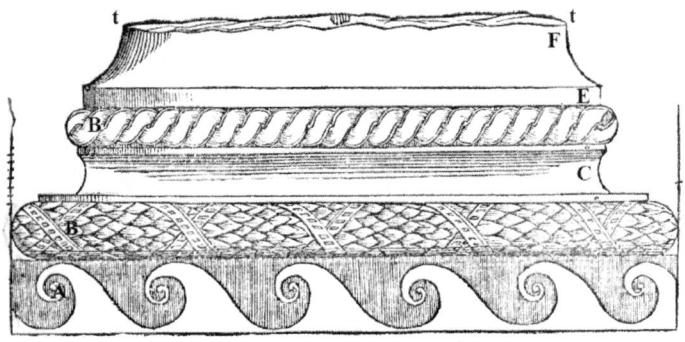

But if there is to be a podium on three sides of the temple, the plinths, bases of the columns, columns, coronæ, and cymatium, may accord with the stylobata, under the bases of the columns. The stylobata should be so adjusted, that, by means of small steps or stools, it may be highest in the middle. For if it be set out level, it will have the appearance of having sunk in the centre. The mode of adjusting the steps (scamilli impares), in a proper manner, will be shewn at the end of the book.

The scamilli being prepared and set, the bases of the columns may be laid, their height being equal to the semidiameter of the column including the plinth, and their projection, which the Greeks call ἔκφορα, one quarter of the diameter of the column. Thus the height and breadth, added together, will amount to one diameter and a half.

If the attic base be used, it must be so subdivided that the upper part be one-third of the thickness of the column, and that the remainder be assigned for the height of the plinth. Excluding the plinth, divide the height into four parts, one of which is to be given to the upper torus; then divide the remaining three parts into two equal parts, one will be the height of the lower torus, and the other the height of the scotia, with its fillets, which the Greeks call τρόχιλος (trochilus).

If Ionic, they are to be set out so that the base may each way be equal to the thickness and three eighths of the column. Its height and that of the plinth the same as the attic base. The plinth is the same height as in that of the attic base, the remainder, which was equal to one-third part of the column's diameter, must be divided into seven parts, three of which are given to the upper torus; the remaining four parts are to be equally divided into two, one of which is given to the upper cavetto, with its astragals and listel, the other to the lower cavetto, which will have the appearance of being larger, from its being next to the plinth. The astragals must be an eighth part of the scotia, and the whole base on each side is to project three sixteenths of a diameter.

The bases being thus completed, we are to raise the columns on them. Those of the pronaos and posticum are to be set up with their axes perpendicular, the angular ones excepted, which, as well as those on the flanks, right and left, are to be so placed that their interior faces towards the cell be perpendicular. The exterior faces will diminish upwards, as above-mentioned. Thus the diminution will give a pleasing effect to the temple.

The shafts of the columns being fixed, the proportions of the capitals are thus adjusted: if pillowed, as in the Ionic, they must be so formed that the length and breadth of the abacus be equal to the diameter of the lower part of the column and one eighteenth more, and the height of the whole, including the volutes, half a diameter. The face of the volutes is to recede within the extreme projection of the abacus one thirty-ninth part of the width of the abacus. Having set out these points on the listel of the abacus at the four angles, let fall vertical lines. These are called catheti. The whole height of the capital is now to be divided into nine parts and a half, whereof one part and a half is the height of the abacus, and the remaining eight are for the eye of the volute.

Within the line dropt from the angle of the abacus, at the distance of one and a half of the parts last found, let fall another vertical line, and so divide it that four parts and a half being left under the abacus, the point which divides them from the remaining three and a half, may be the centre of the eye of the volute; from which, with a radius equal to one half of one of the parts, if a circle be described, it will be the size of the eye of the volute. Through its centre let an horizontal line be drawn, and beginning from the upper part of the vertical diameter of the eye as a centre, let a quadrant be described whose upper part shall touch the under side of the abacus; then changing the centre, with a radius less than the last by half the width of the diameter of the eye, proceed with other quadrants, so that the last will fall into the eye itself, which happen in the vertical line, at a point perpendicularly under that of setting out.

The heights of the parts of the capital are to be so regulated that three of the nine parts and a half, into which it was divided, lie below the level of the astragal on the top of the shaft. The remaining parts are for the cymatium, abacus, and channel. The projection of the cymatium beyond the abacus is not to be greater than the size of the diameter of the eye. The bands of the pillows project beyond the abacus, according to the following rule. Place one point of the compasses in the centre of the eye, and let the other extend to the top of the cymatium, then describing a semicircle, its extreme part will equal the projection of the band of the pillow. The centres, from which the volute is described, should not be more distant from each other than the thickness of the eye, nor the channels sunk more than a twelfth part of their width. The foregoing are the proportions for the capitals of columns which do not exceed fifteen feet in height: when they exceed that, they must be otherwise proportioned, though upon similar principles, always observing that the square of the abacus is to be a ninth part more than the diameter of the column, so that, inasmuch as its diminution is less as its height is greater, the capital which crowns it may also be augmented in height and projection.

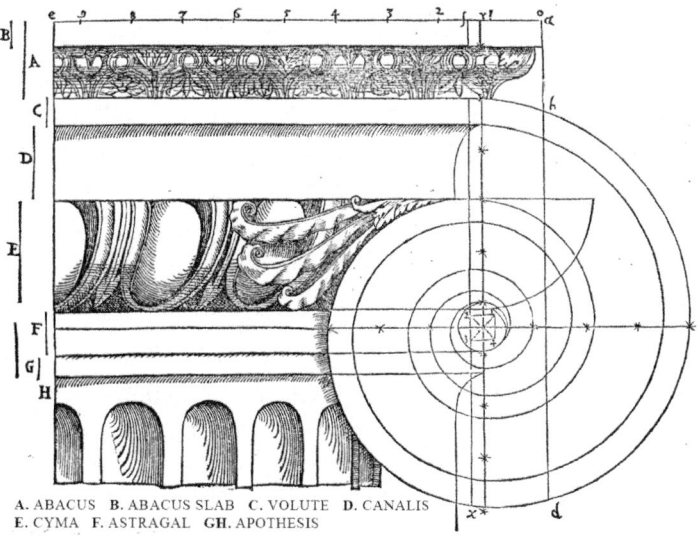

A. ABACUS B. ABACUS SLAB C. VOLUTE D. CANALIS
E. CYMA F. ASTRAGAL GH. APOTHESIS

The method of describing volutes, in order that they may be properly turned and proportioned, will be given at the end of the book. The capitals being completed, and set on the tops of the shafts, not level throughout the range of columns, but so arranged with a gauge as to follow the inclination which the small steps on the stylobata produce, which must be added to them on the central part of the top of the abacus, that the regularity of the epistylia may be preserved: we may now consider the proportion of these epistylia, or architraves. When the columns are at least twelve and not more than fifteen feet high, the architrave must be half a diameter in height. When they are from fifteen to twenty feet in height, the height of the column is to be divided into thirteen parts, and one of them taken for the height of the architrave. So from twenty to twenty-five feet, let the height be divided into twelve parts and a half, and one part be taken for the height of the architrave. Thus, in proportion to the height of the column, is the architrave to be proportioned; always remembering, that the higher the eye has to reach, the greater is the difficulty it has in piercing the density of the air, its power being diminished as the height increases; of which the result is, a confusion of the image. Hence, to preserve a sensible proportion of parts, if in high situations, or of colossal dimensions, we must modify them accordingly, so that they may appear of the size intended. The under side of the architrave is to be as wide as the upper diameter of the column, at the part under the capital; its upper part equal in width to the lower diameter of the column.

Its cymatium is to be one seventh part of the whole height, and its projection the same. After the cymatium is taken out, the remainder is to be divided into twelve parts, three of which are to be given to the lower fascia, four to the next, and five to the upper one. The zophorus, or frieze, is placed over the epistylium, than which it must be one fourth less in height; but if sculptured, it must be one fourth part higher, that the effect of the carving may not be injured. Its cymatium is to be a seventh part of its height, the projection equal to the height.

Above the frieze is placed the dentil-band, whose height must be equal to that of the middle fascia of the architrave, its projection equal to its height. The cutting thereof, which the Greeks call μετοχὴ (metoche), is to be so executed that the width of each dentil may be half its height, and the space between them two-thirds of the width of a dentil. The cymatium is to be one sixth part of its height. The corona, with its cymatium, but without the sima is to be the same height as the middle fascia of the architrave. The projection of the corona and dentils, together is to be equal to the height from the frieze to the top of the cymatium of the corona. It may, indeed, be generally observed, that projections are more beautiful when they are equal to the height of the member.

The height of the tympanum, which crowns the whole work, is to be equal to one ninth part of the extent of the corona, measured from one extremity of its cymatium to the other, and set up in the centre. Its face is to stand perpendicularly over the architrave and the hypotrachelia of the columns. The coronæ over the tympanum are to be equal to that below, without the simæ. Above the coronæ are set the simæ, which the Greeks call ἐπιτιθίδες, whose height must be one-eighth more than that of the corona. The height of the acroteria is to be equal to that of the middle of the tympanum; the central ones one eighth part higher than those at the angles.

All members over the capitals of columns, such as architraves, friezes, coronæ, tympana, crowning members (fastigia), and acroteria, should not be vertical, but inclined forwards, each a twelfth part of its height; and for this reason, that when two lines are produced from the eye, one to the upper part of a member, and the other to its lower part, the upper line or visual ray will be longer than the lower one, and if really vertical, the member will appear to lean backwards;

but if the members are set out as above directed, they will have the appearance of being perpendicular.

The number of flutes in a column is twenty-four. They are to be hollowed, so that a square kept passing round their surface, and at the same time kept close against the arrises of the fillets, will touch some point in their circumference and the arrises themselves throughout its motion. The additional thickness of the flutes and fillets in the middle of the column, arising from the entasis or swelling, will be proportional to the swelling.

On the simæ of the coronæ on the sides of temples, lions' heads should be carved; and they are to be so disposed that one may come over each column, and the others at equal distances from each other, and answering to the middle of each tile. Those which are placed over the columns are to be bored through, so as to carry off the rain-water collected in the gutter. But the intermediate ones must be solid, so that the water from the tiles, which is collected in the gutter, may not be carried off in the intercolumniations, and fall on those passing. Those over the columns will appear to vomit forth streams of water from their mouths. In this book I have done my utmost to describe the proportions of Ionic temples: in that following I shall explain the proportions of Doric and Corinthian temples.

A. EPISTYLIUM
B. CYMATIUM
C. ZOPHORUS
D. CYMATIUM
E. DENTILBAND
F. CYMATIUM
G. CORONA
L. FASTIGIA
K. TYMPANA
I. ACROTERIA
H. SIMAE

DE ARCHITECTURA

BOOK IV
Temples and the Orders of Architecture

INTRODUCTION

Finding, O Emperor, that many persons have left us precepts in Architecture, and volumes of commentaries thereon, not systematically arranged, but mere general principles, little more indeed than scattered hints, I considered it a worthy and useful task, first, to give a general view of the whole subject, and then to dilate in each book on the detail. Thus, Cæsar, I treated in the first book on the duties of an architect, and the sciences in which he should be skilled. In the second, I taught the knowledge of the different materials used in building. The third contained instructions on the arrangement of sacred buildings, their different forms and species, and the distributions appropriate to each sort; confining myself, however, to the use of the Ionic order, which, of the three, from the great delicacy of its proportions, requires the most attention in its use. I shall now, in this book, point out the difference and properties of the Doric and Corinthian Orders.

CHAPTER I.

OF THE ORIGIN OF THE THREE SORTS OF COLUMNS, AND OF THE CORINTHIAN CAPITAL.

The Corinthian Column is, except in its capital, of the same proportion as the Ionic: but the additional height of its capital makes it taller and more graceful; the Ionic capital being but one third of the diameter of the shaft in height, whilst that of the Corinthian is equal to the thickness of the shaft. Thus, the two thirds of the thickness of the shaft, which are added to its height, give it, in that respect, a more pleasing effect.

The other members which are placed on the Columns, are borrowed either from the Doric or Ionic proportions: inasmuch as the Corinthian itself has no regular settled rules for its cornice, and other ornaments, but is regulated by analogy, either from the mutuli in the cornice, or the guttæ in the architrave, or epistylium in the Doric order; or it is set out according to the laws of the Ionic, with a sculptured frieze, dentils and a cornice.

Thus, from the two orders, by the interposition of a capital, a third order arises. The three sorts of columns, different in form, have received the appellations of Doric, Ionic, and Corinthian, of which the first is of the greatest antiquity. For Dorus, the son of Hellen, and the Nymph Orseïs, reigned over the whole of Achaia and Peloponnesus, and built at Argos, an ancient city, on a spot sacred to Juno, a temple, which happened to be of this order. After this, many temples similar to it, sprung up in the other parts of Achaia, though the proportions which should be preserved in it, were not as yet settled.

But afterwards when the Athenians, by the advice of the Delphic oracle in a general assembly of the different states of Greece, sent over into Asia thirteen colonies at once, and appointed a governor or leader to each, reserving the chief command for Ion, the son of Xuthus and Creüsa, whom the Delphic Apollo had acknowledged as son; that person led them over into Asia, and occupied the borders of Caria, and there built the great cities of Ephesus, Miletus, Myus (which was long since destroyed by inundation and its sacred rites and suffrages transferred by the Ionians to the inhabitants of Miletus), Priene, Samos, Teos, Colophon, Chios, Erythræ, Phocæa, Clazomenæ, Lebedos, and Melite. The last, as a punishment of the arrogance of its citizens, was detached from the other states in a war levied pursuant to the directions of a general council; and in its place, as a mark of favor towards king Attalus, and Arsinoë, the city of Smyrna was admitted into the number of Ionian states, which received the appellation of Ionian from their leader Ion, after the Carians and Lelegæ had been driven out. In this country, allotting different spots for sacred purposes, they began to erect temples, the first of which was dedicated to Apollo Panionios, and resembled that which they had seen in Achaia, and they gave it the name of Doric, because they had first seen that species in the cities of Doria.

As they wished to erect this temple with columns, and had not a knowledge of the proper proportions of them, nor knew the way in which they ought to be constructed, so as at the same time to be both fit to carry the superincumbent weight, and to produce a beautiful effect, they measured a man's foot, and finding its length the sixth part of his height, they gave the column a similar proportion, that is, they made its height, including the capital, six times the thickness of the shaft, measured at the base. Thus the Doric order obtained its proportion, its strength, and its beauty, from the human figure.

With a similar feeling they afterwards built the temple of Diana. But in that, seeking a new proportion, they used the female figure as the standard: and for the purpose of producing a more lofty effect, they first made it eight times its thickness in height. Under it they placed a base, after the manner of a shoe to the foot; they also added volutes to its capital, like graceful curling hair hanging on each side, and the front they ornamented with cymatia and festoons in the place of hair. On the shafts they sunk channels, which bear a resemblance to the folds of a matronal garment. Thus two orders were invented, one of a masculine character, without ornament, the other bearing a character which resembled the delicacy, ornament, and proportion of a female.

The successors of these people, improving in taste, and preferring a more slender proportion, assigned seven diameters to the height of the Doric column, and eight and a half to the Ionic. That species, of which the Ionians were the inventors, has received the appellation of Ionic. The third species, which is called Corinthian, resembles in its character, the graceful elegant appearance of a virgin, in whom, from her tender age, the limbs are of a more delicate form, and whose ornaments should be unobtrusive.

The invention of the capital of this order is said to be founded on the following occurrence. A Corinthian virgin, of marriageable age, fell a victim to a violent disorder. After her interment, her nurse, collecting in a basket those articles to which she had shewn a partiality when alive, carried them to her tomb, and placed a tile on the basket for the longer preservation of its contents. The basket was accidentally placed on the root of an acanthus plant, which, pressed by the weight, shot forth, towards spring, its stems and large foliage, and in the course of its growth reached the angles of the tile, and thus formed volutes at the extremities.

Callimachus, who, for his great ingenuity and taste was called by the Athenians Catatechnos, happening at this time to pass by the tomb, observed the basket, and the delicacy of the foliage which surrounded it. Pleased with the form and novelty of the combination, he constructed from the hint thus afforded, columns of this species in the country about Corinth, and arranged its proportions, determining their proper measures by perfect rules.

 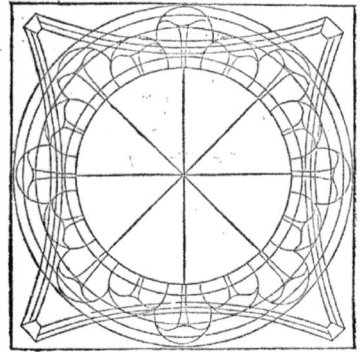

The method of setting out the capital is as follows. Its height, including the abacus, is to be equal to the diameter of the lower part of the column. The width of the abacus is obtained by making its diagonal from opposite angles, equal to twice its height. It will thus have a proper front on each face. The faces of the four sides of the abacus are to be curved inwards from its extreme angles, equal to one ninth of its extent. The thickness of the lower part of the capital must be equal to the diameter of the top of the shaft, exclusive of the apotheosis and astragal. The height of the abacus is a seventh of the height of the whole capital; the remainder is to be divided into three parts, one of which is to be given to the lower leaf, the middle leaf will occupy the space of the next third part, the stalks or caulicoli will be the same height as the last named, out of which the leaves spring for the reception of the abacus. Large volutes are generated from these, which branch out towards the angles. The smaller volutes spread out towards the flowers, which are introduced in the centre of each abacus. Flowers whose diameters are equal to the height of the abacus, are to be placed in the central part of each its faces. By attention to these rules the Corinthian capital will be properly proportioned. Other sorts of capitals are however placed on these columns, which, differing in proportion, and standing on a different sort of shaft, cannot be referred to any other class; but their origin, though the detail be changed, is traced to, and deduced from the Corinthian, the Ionic, and the Doric, their only differences arising from a variation of the arrangement of the sculpture on them.

CHAPTER II.

OF THE ORNAMENTS OF COLUMNS.

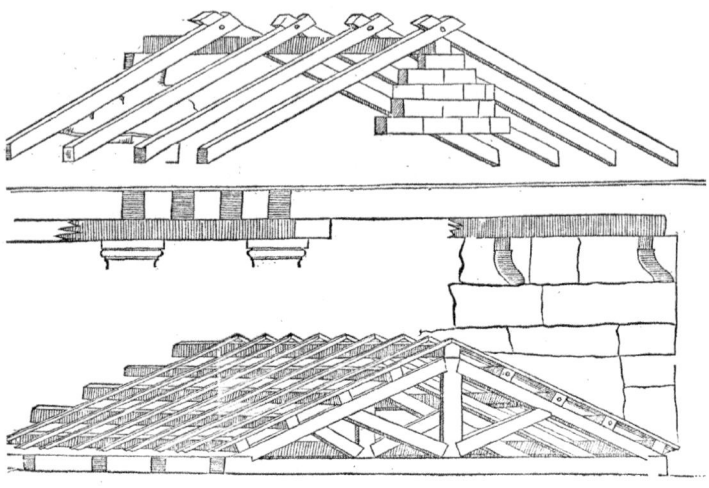

The origin and invention of the different species of columns having been discussed, it is now necessary to say something on the subject of their ornaments, how they originated, and upon what principles and for what purposes they were invented. In all buildings the timber framed work, which has various names, crowns them. The timbers vary as much in their uses as in their names. Those are called bressummers (trabes) which are placed over columns, pilasters (parastatæ), and antæ. In the framing of floors, beams (tigna) and boards (axes) are used. If the span of a roof be large, a ridge piece (columen) is laid on the top of the king post (columna, whence is derived the word column), and a tye beam (transtrum) and struts (capreoli) will be necessary. If the roof be of moderate span, the ridge piece (columen), and rafters (cantherii), of sufficient projection at their feet to throw the water off the walls, will answer the purpose. On the rafters are laid purlines (templa), and again on these, to receive the tiles, are placed common rafters (asseres), which must be of sufficient length to cover the walls and protect them.

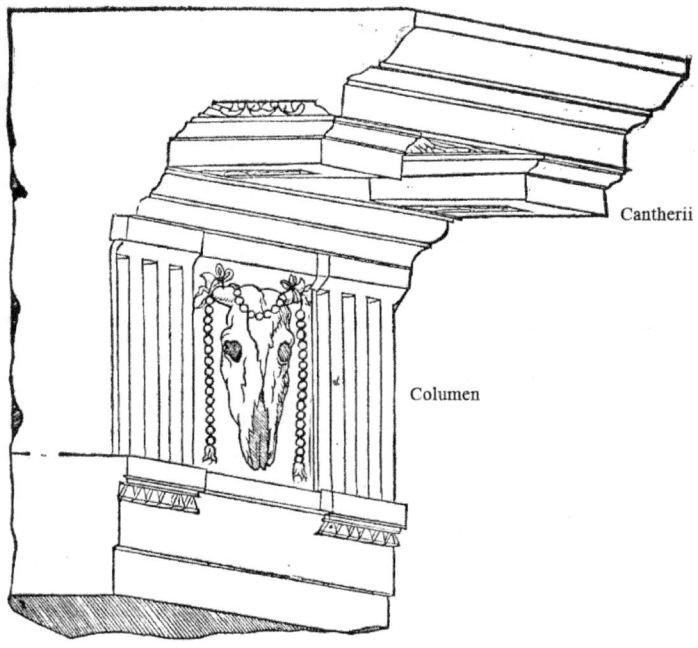

Thus each piece has its proper place, origin, and purpose. Hence, following the arrangement of timber framing, workmen have imitated, both in stone and marble, the disposition of timbers in sacred edifices, thinking such a distribution ought to be attended to; because some ancient artificers, having laid the beams so that they ran over from the inner face of the walls, and projected beyond their external face, filled up the spaces between the beams, and ornamented the cornices and upper parts with wood-work elegantly wrought. They then cut off the ends of the beams that projected over the external face of the wall, flush with its face; the appearance whereof being unpleasing, they fixed, on the end of each beam so cut, indented tablets, similar to the triglyphs now in use, and painted them with a waxen composition of a blue colour, so that the ends of the beams in question might not be unpleasant to the eye. Thus the ends of the timbers covered with tablets, indented as just mentioned, gave rise to the triglyph and metopa in the Doric order.

Others, in subsequent works, suffered the rafters' feet above each triglyph, to run over, and hollowed out the projecting inferior surface. Thus, from the arrangement of beams, arose the invention of triglyphs; and, from the projection of the rafters, the use of mutuli under the corona. On which latter account it is observable, that in works of stone and marble the carving of the mutuli is inclined, in imitation of the feet of rafters, whose slope is necessary to carry off the water. Hence we have the imitation of the earliest works to account for the Doric triglyph and mutulus, and not, as some have erroneously said, from the circumstance of triglyphs being introduced as windows; which could not be the case, inasmuch as they are placed on external angles, and immediately over columns, in both which situations windows would be absurd, in the highest degree, for the tye at the angles of buildings would be entirely destroyed, if occupied by windows; and therefore the dentils of the Ionic orders might as properly be seen to occupy the places of windows, if the spaces occupied by triglyphs have an origin of such a nature. The intervals, moreover, between dentils, as well as those between triglyphs, are called metopæ. Besides, the Greeks, by the word ὄπαι, signify the beds of the beams, which we call cava columbaria: thus the space between two beams obtained the name of a metopa.

As in works of the Doric order triglyphs and mutuli were first used, so in Ionic works the use of dentils was first introduced; for as the mutuli bear a resemblance to the projecting feet of the principal rafters, so, in the Ionic order, the dentils imitate the projection of the common rafters. Hence the Greeks never placed dentils below the mutuli, because the feet of common rafters cannot be below those of principal rafters. For a design must be anomalous, when that which ought to be above the principal rafters is placed below them. The antients, therefore, neither approved nor used mutuli nor dentils in the cornices of their pediments, but coronæ simply; because neither principal nor common rafters tail on the front of a pediment, neither can they project beyond it, their direction being towards the eaves. Their opinion, therefore, evidently was, that a distribution would not be correct in a copy which could not exist in the prototype.

For the perfection of all works depends on their fitness to answer the end proposed, and on principles resulting from a consideration of Nature herself, and they approved those only which, by strict analogy, were borne out by the appearance of utility. Their principles were thus established, and they have left us the symmetry and proportion of each order. Following their steps, I have already spoken of the Ionic and Corinthian orders: I shall now proceed to give a succinct account of the Doric order, and its most approved proportion.

CHAPTER III.

OF THE DORIC PROPORTIONS.

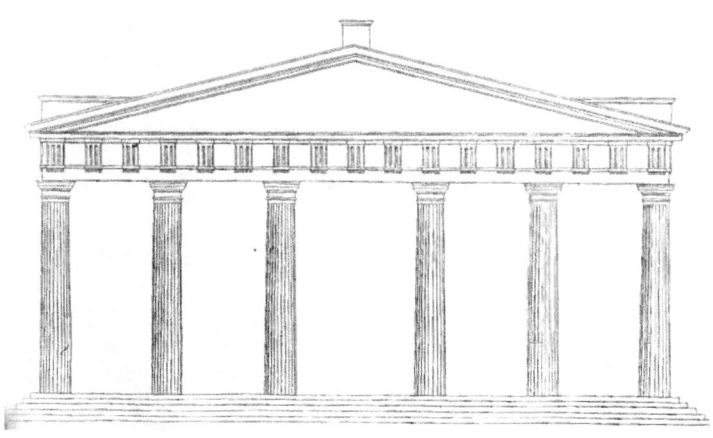

Some ancient architects have asserted that sacred buildings ought not to be constructed of the Doric order, because false and incongruous arrangements arise in the use of it. Such were the opinions of Tarchesius, Pitheus, and Hermogenes. The latter, indeed, after having prepared a large quantity of marble for a Doric temple, changed his mind, and, with the materials collected, made it of the Ionic order, in honour of Bacchus. It is not because this order wants beauty, antiquity (genus), or dignity of form, but because its detail is shackled and inconvenient, from the arrangement of the triglyphs, and the formation of the sofite of the corona (lacunaria).

It is necessary that the triglyphs stand centrally over the columns, and that the metopæ which are between the triglyphs should be as broad as high. Over the columns, at the angles of the building, the triglyphs are set at the extremity of the frieze, and not over the centre of the columns.

In this case the metopæ adjoining the angular triglyphs are not square, but wider than the others by half the width of the triglyph. Those who resolve to make the metopæ equal, contract the extreme intercolumniation half a triglyph's width. It is, however, a false method, either to lengthen the metopæ or to contract the intercolumniations; and the ancients, on this account, appear to have avoided the use of the Doric order in their sacred buildings.

I will, however, proceed to explain the method of using it, as instructed therein by my masters; so that if any one desire it, he will here find the proportions detailed, and so amended, that he may, without a defect, be able to design a sacred building of the Doric order. The front of a Doric temple, when columns are to be used, must if tetrastylos, be divided into twenty-eight parts; if hexastylos, into forty-four parts; one of which parts is called a module, by the Greeks ἐμβάτης: from the module so found the distribution of all the parts is regulated.

The thickness of the columns is to be equal to two modules, their height equal to fourteen. The height of the capital one module, its breadth one module and a sixth. Let the height of the capital be divided into three parts; then one of those parts is to be assigned for the abacus and its cymatium, another for the echinus, with its fillets; the third for the hypotrachelium. The diminution of the column is to be as directed for the Ionic order in the third book. The architrave or epistylium, with its tænia and guttæ, is to be one module in height; the tænia is the seventh part of a module; the length of the guttæ under the tænia plumb with the triglyphs, and including the fillet, the sixth part of a module. The width of the soffit of the architrave is to correspond with the thickness of the column at the hypotrachelium. Over the architrave triglyphs are placed, with metopæ one module and a half high, and one module wide on the face. They are to be distributed so, that as well over the columns at the angles, as

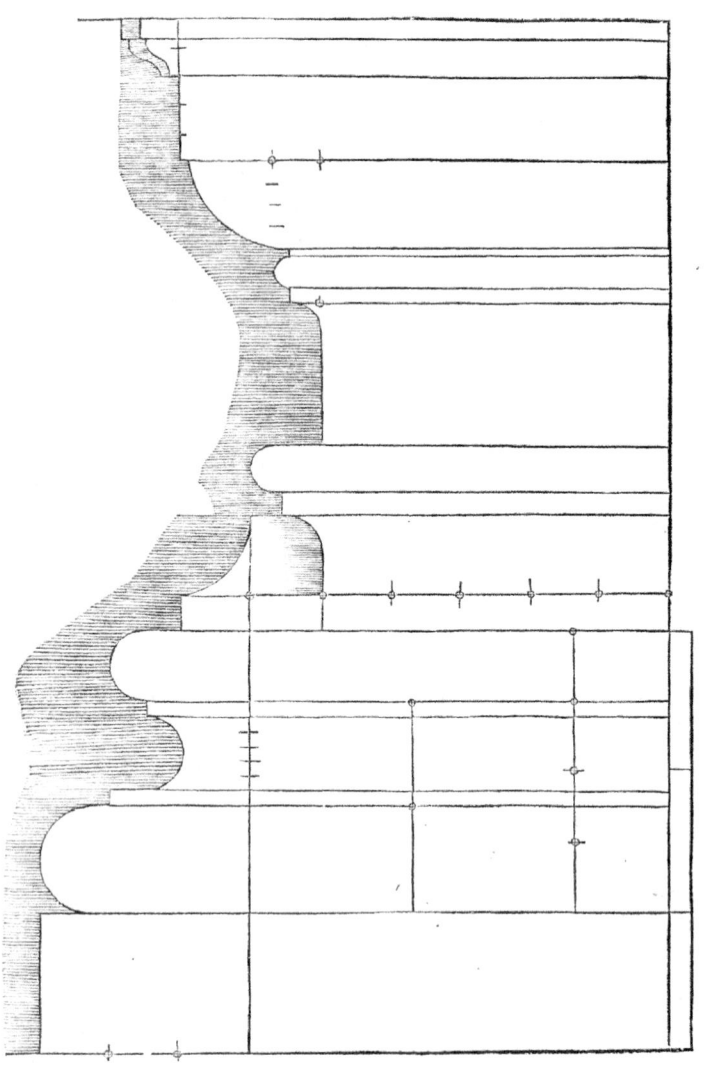

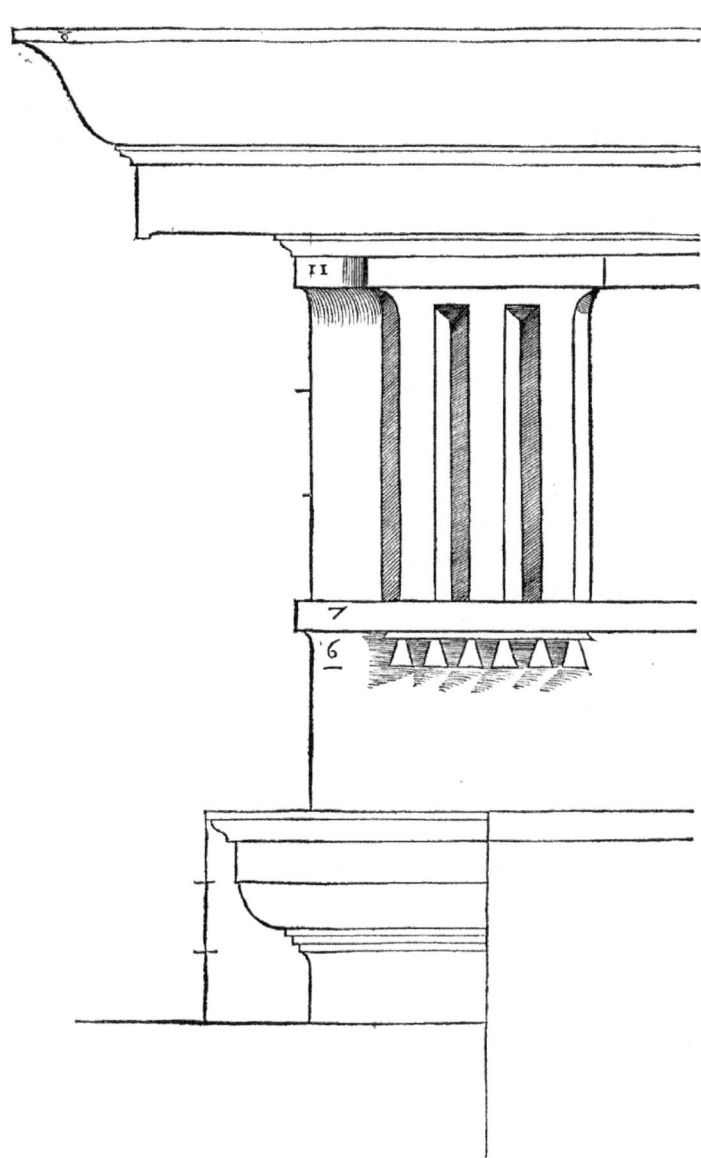

over the intermediate columns, they may stand above the two central quarters of the columns. Two are to be placed in each intercolumniation, except in the central one of the pronaos and posticum, in which three are to be set; because, by making the middle intercolumniations wider, a freer passage will be given to those who approach the statues of the gods.

The width of a triglyph is divided into six parts, of which five are left in the middle, and of the two halves of the remaining part, one is placed on the right and the other on the left extremity. In the centre a flat surface is left, called the femur (thigh), by the Greeks μηρὸς, on each side of which channels are cut, whose faces form a right angle; and on the right and left of these are other femora; and, lastly, at the angles are the two half channels. The triglyphs being thus arranged, the metopæ, which are the spaces between the triglyphs, are to be as long as they are high. On the extreme angles are semi-metopæ half a module wide. In this way all the defects in the metopæ, intercolumniations, and lacunaria, will be remedied.

The capitals of the triglyphs are to be made the sixth part of a module. Over the capitals of the triglyphs the corona is to be laid, whose projection is one half and a sixth part of a module, with a Doric cymatium over it, and another above it, so that, with the cymatia, the corona is one half of a module high. In the soffit of the corona, perpendicularly over the triglyphs and centres of the metopæ, are arranged guttæ and sinkings. The former, so as to have six guttæ appearing in front, and three on the return: the remaining spaces, which occur from the increased width of the metopæ beyond that of the triglyphs, are left plain or sculptured with representations of thunderbolts, and near the edge of the corona a channel is cut, called a scotia. The remaining parts, the tympana, simæ, and coronæ, are to be executed similar to those described for Ionic buildings.

The above is the method used in diastyle works. If the work be systyle, with a monotriglyph: the front of the building, when tetrastylos, is to be divided into twenty-three parts; when hexastylos, into thirty-five: of these, one part is taken for a module; according to which, as above directed, the work is to be set out.

Thus, over the epistylia are two metopæ and one triglyph, and in the angles a space will be left equal to half a triglyph. The middle part, under the pediment, will be equal to the space of three triglyphs and three metopæ, in order that the central intercolumniation may give room to those approaching the temple, and present a more dignified view of the statue of the god. Over the capitals of the triglyphs a corona is to be placed, with a Doric cymatium below, as above described, and another above. The corona, also, together with the cymatia, is to be half a module high. The soffit of the corona, perpendicularly over the triglyphs and centres of the metopæ, is to have guttæ and sinkings, and the other parts as directed for the diastyle.

It is necessary that the columns should be wrought in twenty faces, which, if plane, will have twenty angles; but if channelled, they are to be so formed, that a square being described, whose side is equal to that of the channel or flute, if, in the middle of the square, the point of a pair of compasses be placed, and a segment of a circle be drawn, touching the angles of the square, such segment will determine their sinking. Thus is the Doric column properly chamfered.

In respect of the additional thickness in the middle thereof, as mentioned in the third book, respecting Ionic columns, reference must be made to that place. As the external symmetry of Corinthian, Doric, and Ionic edifices has been explained, it is necessary to give directions for the interior arrangements of the cell and pronaos.

CHAPTER IV.

OF THE INTERIOR OF THE CELL AND THE ARRANGEMENT OF THE PRONAOS.

The length of a temple must be twice its width. The cell itself is to be in length one fourth part more than the breadth, including the wall in which the doors are placed. The remaining three parts run forward to the antæ of the walls of the pronaos, which antæ are to be of the same thickness as the columns. If the temple be broader than twenty feet, two columns are interposed between the two antæ, to separate the pteroma from the pronaos. The three intercolumniations between the antæ and the columns may be enclosed with fence work, either of marble or of wood, so, however, that they have doors in them for access to the pronaos.

If the width be greater than forty feet, columns opposite to those which are between the antæ, are placed towards the inner part, of the same height as those in front, but their thickness is to be diminished as follows. If those in front are an eighth part of their height in thickness, these are to be one ninth; and if the former are a ninth, or a tenth, the latter are to be proportionally diminished. For where the air does not play round them, the diminution thus made will not be perceived; lest, however, they should appear slenderer, when the flutes of the external columns be twenty-four in number, these may have twenty-eight, or even thirty-two. Thus, what is taken from the absolute mass of the shaft, will be imperceptibly aided by the number of the flutes, and though of different thicknesses, they will have the appearance of being equal.

This arises from the eye embracing a greater number of surfaces, and thence producing on the mind the effect of a larger body. For if two columns, equally thick, one of them without flutes, and the other fluted, are measured round with lines, and the line is passed over the flutes and their fillets, though the columns are of equal thickness, the lines which girt them will not be equal, for that which passes over the fillets and flutes will of course be the longest. This being the case, it is not improper in confined and enclosed situations to make the columns of slenderer proportions, when we have the regulation of the flutes to assist us.

The thickness of the walls of the cell must depend on the magnitude of the work, taking care, however, that the antæ are the same thickness as the columns. If built in the ordinary way, they are to be of small stones, very carefully laid, but if of square stone or marble, the pieces should be chiefly small and of equal size, because then, the upper stones coming over the middle of the joint below them, bind the work together and give it strength; fillets of lime used in pointing the joints and beds give the work an agreeable appearance.

CHAPTER V.

OF THE DIFFERENT ASPECTS OF TEMPLES.

If there be nothing to prevent it, and the use of the edifice allow it, the temples of the immortal gods should have such an aspect, that the statue in the cell may have its face towards the west, so that those who enter to sacrifice, or to make offerings, may have their faces to the east as well as to the statue in the temple. Thus suppliants, and those performing their vows, seem to have the temple, the east, and the deity, as it were, looking on them at the same moment. Hence all altars of the gods should be placed towards the east.

But if the nature of the place do not permit this, the temple is to be turned as much as possible, so that the greater part of the city may be seen from it. moreover, if temples be built on the banks of a river, as those in Egypt on the Nile, they should face the river. So, also, if temples of the gods be erected on the road side, they should be placed in such a manner that those passing by may look towards them, and make their obeisance.

CHAPTER VI.

OF THE PROPORTIONS OF THE DOORS OF TEMPLES.

The following are the rules for door-ways of temples, and for their dressings (antepagmenta). First the species is to be considered: this is Doric, Ionic, or Attic. The Doric is constructed with these proportions. The top of the cornice, which is above the upper dressing, is to be level with the top of the capitals in the pronaos. The aperture of the door is determined as follows. The height from the pavement to the lacunaria is to be divided into three parts and a half, of which two constitute the height of the doors. The height thus obtained is to be divided into twelve parts, of which five and a half are given to the width of the bottom part of the door. This is diminished towards the top, equal to one third of the dressing, if the height be not more than sixteen feet. From sixteen feet to twenty-five the upper part of the opening is contracted one fourth part of the dressing. From twenty-five to thirty feet the upper part is contracted one-eighth of the dressing. Those that are higher should have their sides vertical.

The thickness of the dressings in front is to be equal to one-twelfth of the height of the door, and they are to diminish towards the top a fourteenth part of their width. The height of the architrave is to be equal to the upper part of the dressing. The cymatium is to be a sixth part of the dressing; its projection equal to its thickness. The cymatium is to be sculptured in the Lesbian form, with an astragal. Above the cymatium of the architrave of the dressing (supercilium), the frieze (hyperthyrum), is placed, and it is to have a Doric cymatium, with a Lesbian astragal, in low relief. Over this the corona is placed, unornamented, and with a cymatium. Its projection is to equal the height of the supercilium placed over the architrave of the dressing. On the right and left, projectures are made; and the cymatia of the dressings are connected by a mitre.

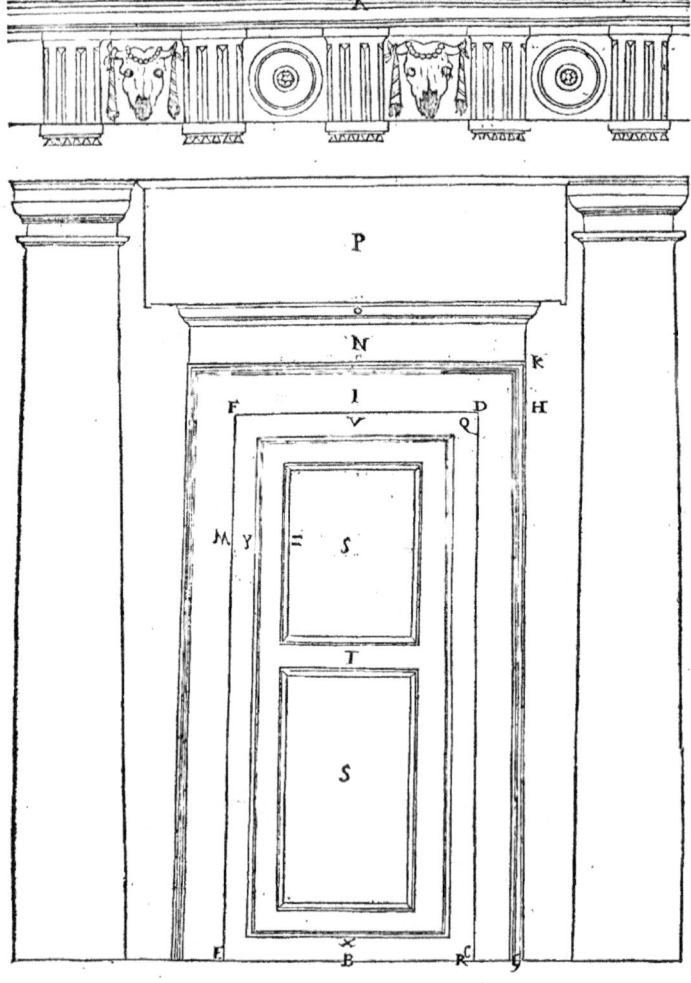

A.B. HEIGHT FROM PAVEMENT TO LACUNARIA C.D. LIGHT HEIGHT C.E. INFERIOR LIGHT WIDTH
D.F. SUPERIOR LIGHT WIDTH C.G INFERIOR DRESSING WIDTH D.H. SUPERIOR DRESSING WIDTH
I. SUPERCILIUM K. CYMATIUM M. ANTEPAGMENTA N. HYPERTHYRUM O. DORIC CYMATIUM
P. CORONA WITH CYMATIUM Q.R. HEIGHT OF ANTEPAGMENTA S. TYMPANA T. IMPAGES
V. SCAPI CARDINALES X. IMPAGES Y.Z. CYMATIUM

If the doors are Ionic, their height is to be regulated as in those that are Doric. Their width is found by dividing the height into two parts and a half, and taking one and a half for the width below. The diminution is to be as in the Doric door-way. The width of the dressings is to be a fourteenth part of the height of the aperture; the cymatium a sixth part of their width; the remainder, deducting the cymatium, is to be divided into twelve parts, three of which are given to the first fascia, with the astragal, four to the second, and five to the third. The fasciæ, with the astragal, run quite round the dressings.

The upper members of the door-way are the same as those of the Doric. The trusses (ancones), or prothyrides, which are carved on the right and left, reach to the bottom of the level of the architrave, exclusive of the leaf. Their width on the face is one-third of the dressing, and at the bottom one fourth part less. The wooden doors are to be so put together, that the hinge styles (scapi cardinales) may be one-twelfth of the height of the aperture. The pannels (tympana) between the styles are to be three out of twelve parts in width.

The arrangement of the rails is to be such, that when the height is divided into five parts, two are given to the upper and three to the lower rail. In the centre the middle rails (medii impages) are placed; the others are disposed above and below. The width of the rail is to be one-third of the pannel, and its cymatium a sixth part of the rail itself. The width of the inner styles is one half of the rail, and the raising (replum) four sixths of the rail. The styles nearest the dressings are made one half of the rail. If the doors are folding, the height remains the same, but the width is to be increased. If in four folds, the height is to be increased.

The Attic doors are made of the same proportion as the Doric, except that, in the dressings, the fasciæ return within the cymatium; and these are proportioned so, that exclusive of the cymatium, they are to be two sevenths. These doors are not to be inlaid (cerostrata), nor in two folds, but single folded, and to open outwards. I have explained, to the best of my power, the proportions used in setting out Doric, Ion-

I. CORONA f. ANCONE d. FRIEZE (HYPERTHYRUM) c. LEAF e CYMATIA I.E. COLLUMN'S SHAFT
g. CYMATIUM h. REPLUM A B. LACUNARIA HEIGHT D. CORONA G. FRIEZE (HYPERTHYRUM)
H. CYMATIUM M. TYMPANA N. IMPAGES O. SCAPI C. FRIEZE (HYPERTHYRUM)

ic, and Corinthian temples, according to the approved methods. I shall now treat of the arrangement of Tuscan temples, and how they ought to be built.

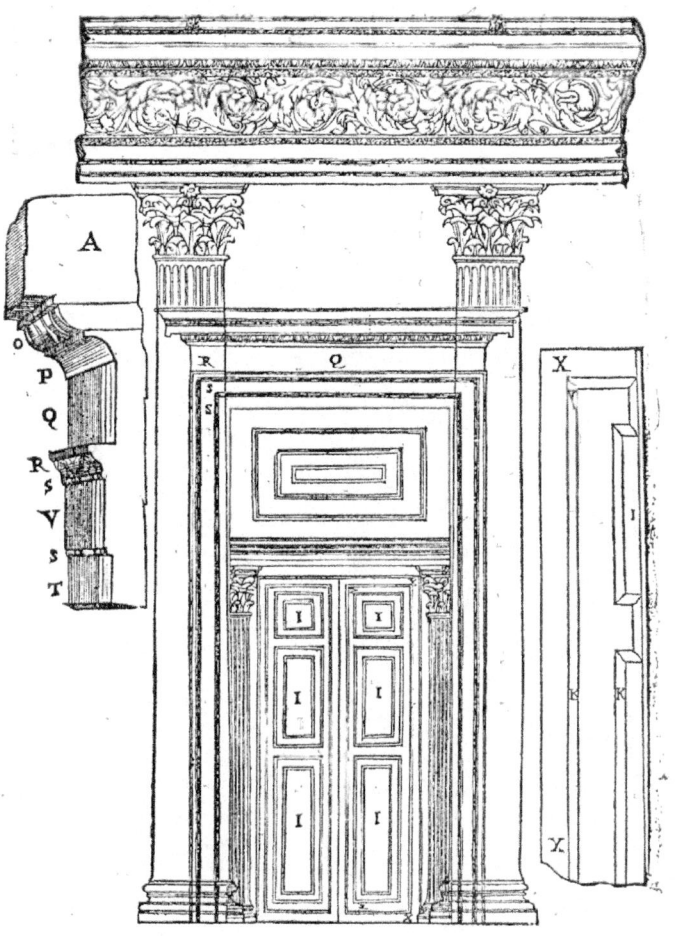

A. CORONA O. CYMA REVERSA P. DORIC CYMA Q. HYPERTHYRUM
R. ANTEPAGMENTA CYMATIUM S. ASTRAGAL T. FIRST FASCIA s. SECOND FASCIA
V. THIRD FASCIA X X. SCAPI Y. CYMATIUM Z. REPLUM I. TYMPANUM K K. IMPAGES

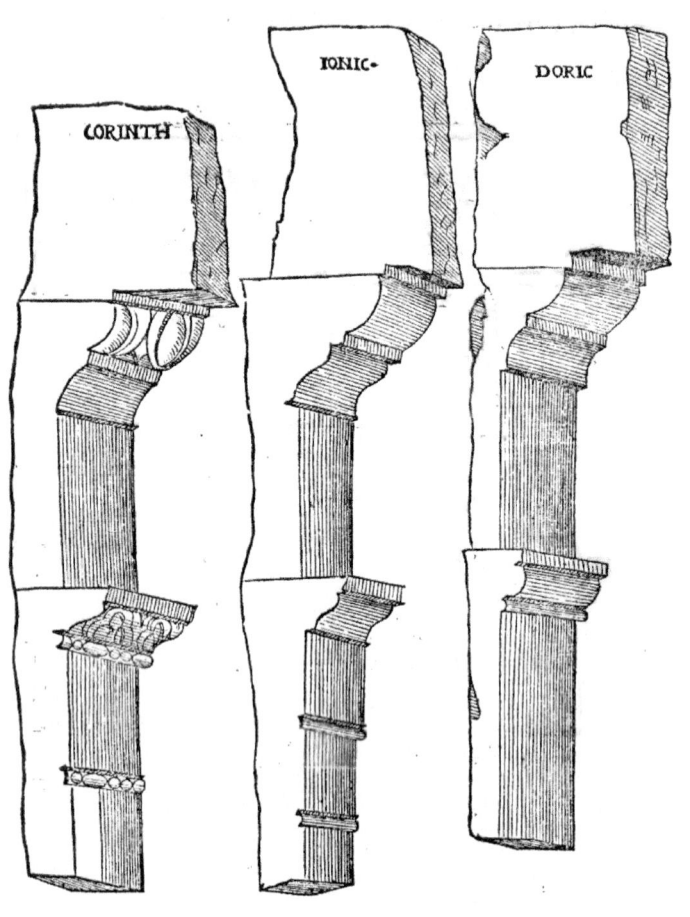

CHAPTER VII.

OF THE TUSCAN PROPORTIONS: OF CIRCULAR TEMPLES, AND OTHER SPECIES

The length of the site of the temple intended, must be divided into six parts, wherefrom subtracting one part, the width thereof is obtained. The length is then divided into two parts, of which the furthest is assigned to the cell, that next the front to the reception of the columns.

The above width is to be divided into ten parts, of which, three to the right and three to the left are for the smaller cells, or for the alæ, if such are required: the remaining four are to be given to the central part. The space before the cells in the pronaos, is to have its columns so arranged, that those at the angles are to correspond with the antæ of the external walls: the two central ones, opposite the walls, between the antæ and the middle of the temple, are to be so disposed, that between the antæ and the above columns, and in that direction, others may be placed. Their thickness below is to be one seventh of their height: their height one third of the width of the temple, and their thickness at top is to be one fourth less than their thickness at bottom.

Their bases are to be half a diameter in height. The plinths, which are to be circular, are half the height of the base, with a torus and fillet on them as high as the plinth. The height of the capital is to be half a diameter. The width of the abacus is equal to the lower diameter of the column. The height of the capital must be divided into three parts, of which one is assigned to the plinth or abacus, another to the echinus, the third to the hypotrachelium, with its apophyge.

Over the columns coupled beams are laid of such height as the magnitude of the work may require. Their width must be equal to that of the hypotrachelium at the top of the column, and they are to be so coupled together with dovetailed

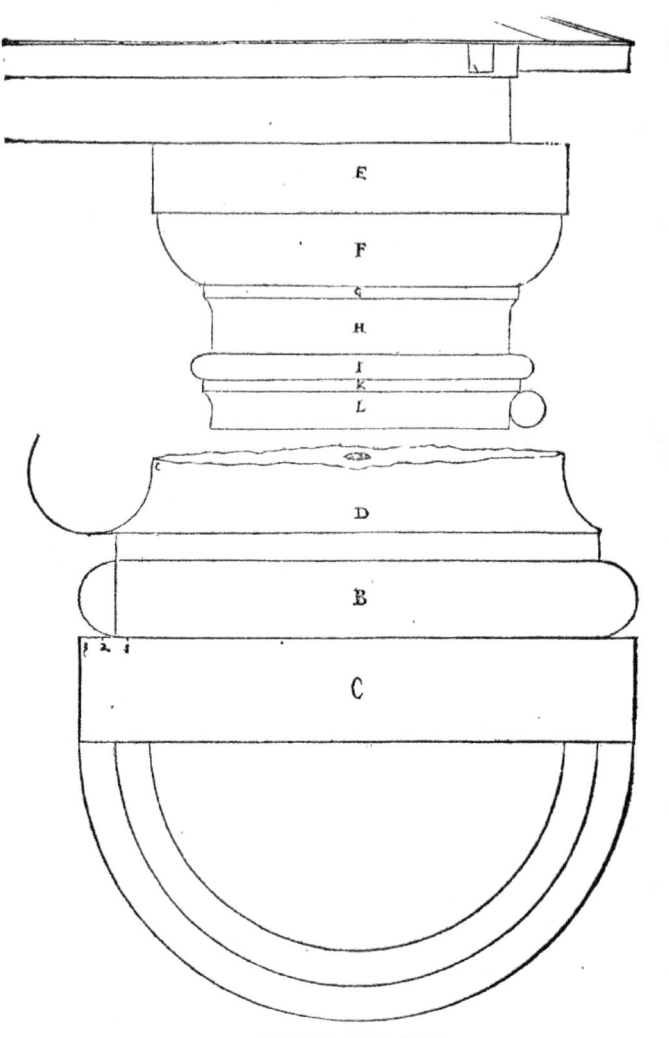

TUSCAN CAPITAL PARTS
E. ABACUS F. ECHINUS G. ANNULUS H I K L. HYPOTRACHELIUM APOPHAGES
B. TORUS C. PLINTHUS

dowels as to leave a space of two inches between them. For if they are laid touching each other, and the air does not play round them, they heat and soon rot. Above the beams and walls the mutuli project one fourth the height of the column. In front of these members are fixed, and over them the tympanum of the pediment, either of masonry or timber.

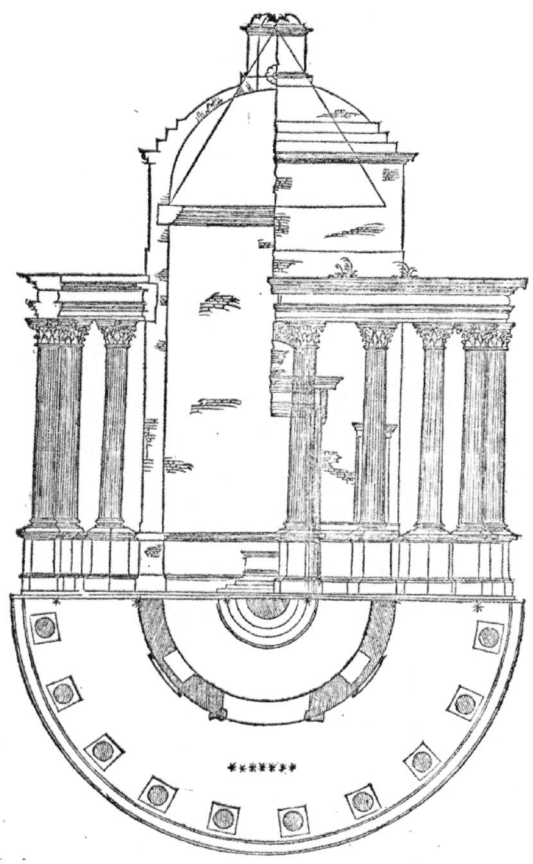

Above the pediment the ridge-piece (columen), rafters (cantherii), and purlines (templa), are distributed so that the water may drip therefrom on three sides.

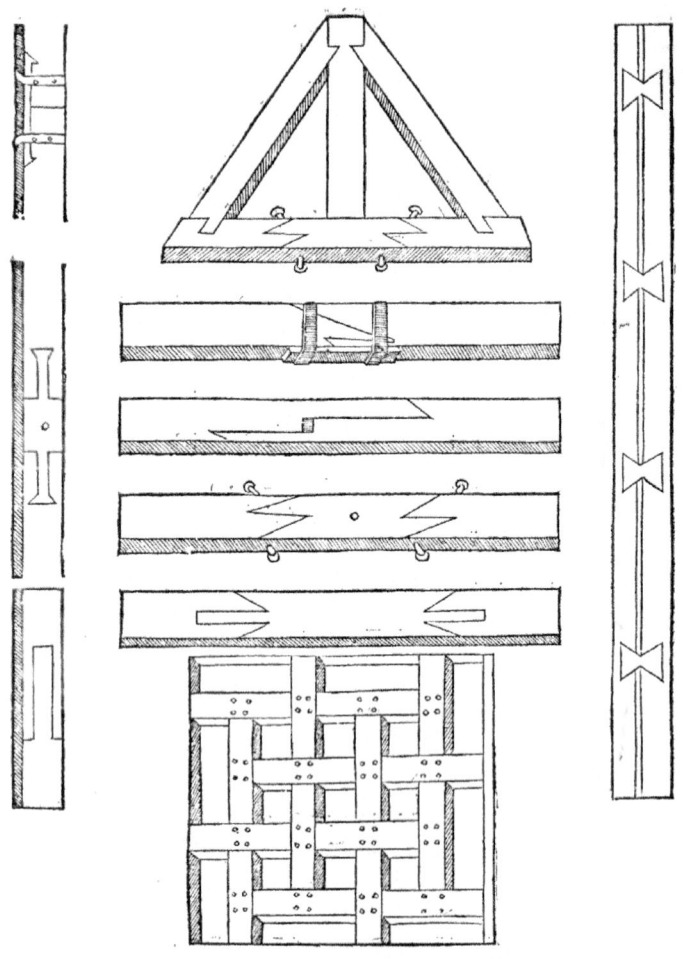

CHAPTER VIII.

OF THE ORGANISATION OF ALTARS

Circular temples are also constructed, of which some are monopteral, having columns without a cell; others are called peripteral. Those without a cell have a raised floor (tribunal), and an ascent thereto equal to one third of their diameter. On the pedestals (stylobatæ) columns are raised, whose height is equal to the diameter which the pedestal occupies, and their thickness, including the bases and capitals, one tenth part of their height. The height of the architrave is half a diameter; the frieze and members over it are to be proportioned according to the directions to that effect which have been given in the third book.

But if the building be peripteral, two steps, and then the pedestals are built thereunder; the wall of the cell is raised at a distance from the pedestals of about one fifth of the whole diameter, and in the middle is left an opening for the door. The clear diameter of the cell within the walls, is to be equal to the height of the columns above the pedestals. The columns round the cell are proportioned as above directed.

In the centre of the roof, the height of it is equal to half the diameter of the work, exclusive of the flower. The flower without the pyramid is to equal in dimensions the capitals of the columns. The other parts are to be similar in proportions and symmetry to those already described.

Other species of temples are also erected, regulated on the same principles, but with a different arrangement of parts, such as the temple of Castor in the Circus Flaminius, and of Beardless Jupiter (Vejovis), between the two groves. As also, though more ingeniously contrived, that of Diana Aricina, with columns on each flank of the pronaos. The first temples built similar to that of Castor in the Circus, were those of

Minerva on the Acropolis of Athens, and of Pallas at Sunihum in Attica, the proportions of which are similar. The length of the cells is double their breadth, and in other respects, those symmetries which are used in the fronts are preserved on the sides.

Others, with an arrangement of columns similar to that observed in Tuscan temples, transfer it to Corinthian and Ionic designs; for in some examples, instead of the antæ which run out from the pronaos, two columns are substituted, and thus Tuscan and Greek principles are mixed.

Others removing the walls of the cell, and placing them between the intercolumniations of the pteroma, give more space to the cell by their removal, and by preserving in other respects the same proportions and symmetry, seem to have invented another species which may be called pseudoperipteral. These different sorts of temples are dependent on the sacrifices performed in them; for temples to the gods are not all to be constructed in the same manner, the worship and sacred rites of each being different.

I have, according to the rules taught to me, explained the different principles on which temples are constructed, the different orders and symmetry of their detail, wherein and how they respectively differ; and this I have written to the best of my ability. I shall now describe the altars of the immortal gods, and their situation as adapted to sacrifices.

DE ARCHITECTURA

BOOK V

Civil Buildings

INTRODUCTION

Those, O Emperor, who at great length have explained their inventions and doctrines, have thereby given to their writings an extended and singular reputation. Would that such were the case with my labours, so that amplification might bring reputation with it. That, however, I believe is not probable, since a treatise on Architecture is not like History or Poetry. History interests the reader by the various novelties which occur in it; Poetry, on the other hand, by its metre, the feet of its verses, the elegant arrangement of the words, the dialogue introduced into it, and the distinct pronunciation of the lines, delighting the sense of the hearer, leads him to the close of the subject without fatigue.

This cannot be accomplished in Architectural works, because the terms, which are unavoidably technical, necessarily throw an obscurity over the subject. These terms, moreover, are not of themselves intelligible, nor in common use; hence if the precepts which are delivered by authors extend to any length, and are otherwise explained than in few and perspicuous expressions, the mind of the reader is bewildered by the quantity and frequent recurrence of them. These reasons induce me to be brief in the explanation of unknown terms, and of the symmetry of the parts of a work, because the matter may thereby be more easily committed to and retained by the memory.

I am moreover inclined to be concise when I reflect on the constant occupation of the citizens in public and private affairs, so that in their few leisure moments they may read and understand as much as possible. Pythagoras and his followers wrote the precepts of their doctrines in cubical arrangement, the cube containing two hundred and sixteen verses, of which they thought that not more than three should be allotted to any one precept.

A cube is a solid, with six equal square faces, which, however it falls, remains steady and immoveable till removed by force: such are the dice which are thrown on a table by gamesters. From this circumstance they seem to have adopted the cube, since like the cube, this number of verses makes a more lasting impression on the memory. The Greek comic poets have also divided the action of their stories, by the interposition of the chorus to ease the principal actors, so that a cubical proportion is observed.

Since the ancients therefore used these methods, founded on the observance of natural effects, seeing that the subject I treat of will be new and obscure to many, I thought it would be preferable to divide it into small portions, that it might more easily strike the understanding of the reader. The subjects also are so arranged, that those of the same nature are classed together. Thus, O Cæsar, I explained the proportions of temples in the third and fourth books; in this I intend to describe the arrangement of public buildings; and that of the forum first, because therein public no less than private affairs are regulated by the magistrates.

CHAPTER I.

OF THE FORUM AND BASILICA

The Greeks make their forum square, with a spacious and double portico, ornamenting it with columns placed at narrow intervals, and stone or marble epistylia, and forming walks above on the timber framed work. In the cities of Italy, however, this practice is not followed, because the ancient custom prevails of exhibiting the shows of gladiators in the forum.

Hence, for the convenience of the spectators, the intercolumniations must be wider; and the bankers' shops are situated in the surrounding porticos with apartments on the floors over them, which are constructed for the use of the parties, and as a depôt of the public revenue. The size of the forum is to be proportioned to the population of the place, so that it be not too small to contain the numbers it should hold, nor have the appearance of being too large, from a want of numbers to occupy it. The width is obtained by assigning to it two-thirds of its length, which gives it an oblong form, and makes it convenient for the purpose of the shows.

The upper columns are to be made one-fourth less than those below; and that because the latter being loaded with a weight, ought to be the stronger: because, also, we should follow the practice of nature, which, in straight growing trees, like the fir, cypress, and pine, makes the thickness at the root greater than it is at top, and preserves a gradual diminution throughout their height. Thus, following the example of nature, it is rightly ordered that bodies which are uppermost should be less than those below, both in respect of height and thickness.

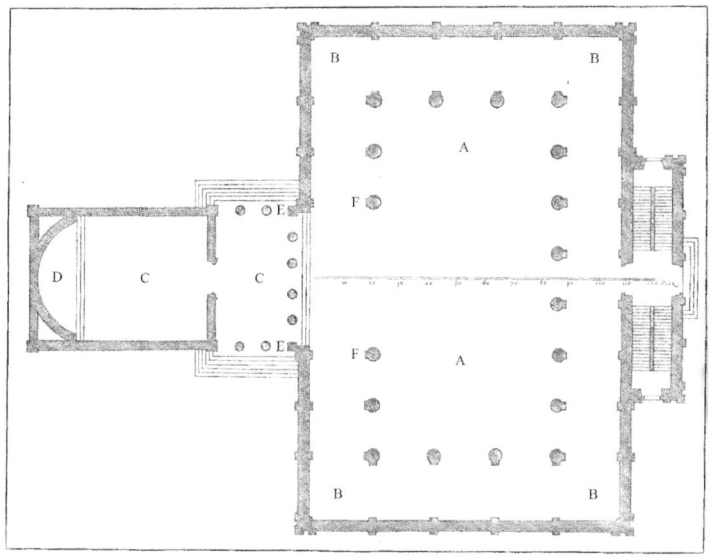

FANO BASILICA

A. NAVE B. WINGS C. AUGUSTUS TEMPLE D. TRIBUNAL E. ANTAE F. THIRD COLLUMNS

The basilica should be situated adjoining the forum, on the warmest side, so that the merchants may assemble there in winter, without being inconvenienced by the cold. Its width must not be less than a third part, nor more than half its length, unless the nature of the site prevent it, and impose a different proportion; if, however, that be longer than necessary, a chalcidicum is placed at the extremity, as in the Julian basilica on the Aquiline.

The columns of basilicæ are to be of a height equal to the breadth of the portico, and the width of the portico one-third of the space in the middle. The upper columns, as herein above described, are to be less than those below. The parapet between the upper columns should be made one-fourth less than those columns, so that those walking on the floor of the basilica may not be seen by the merchants. The proportions of the architrave, frieze, and cornice may be learnt from what has been said on columns in the third book.

Basilicæ, similar to that which I designed and carried into execution in the Julian colony of Fano, will not be deficient either in dignity or beauty. The proportions and symmetry of this are as follow. The middle vault, between the columns, is one hundred and twenty feet long, and sixty feet wide. The portico round it, between the walls and columns, is twenty feet wide. The height of the columns, including the capitals, is fifty feet, their thickness five feet, and they have pilasters behind them twenty feet high, two feet and a half wide, and one and a half thick, supporting beams which carry the floor of the portico. Above these, other pilasters are placed, eighteen feet high, two feet wide, and one foot thick, which also receive timbers for carrying the rafters of the portico, we roof is lower than the vault.

The spaces remaining between the beams, over the pilasters and the columns, are left open for light in the intercolumniations. The columns in the direction of the breadth of the vault are four in number, including those on the angles right and left; lengthwise, in which direction it joins the forum, the number is eight, including those at the angles; on the opposite side, including all the angular columns, there are six columns, because the two central ones on that side are omitted, so that the view of the pronaos of the temple of Augustus may not be obstructed: this is placed in the middle of the side wall of the basilica, facing the centre of the forum and the temple of Jupiter.

The tribunal is in the shape of a segment of a circle; the front dimension of which is forty-six feet, that of its depth fifteen feet; and is so contrived, that the merchants who are in the basilica may not interfere with those who have business before the magistrates. Over the columns round the building architraves are placed. These are triple, each of them two feet in size, and are fastened together. At the third column, on the inside, they return to the antæ of the pronaos, and are carried on to meet the segment on the right and left.

ELEVATION OF VITRUVIUS' BASILICA

A. BEAMS WHICH COMPOSE THE ARCHITRAVE B. PIER C.THIRD COLUMN AT THE INSIDE
K, D. ARCHITRAVES THAT START FROM THE THIRD COLUMNS TO THE TEMPLES ANTAE
E. RAFTER F. TIE BEAM G. STRUT

Over the architraves, upright with the capitals, piers are built three feet high and four feet square, on which are laid beams well wrought, joined together in two thicknesses of two feet each, and thereon the beams and rafters are placed over the columns, antæ, and walls of the pronaos, carrying one continued ridge along the basilica, and another from the centre thereof, over the pronaos of the temple.

Thus the two-fold direction of the roof gives an agreeable effect outside, and to the lofty vault within. Thus the omission of the cornices and parapets, and the upper range of columns, saves considerable labour, and greatly diminishes the cost of the work; and the columns in one height brought up to the architrave of the arch, give an appearance of magnificence and dignity to the building.

CHAPTER II.

OF THE TREASURY, PRISON AND CURIA

The treasury, prison, and curia are to adjoin the forum, to which their dimensions are to be proportionate. First of the curia, which must be suitable to the importance of the community or state. If square, its height is to be once and a half its width; but if oblong, the length and width must be added together, and one half of their sum assigned for the height up to the lacunaria.

The walls, moreover, at half their height, are to have cornices run round them of wood or plaster. For if such be not provided, the voices of the disputants meeting with no check in their ascent, will not be intelligible to the audience. But when the walls are encircled round with cornices, the voice, being thereby impeded, will reach the ear before its ascent and dissipation in the air.

CHAPTER III.

OF THE THEATRE, AND OF ITS HEALTHY SITUATION

When the forum is placed, a spot as healthy as possible is to be chosen for the theatre, for the exhibition of games on the festival days of the immortal gods, according to the instructions given in the first book respecting the healthy disposition of the walls of a city. For the spectators, with their wives and children, delighted with the entertainment, sit out the whole of the games, and the pores of their bodies being opened by the pleasure they enjoy, are easily affected by the air, which, if it blows from marshy or other noisome places, infuses its bad qualities into the system. These evils are avoided by the careful choice of a situation for the theatre, taking especial precaution that it be not exposed to the south; for when the sun fills the cavity of the theatre, the air confined in that compass being incapable of circulating, by its stoppage therein, is heated, and burns up, extracts, and diminishes the moisture of the body. On these accounts, those places where bad air abounds are to be avoided, and wholesome spots to be chosen.

The construction of the foundations will be more easily managed, if the work be on a hill; but if we are compelled to lay them on a plain, or in a marshy spot, the piling and foundations must be conducted as described for the foundations of temples in the third book. On the foundations, steps (gradationes) are raised, of stone and marble.

The number of passages (præcinctiones) must be regulated by the height of the theatre, and are not to be higher than their width, because if made higher, they will reflect and obstruct the voice in its passage upwards, so that it will not reach the upper seats above the passages (præcinctiones), and the last syllables of words will escape. In short, the building should be so contrived, that a line drawn from the first to the last step should touch the front angle of the tops of all the seats; in which case the voice meets with no impediment.

The entrances (aditus) should be numerous and spacious; those above ought to be unconnected with those below, in a continued line wherever they are, and without turnings; so that when the people are dismissed from the shows, they may not press on one another, but have separate outlets free from obstruction in all parts. A place which deadens the sound must be carefully avoided; but, on the contrary, one should be selected in which it traverses freely. This will be effected, if a place is chosen wherein there is no impediment to sound.

The voice arises from flowing breath, sensible to the hearing through its percussion on the air. It is propelled by an infinite number of circles similar to those generated in standing water when a stone is cast therein, which, increasing as they recede from the centre, extend to a great distance, if the narrowness of the place or some obstruction do not prevent their spreading to the extremity; for when impeded by obstructions, the first recoil affects all that follow.

In the same manner the voice spreads in a circular direction. But, whereas the circles in water only spread horizontally, the voice, on the contrary, extends vertically as well as horizontally. Wherefore, as is the case with the motion of water, so with the voice, if no obstacle disturb the first undulation, not only the second and following one, but all of them will, without reverberation, reach the ears of those at bottom and those at top.

On this account the ancient architects, following nature as their guide, and reflecting on the properties of the voice, regulated the true ascent of steps in a theatre, and contrived, by musical proportions and mathematical rules, whatever its effect might be on the stage (scena), to make it fall on the ears of the audience in a clear and agreeable manner. Since in brazen or horn wind instruments, by a regulation of the genus, their tones are rendered as clear as those of stringed instruments, so by the application of the laws of harmony, the ancients discovered a method of increasing the power of the voice in a theatre.

CHAPTER IV.

OF HARMONY

Harmony is an obscure and difficult musical science, but most difficult to those who are not acquainted with the Greek language; because it is necessary to use many Greek words to which there are none corresponding in Latin. I will therefore explain, to the best of my ability, the doctrine of Aristoxenus, and annex his diagram, and will so designate the place of each tone, that a person who studiously applies himself to the subject may very readily understand it.

The inflexion of the voice is two-fold; first, when it is monotonous, second, when it proceeds by intervals. The first is not limited by cadences at the close, nor in any other place; no perceptible difference of tone being discoverable between its beginning and its ending, the time between each sound is however distinctly marked, as in speaking, when we pronounce the words, sol, lux, flos, nox. Herein the ear does not perceive any difference of tone between the beginning and the ending, by the voice rising higher or descending lower; neither, that from a high pitch it becomes lower, nor the contrary. But when the voice moves by intervals, it is differently inflected, being sometimes at a high pitch, and sometimes at a low one, and ing at different times on different tones; by doing which with quickness and facility, it appears unfixed. Thus in singing, the variety of inflexion produces an air. In short, by the use of different intervals, the tones are so marked and determined, that we perceive the pitch at which it begins, and that at which it finishes, though the intermediate tones are not heard.

There are three sorts of modulation, the enharmonic (ἁρμονία), the chromatic (χρῶμα), and the diatonic (διάτονος), so called by the Greeks. The enharmonic is so constructed by art, as to be full of majesty and pathos. The chromatic by the skilful contrivance and closeness of its intervals has more sweetness. The diatonic, whose intervals are more simple, is most natural. The disposition of the tetrachords, in these genera, are dissimilar. The enharmonic tetrachord consists of two dieses, and two whole tones; a diesis being the fourth part of a tone, and two of them consequently equal to a semitone. In the chromatic tetrachord, there are two consecutive semitones, and the third interval contains three semitones. The diatonic tetrachord has two consecutive tones, and an interval of a semitone. Thus in each genus, the whole tetrachord is equal to two whole tones and a semitone. But the intervals in each genus, differ when considered separately.

For nature has made the divisions of tones, semitones, and tetrachords, and has established those proportions of the intervals, by which workmen are guided in making and assigning their just proportions to instruments.

Each genus consists of eighteen sounds, which the Greeks call φθόγγοι (phthongi). Of these, eight sounds in each of the genera, vary neither in sound nor situation. The remaining ten in each are not common to the other two genera. Those which do not vary, contain between them the variable sounds, and are the limits of the tetrachords in all the genera. Their names are as follow: proslambanomenos, hypatè hypatôn, hypatè mesôn, mesè, netè synèmmenôn, paramesè, netè diezeugmenôn, netè hyperbolæôn. The variable, which lie between those that are not variable, change their places according to the genus. Their names are parhypatè hypatôn, lichanos hypatôn, parhypatè mesôn, lichanos mesôn, tritè synèmmenôn, paranetè synèmmenôn, tritè diezeugmenôn, paranetè diezeugmenôn, tritè hyperbolæôn, paranetè hyperbolæôn.

Those sounds which shift their places, change also their nature, and are at different intervals, as, for instance, the interval between hypatè and parhypatè, which in the enharmonic genus is only a diesis or quarter tone, is in the chromatic genus a semitone. So the lichanos is only a semitone distant from the hypatè in the enharmonic genus; whereas in the chromatic it is two semitones distant, and in the diatonic three semitones. Thus, the ten sounds, by their situation in the different genera, make three different sorts of melody.

There are five tetrachords. The Greeks call the lowest ὕπατον (hypaton); the second, which is in the middle, μέσον (meson). The third, which is joined to the two preceding, is called συνημμένον (synèmmenon). The fourth, which is disjoined, called διεζευγμένον (diezeugmenon). The fifth, which is the highest, the Greeks call ὑπερβόλαιον (hyperbolæon). The natural consonances, which the Greeks call συμφωνίαι (symphoniæ), are six in number; diatessarôn (fourth), diapente (fifth), diapasôn (octave), diapasôn with diatessarôn(eleventh), diapasôn with diapente (twelfth), and disdiapasôn (fifteenth).

These names are given them from the number of tones which the voice passes through in going to them, counting that on which the voice begins as one; thus, moving through them to the fourth sound is called diatessarôn; to the fifth, diapente. to the eighth diapasôn, to the eleventh diapasôn with diatessarôn, to the twelfth diapasôn with diapente, to the fifteenth disdiapasôn.

For between two intervals, either in a melody sung by a voice, or played on a stringed instrument, neither with the third, sixth nor seventh can there be consonances, but only, as above shewn, with the diatessarôn and diapente up to the diapasôn do natural consonances arise, and those are produced by an union of those sounds which the Greeks call φθόγγοι (phthongi).

CHAPTER V.

OF THE VASES USED IN THE THEATRE

On the foregoing principles, the brazen vases are to be made with mathematical proportions, depending on the size of the theatre. They are formed so, as when struck, to have sounds, whose intervals are a fourth, fifth, and so on consecutively to a fifteenth. Then, between the seats of the theatre, cavities having been prepared, they are disposed therein in musical order, but so as not to touch the wall in any part, but to have a clear space round them and over their top: they are fixed in an inverted position, and on the side towards the scene are supported by wedges not less than half a foot high: and openings are left towards the cavities on the lower beds of the steps, each two feet long, and a half a foot wide.

The following is the rule for determining the situations of these vases. If the theatre be of moderate size they must be ranged round at half its height. Thirteen cavities are prepared at twelve equal distances from each other, so that those tones above-named, producing netè hyperbolæon, are to be placed in the cavities at the extreme ends; second, from the ends, the vessels are to be of the pitch of netè diezeugmenon, bearing an interval of one fourth from the last mentioned. The third netè paramesôn, an interval of another fourth. The fourth, netè synemmenôn, another fourth. The fifth, mesè, a fourth. The sixth, hypatè mesôn, a fourth: in the centre of the range, hypatè hypatôn, a fourth.

By the adoption of this plan, the voice which issues from the scene, expanding as from a centre, and striking against the cavity of each vase, will sound with increased clearness and harmony, from its unison with one or other of them. If, however, the theatre be on a larger scale, the height is to be divided into four parts, so that three ranges of cavities may be provided, one for harmonic, the second for chromatic, and the third for diatonic vases. That nearest the bottom is for the harmonic genus as above described, for a lesser theatre.

In the middle range on the extremities, vases producing the chromatic hyperbolæon are placed: in the second cavities the chromatic diezeugmenon, a fourth from the last: in the third, at another interval of a fourth, the chromatic synèmmenon: in the fourth, the chromatic meson, another fourth: in the fifth, the chromatic hypaton, another fourth: in the sixth, the paramesè, which is a fifth to the chromatic hyperbolæon, and a fourth to the chromatic meson.

In the centre none are to be placed, because no other sound in the chromatic genus can be in consonance therewith. In the upper division and range of the cavities, the vases on the extremities are constructed to produce the tones of the diatonic hyperbolæon: in the next cavities, those of the diatonic diezeugmenon, a fourth: in the third, of the diatonic synèmmenon, a fourth: in the fourth, of the diatonic meson, a fourth: in the fifth, of the diatonic hypaton, a fourth: in the sixth, proslambanomenos, a fourth: in the centre, mesè, between which and proslambanomenos is an octave, and a fifth between it and the diatonic hypaton.

He who is desirous of more fully understanding these matters, must refer to the musical diagram at the end of the book, which is that left to us by Aristoxenes, who with much intelligence and labour, formed a general scale of the tones. Hence, he who carefully attends to these rules, to the nature of the voice, and to the taste of the audience, will easily learn the method of designing theatres with the greatest perfection.

Some one may perchance urge, that many theatres are yearly built in Rome, without any regard to these matters. But let him not be herein mistaken, inasmuch as all public theatres which are constructed of wood, have many floors, which are necessarily conductors of sound. This circumstance may be illustrated, by consideration of the practice of those that sing to the harp, who when they wish to produce a loud effect, turn themselves to the doors of the scene, by the aid of which their voice is thrown out. But when theatres are constructed of solid materials, that is of rubble, squared stones or marble, which are not conductors of sound, it is necessary to build them according to the rules in question.

If it be asked what theatre in Rome can be referred to as an example of their utility, we cannot produce one, but such may be seen in some of the provinces of Italy, and many in the Grecian States. We moreover know that L. Mummius on the destruction of the theatre at Corinth, brought to Rome some of its brazen vases, and dedicated them as spoils at the temple of Luna. Many clever architects who have built theatres in small cities, from the want of other, have made use of earthen vessels, yielding the proper tones, and have introduced them with considerable advantage.

CHAPTER VI.

OF THE SHAPE OF THE THEATRE

The form of a theatre is to be adjusted so, that from the centre of the dimension allotted to the base of the perimeter a circle is to be described, in which are inscribed four equilateral triangles, at equal distances from each other, whose points are to touch the circumference of the circle. This is the method also practiced by astrologers in describing the twelve celestial signs, according to the musical division of the constellations. Of these triangles, the side of that which is nearest the scene will determine the face thereof in that part where it cuts the circumference of the circle. Then through the centre a line is drawn parallel to it, which will separate the pulpitum of the pros from the orchestra.

Thus the pulpitum will be more spacious than that of the Greeks, and be the better, on account of our actors remaining chiefly on the scena. In the orchestra, seats are assigned to the senators, and the height of its pulpitum must not exceed five feet, so that those who sit in the orchestra may be enabled to see all the motions of the actors. The portions between the staircases (cunei) of the theatre are so divided that the angles of the triangles, which touch the circumference, point to the directions of the ascents and steps between the cunei, on the first præcinction or story. Above these the steps are placed alternately, and form the upper cunei in the middle of those below.

The angles thus pointing to staircases will be seven in number, the remaining five will mark certain points on the PU. That in the middle, for instance, will mark the situation of the royal doors, those on the right and left, the doors of guests, and those at the extremities, the points at which the road turns off. The seats (gradus) on which the spectators sit are not to be less than twenty inches in height, nor more than twenty-two. Their width must not be more than two feet and a half, nor less than two feet.

CHAPTER VII.

OF THE PORTICO AND OTHER PARTS OF THE THEATRE

The roof of the portico, which is on the last step, should be on a level with the top of the scene; by which arrangement the voice will extend and be distinct to those on the upper seats and roof. For if it be not equally high, where that height is deficient, the voice, first striking thereon, will be stopped.

One sixth part of the diameter of the orchestra is taken between the lowest steps, and level with that dimension the lower seats are disposed. A continuation of this line on the scene marks the height of the entrances: for thus proportioned, they will be of sufficient altitude.

The length of the scene must be double the diameter of the orchestra. The height of the podium, or pedestal, with its cornice and base, from the level of the pulpitum, is a twelfth part of the diameter of the orchestra. The columns on the podium, with their capitals and bases, are to be one-fourth of its diameter high. The architraves and cornices of those columns one-fifth of their height. The upper pedestal, including the base and cornice, half the height of the lower pedestal. The columns on this pedestal one-fourth less in height than the lower columns. The architrave and its cornice a fifth of the columns. If there is to be a third order, the upper pedestal is to be half the height of that under the middle order, and the architrave and cornice a fifth of the columns.

It is not, however, possible to produce the same effect in every theatre by the same proportions; but it behoves the architect to consider the proportions which symmetry requires, and those adapted to the nature of the place or the size of the work. Some things there are which their use re-

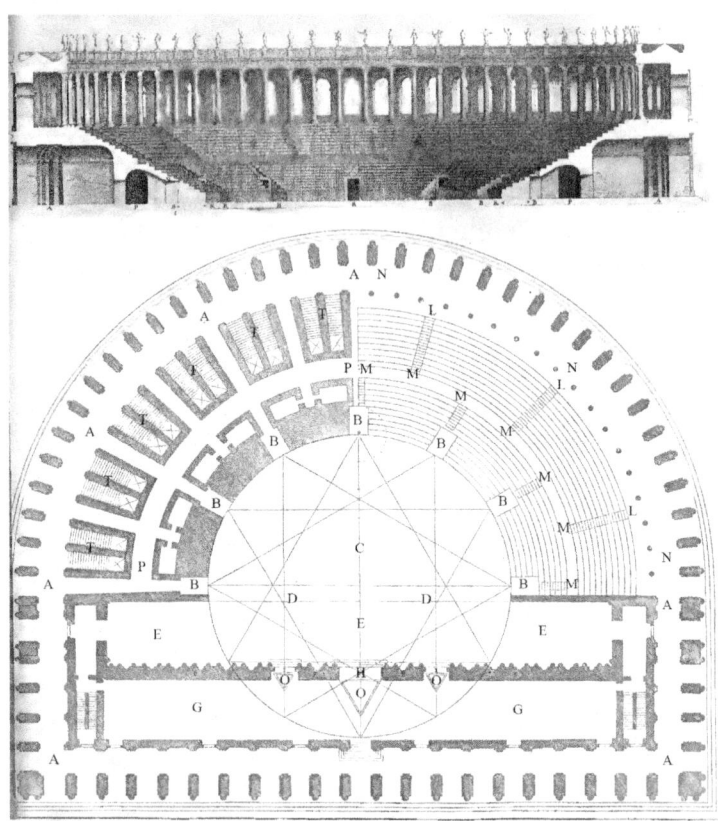

A. PORTICO B. PASSAGES TO ENTER THE ORCHESTRA DCD C. MIDDLE OF THE ORCHESTRA
D. BOUNDARY OF THE PROSCENIUM E. PROSCENIUM / PULPITUM
DI. WIDTH OF THE PROSCENIUM F. FRONT OF THE SCENE G. POSTSCENIUM H. ROYAL DOOR
I. GUEST DOOR LM. STAIRS MB. STAIRS N. ROOF OF THE PORTICO
O. TURNING TRIANGULAR MACHINES P. PASSAGES T. STAIRS OF THE PORTICO ROOF

quires of the same size in a large as in a small theatre; such as the steps, præcinctions, parapets, passages, stairs, pulpita, tribunals, and others which occur; in all which, the necessity of suiting them to their use, makes it impossible to form them symmetrically. So, also, if the materials are not provided in sufficient quantity, such as marble, wood, and the like, the diminution of or addition to the dimensions, so that it be not too much, and made with judgment, may be permitted: and this will be easily managed by an architect who is a man of experience, and who possesses ingenuity and talent.

The parts of the scene are to be so distributed, that the middle door may be decorated as one of a royal palace; those on the right and left, as the doors of the guests. Near these are the spaces destined to receive the decorations; which places the Greeks call περιάκτοι, from the turning triangular machines. Each of these machines has three species of decoration, which, when the subject changes, or on the appearance of a god, are moved round with sudden claps of thunder, and alter the appearance of the decoration. Near these places the turnings run out, which give entrance to the scene from the forum and from the country.

CHAPTER VIII.

OF THE THREE SORTS OF SCENES, AND OF THE THEATRES OF THE GREEKS

There are three sorts of scenes, the Tragic, the Comic, and the Satyric. The decorations of these are different from each other. The tragic scenes are ornamented with columns, pediments, statues, and other royal decorations. The comic scene represents private buildings and galleries, with windows similar to those in ordinary dwellings. The satyric scene is ornamented with trees, caves, hills, and other rural objects in imitation of nature.

In the theatres of the Greeks the design is not made on the same principles as those above mentioned. First, as to the general outline of the plan: whereas, in the Latin theatre, the points of four triangles touch the circumference, in the theatres of the Greeks the angles of three squares are substituted, and the side of that square which is nearest to the place of the scene, at the points where it touches the circumference of the circle, is the boundary of the proscenium. A line drawn parallel to this at the extremity of the circle, will give the front of the scene. Through the centre of the orchestra, opposite to the proscenium, another parallel line is drawn touching the circumference on the right and left, then one foot of the compasses being fixed on the right hand point, with a radius equal to the distance from the left point, describe a circle on the right hand side of the proscenium, and placing the foot of the compasses on the left hand point, with the distance of the right hand interval, describe another circle on the left side of the proscenium.

Thus describing it from three centres, the Greeks have a larger orchestra, and their scene is further recessed. The pulpitum, which they call λογεῖον, is less in width: wherefore, among them, the tragic and comic performers act upon the scene; the rest going through their parts in the orchestra. Hence the performers are distinguished by the names of Scenici and Thymelici. The height of the pulpitum is not less than ten feet, nor more than twelve. The directions of the stairs, between the cunei and seats, are opposite to the angles of the squares on the first præcinction. Above it the other stairs fall in the middle between the lower ones, and so on according to the number of præcinctions.

When these matters are arranged with great care and skill, particular attention must be bestowed on the choice of a place where the voice falls smoothly, and reaches the ear distinctly without an echo. Some places are naturally unfavourable to the diffusion of the voice. Such are the dissonant, which in Greek are called κατηχοῦντες; the circumsonant, which the Greeks call περιηχοῦντες; the resonant, which they call ἀντηχοῦντες; and the consonant, which they call συνηχοῦντες. The dissonant places are those in which the voice, rising first upwards, is obstructed by some hard bodies above, and, in its return downwards, checks the ascent of its following sounds.

The circumsonant are those where the voice, wandering round, is at last retained in the centre, where it is dissipated, and, the final syllables being lost, the meaning of words is not distinguished. The resonant are those in which the voice, striking against some hard body, is echoed in the last syllables so that they appear doubled. Lastly, the consonant are those in which the voice, aided by something below, falls on the ear with great distinctness of words. Hence, if due care be taken in the choice of the situation, the effect of the voice will be improved, and the utility of the theatre increased. The differences of the figures consist in this, that those formed by means of squares are used by the Greeks, and those formed by means of triangles by the Latins. He who attends to these precepts will be enabled to erect a theatre in a perfect manner.

CHAPTER IX.

OF THE PORTICOS AND PASSAGES BEHIND THE SCENES

Behind the scenes porticos are to be built; to which, in case of sudden showers, the people may retreat from the theatre, and also sufficiently capacious for the rehearsals of the chorus: such are the porticos of Pompey, of Eumenes at Athens, and of the temple of Bacchus; and on the left passing from the theatre, is the Odeum, which, in Athens, Pericles ornamented with stone columns, and with the masts and yards of ships, from the Persian spoils. This was destroyed by fire in the Mithridatic war, and restored by king Ariobarzanes. At Smyrna was the Strategeum: at Tralles were porticos on each side over the stadium, as in the scenes of theatres. In short, in all cities which possess skilful architects, porticos and walks are placed about the theatre, which ought to be constructed double, with their exterior columns of the Doric order, whose architraves, and cornices are to be wrought after the Doric method. Their width is to be thus proportioned: the height of the exterior columns is equal to the distance from the lower part of the shaft of the exterior columns to that of those in the middle, and from them to the walls which surround the walks of the portico is an equal distance. The middle range of columns is one fifth part higher than the exterior range; and is of the Ionic or Corinthian order.

The proportions and symmetry of these columns are not to be guided by the rules delivered for those of sacred buildings. For the style used in the temples of the gods should be dignified; whereas, in porticos and similar works, it may be of a lighter character. If, therefore, the columns be of the Doric order, their height, including the capitals, is to be divided into fifteen parts, of which one is taken as a module. By this all the work is set out, making the thickness of the lower part of the column equal to two modules. The intercolumniation is of five modules and a half. The height of a column, exclusive of the capital, fourteen modules; the height of the capital one module, the width of it two modules and a sixth. The proportions of the rest of the work are to be the same as those described for sacred buildings in the fourth book.

If Ionic columns be used, the shaft, exclusive of the base and capital, is to be divided into eight parts and a half, of which one is assigned to the thickness of the column. The base, with its plinth, is half a module high; and the formation of the capital is to be as shewn in the third book. If Corinthian, the shaft and base are to be the same as the Ionic; but the capital is to be proportioned as directed in the fourth book; and the addition on the pedestal is made by means of the scamilli impares, mentioned in the third book. The architraves, coronæ, and all the other parts, are set out in proportion to the columns as explained in the foregoing books.

The central space between the porticos should be ornamented with verdure, inasmuch as hypæthral walks are very healthy; first, in respect of the eyes, because the air from green plants being light and volatile, insinuates itself into the body when in motion, clears the sight, and, removing the gross humours from the eyes, leaves the vision clear and distinct. Moreover, when the body is heated by the exercise of walking, the air, extracting its humours, diminishes corpulency, dissipating that which is superabundant in the body.

That this is the case, may be proved by observing, that from fountains in covered places, or those which are under ground, no moist vapours rise; whilst in open places exposed to the air, when the rising sun darts his rays upon the earth, he raises the vapours from humid and marshy places, and, gathering them into masses, carries them into the air. If, therefore, in open places, the noxious humours of bodies are

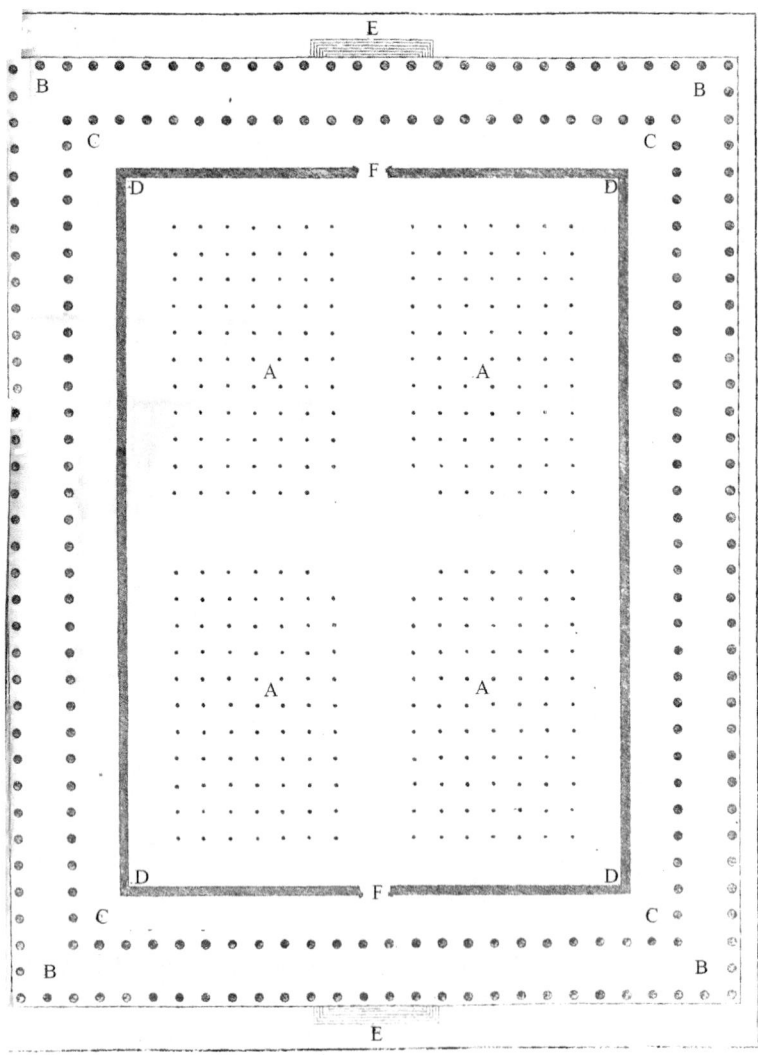

PLAN OF PASSAGES AND PORTICOS BEHIND THE THEATER SCENES
A. PASSAGE **B.** OUTER PORTICO **C.** INNER PORTICO
D. SURROUNDING PASSAGE WALLS **E.** PORCH **F.** DOOR

carried off by the air, as they are from the earth by means of clouds, there can be no doubt of the necessity of making spacious and pleasant walks open to the air in every city.

That they may always be dry and free from mud, the following method must be adopted. They must be dug out and drained to the lowest possible level; and on the right and left sewers must be constructed; and in the walls thereof, towards the walk, drains are laid, with an inclination to the sewer. When this is done, the place is filled in with coals; over which the walks are strewed with gravel, and levelled. Thus, from the natural porosity of the coals, and the inclination of the drains towards the sewer, the quantity of water is carried off, and the Vs remain dry and unaffected by the moisture.

In these places the ancients also made depôts for the reception of things necessary for the use of the city. For in case of the city being under blockade, all things are more easily provided than wood. Salt is with facility laid in beforehand; corn, from the public or private stores, is soon collected; and the want of that is remedied by the use of garden herbs, flesh, or pulse. Water is obtained either by digging new wells, or by collecting it from the roofs of buildings; but wood, which is absolutely necessary for cooking the food, is provided with difficulty and trouble; and that which is slowly procured is quickly consumed.

In such times these walks are opened, and an allowance distributed to the tribes, according to their numbers. Thus they are conducive to two good purposes; to health in time of peace, and to preservation in time of war. If walks are provided after these directions not only behind the scene of the theatre, but also adjoining the temples of all the gods, they will be of great utility in every city. As they have been sufficiently explained, the method of arranging the different parts of baths will now follow.

CHAPTER X.

OF THE ARRANGEMENT AND PARTS OF BATHS

First, as warm a spot as possible is to be selected, that is to say, one sheltered from the north and north-east. The hot and tepid baths are to receive their light from the winter west; but, if the nature of the place prevent that, at all events from the south, because the hours of bathing are principally from noon to evening. Care must be taken that the warm baths of the women and men adjoin, and have the same aspect; in which case the same furnace and vessels will serve both. The caldrons over the furnaces are to be three in number, one for hot water, another for tepid water, and a third for cold water: and they must be so arranged, that the hot water which runs out of the heated vessel, may be replaced by an equal quantity from the tepid vessel, which in like manner is supplied from the cold vessel, and that the arched cavities in which they stand may be heated by one fire.

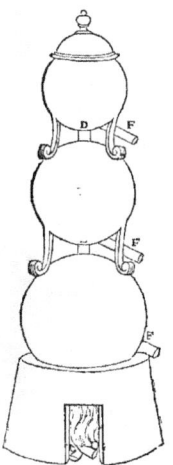
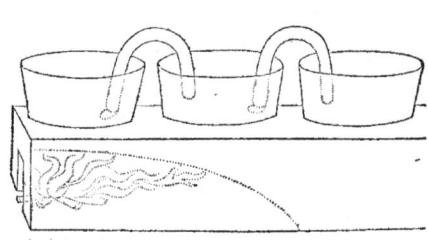

The floors of the hot baths are to be made as follows. First, the bottom is paved with tiles of a foot and a half inclining towards the furnace, so that if a ball be thrown into it, it will not remain therein, but roll back to the mouth of the furnace; thus the flame will better spread under the floor. Upon this, piers of eight inch bricks are raised, at such a distance from each other, that tiles of two feet may form their covering. The piers are to be two feet in height, and are to be laid in clay mixed with hair, on which the above-mentioned two feet tiles are placed, which carry the pavement.

The ceilings, if of masonry, will be preferable; if, however, they are of timber, they should be plastered on the under side, which must be done as follows. Iron rods, or arcs, are prepared and suspended by iron hooks to the floor as close as possible. These rods or arcs are at such distances from each other, that tiles, without knees, may rest on and be borne by every two ranges, and thus the whole vaulting depending on the iron may be perfected. The upper parts of the joints are stopped with clay and hair. The under side towards the pavement is first plastered with pounded tiles and lime, and then finished with stucco or fine plastering. If the vaulting of hot baths is made double it will be better, because the moisture of the steam cannot then affect the timber, but will be condensed between the two arches.

The size of baths must depend on the number of persons who frequent them. Their proportions are as follow: their width is to be two thirds of their length, exclusive of the space round the bathing vessel (schola labri) and the gutter round it (alveus). The bathing vessel (labrum) should be lighted from above, so that the bye standers may not cast any shadow thereon, and thereby obstruct the light. The schola labri ought to be spacious, so that those who are waiting for their turn may be properly accommodated. The width of the alveus between the wall of the labrum and the parapet must not be less than six feet, so that it may be

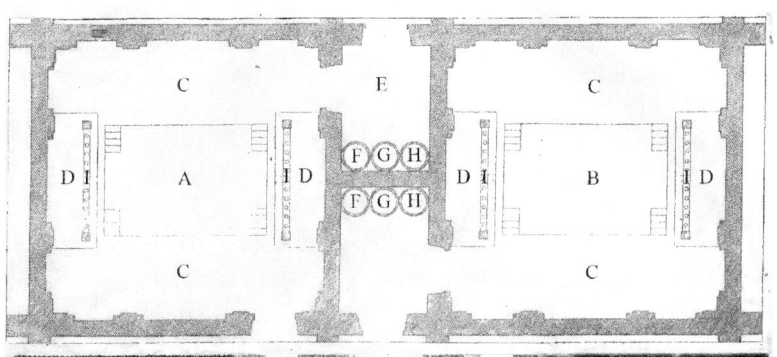

PLAN OF THE ANCIENT BATHS
A. MEN BATHS **B.** WOMEN BATHS **C.** RESTING ROOM **D.** CORRIDORS
E. VASE ROOM **F.** HOT WATER VASE **G.** MILD WATER VASE
H. COLD WATER VASE **I.** ARMREST

commodious after the reduction of two feet, which are allotted to the lower step and the cushion.

The laconicum and sudatories are to adjoin the tepid apartment, and their height to the springing of the curve of the hemisphere is to be equal to their width. An opening is left in the middle of the dome from which a brazen shield is suspended by chains, capable of being so lowered and raised as to regulate the temperature. It should be circular, that the intensity of the flame and heat may be equally diffused from the centre throughout.

CHAPTER XI.

OF THE PALÆSTRA

Though not used by the people of Italy, it seems proper that I should explain the form of the palæstra, and describe the mode in which it was constructed by the Greeks. The square or oblong peristylia of palestræ, have a walk round them which the Greeks call δίαυλος, two stadia in circuit: three of the sides are single porticos: the fourth, which is that on the south side, is to be double, so that when showers fall in windy weather, the drops may not drive into the inner part of it.

In the three porticos are large recesses (exedræ) with seats therein, whereon the philosophers, rhetoricians, and others who delight in study, may sit and dispute. In the double portico the following provision is to be made: the ephebeum is to be in the middle, which is in truth nothing more than a large exedra with seats, and longer by one third than its width, on the right is the coriceum, immediately adjoining which is the conisterium, near which, in the angle of the portico, is the cold bath, which the Greeks call λουτρόν. On the left of the ephebeum is the elæothesium, adjoining that is the frigidarium, whence a passage leads to the propigneum in the angle of the portico. Near, but more inward, on the side of the frigidarium, is placed the vaulted sudatory, whose length is double its width; on one side of this is the laconicum, constructed as before described: on the other side is the hot bath.

The peristylia of the palæstra are to be carefully set out as above mentioned. Exteriorly three porticos are constructed, one through which those who come out of the palæstra pass; and stadial ones on the right and left, of which, that towards the north is double, and of considerable width. The other is single, and so formed that as well on the side next the wall, as on that where the columns stand, there are margins for paths of not less than ten feet, the centre part is sunk one foot and a half from the path, to which there is an ascent of two steps; the sunken part is not to be less than twelve feet in width. Thus, those who in their clothing walk round the paths, will not be incommoded by the anointed wrestlers who are practising.

This species of portico is called xystus (ξυστὸς) by the Greeks; for the wrestlers exercise in covered stadia in the winter time. Xysti ought, between the two porticos, to have groves or plantations, with walks between the trees and seat of cemented work. On the sides of the xystus and double portico are open walks which the Greeks call περιδρόμιδες, but with us they are termed xysti, on which the athletæ exercise themselves, when the weather is fine, in the winter. Behind the xystus the stadium is set out, of such dimensions that a great number of people may commodiously behold the contending wrestlers. I have now given rules for the proper distribution of such buildings as are within the walls.

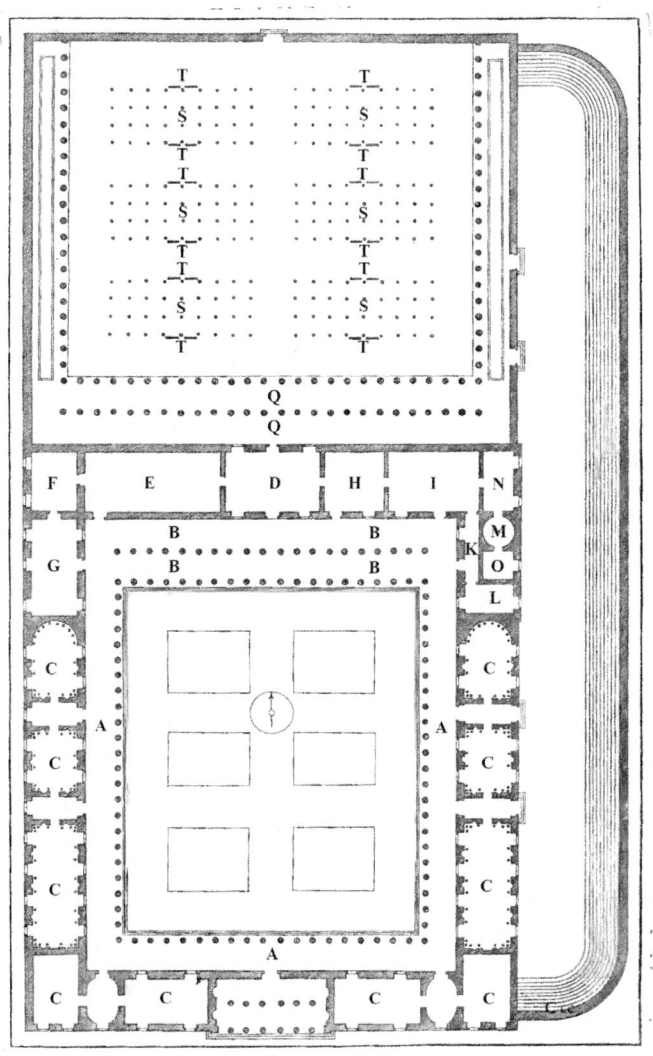

PLAN OF THE PALÆSTRA

A. SIMPLE PORTICO **B.** DOUBLE PORTICO **C.** RECESSES **D.** EPHEBEUM
E. CORICEUM **F.** CONISTERIUM **G.** COLD BATH **H.** ELÆOTHESIUM
I. FRIGIDARIUM **K.** PASSAGE **L.** PROPIGNEUM **M.** LACONICUM
N. STOVE **O.** WARM BATH **Q.** DOUBLE PORTICO **S.** TREES
T. CEMENTED SEATS

CHAPTER XII.

OF HARBOURS AND OTHER BUILDINGS IN WATER

I must not omit to speak of the formation of harbours, but explain in what manner ships are secured therein in stormy weather. If they are naturally well situated, and have rocks or long promontories jutting out, which from the shape of the place, form curves or angles, they are of the greatest utility; because, in that case, nothing more is necessary than to construct porticos and arsenals round them, or passages to the markets; and then erect a tower on each side, wherefrom chains may be suspended across by means of machinery.

But, if the place be not thus fitted by nature, nor secure for ships in stormy weather, and there be no river there to prevent it, but on one side there is a proper shore, then on the other side, by means of building or heaps of stones, a projection is run out, and in this the enclosures of harbours are formed. Building in the sea is thus executed. That powder is procured, which is found in the country between Cumæ and the promontory of Minerva, and is mixed with the water in the proportion of two parts thereof to one of lime.

Then, in the place selected, dams are formed in the water, of oaken piles tied together with chain pieces, which are driven firmly into the bottom. Between the ranges of piles, below the level of the water, the bed is dug out and levelled, and the work carried up with stones and mortar, compounded as above directed, till the wall fills the vacant space of the dam. If, however, from the violence of the waves and open sea the dams cannot be kept together, then on the edge of the main land, a foundation for a wall is constructed of the greatest possible strength; this foundation is laid horizontally, throughout rather less than half its length; the remainder, which is towards the shore, is made to overhang.

Then, on the side towards the water, and on the flanks round the foundation, margins, projecting a foot and a half, are brought up to the level already mentioned. The overhanging part is filled up underneath with sand, brought up level with the foundation. On the level bed thus prepared, as large a pier as possible is built, which must remain for at least two months to set. The margin which incloses the sand is then removed, and the sand being washed away by the action of the waves causes the fall of the mass into the sea, and by a repetition of this expedient the work may be carried forward into the sea.

When the place does not afford the powder named, the following method is to be adopted. Double dams are constructed, well connected with planks and chain pieces, and the cavity between them is filled up with clay and marsh weeds well rammed down. When rammed down and squeezed as close as possible, the water is emptied out with screw pumps or water wheels, and the place is emptied and dried, and the foundations excavated. If the bottom be of loose texture, it must be dug out till a solid bottom is come to, wider than the wall about to be erected, and the wall is then built of stone, lime, and sand.

But if the bottom be very soft, alder, olive, or oak piles, previously charred, must be driven, and the intervals between them filled with coals, as directed above for the foundations of theatres and walls. The wall is then raised with squared stones, the joints of which are to be as long as possible, in order that the middle stones may be well tied in. The inside of the wall is then filled with rubble or masonry; and on this, even a tower might be erected.

When this is completed, the arsenals are to be constructed chiefly with a northern aspect; for if they are to the south, the heat will generate and nourish the rot, the worm, the ship worm, and other noxious insects; and timber should be sparingly used in these buildings on account of fire. No rule can be given for the size, but they must be suited to receive the largest ships, so that, if drawn ashore, there may be plenty of room for them. In this book, as far as it has occurred to me, I have treated of the public buildings necessary for the use of a city: in that following, I shall treat of the convenience and symmetry of private houses.

DE ARCHITECTURA

BOOK VI

Domestic buildings

INTRODUCTION

Aristippus, the Socratic philosopher, shipwrecked on the coast of Rhodes, perceiving some geometrical diagrams thereon, is reported to have exclaimed to his companions, "Be of good courage, I see marks of civilization:" and straightway making for the city of Rhodes, he arrived at the Gymnasium; where, disputing on philosophical subjects, he obtained such honours, that he not only provided for himself, but furnished clothing and food to his companions. When his companions had completed their arrangements for returning home, and asked what message he wished to send to his friends, he desired them to say: that the possessions and provision to be made for children should be those which can be preserved in case of shipwreck; inasmuch as those things are the real supports of life which the chances of fortune, the changes of public affairs, and the devastation of war, cannot injure. Thus, also, Theophrastus, following up the sentiment that the learned ought to be more honoured than the rich, says, "that the learned man is the only person who is not a stranger in foreign countries, nor friendless when he has lost his relations; but that in every state he is a citizen, and that he can look upon a change of fortune without fear. But he who thinks himself secured by the aid of wealth, and not of learning, treads on slippery ground, and leads an unstable and insecure life."
Epicurus also says, that fortune is of little assistance to the wise, since all that is of consequence or necessary may be obtained by the exercise of the mind and understanding. The poets, not less than the philosophers, have argued in this way; and those who formerly wrote the Greek comedies delivered the same sentiments in verse; as Euchrates, Chionides, Aristophanes, and, above all, Alexis, who said, that the Athenians deserved particular commendation, since, inasmuch as the laws of all the Greeks make it imper-

ative on children to support their parents, those of the Athenians are only obligatory on those children who have been instructed, by the care of their parents, in some art. Such as possess the gifts of fortune are easily deprived of them: but when learning is once fixed in the mind, no age removes it, nor is its stability affected during the whole course of life.

I therefore feel myself under infinite obligations, and am grateful to my parents, who, adopting the practice of the Athenians, took care that I should be taught an art, and one of such a nature that it cannot be practised without learning and a general knowledge of the sciences. Since, then, by my parents' care, and by the instruction of masters, I had the means afforded me of acquiring knowledge, and was naturally delighted with literary and philosophical subjects, I laid up those stores in my mind, from the use of which I enjoy the advantage of wanting no more, and the value of riches consists in having nothing to wish for. But some thinking, perhaps, lightly of these things, suppose those only are wise who have plenty of money. Hence, many, aiming at that end alone, have, by the aid of their assurance, acquired notoriety from their riches.

But I, Cæsar, have not sought to amass wealth by the practice of my art, having been rather contented with a small fortune and reputation, than desirous of abundance accompanied by a want of reputation. It is true that I have acquired but little; yet I still hope, by this publication, to become known to posterity. Neither is it wonderful that I am known but to a few. Other architects canvass, and go about soliciting employment, but my preceptors instilled into me a sense of the propriety of being requested, and not of requesting, to be entrusted, inasmuch the ingenuous man will blush and feel shame in asking a favour; for the givers of a favour and not the receivers, are courted. What must he suspect who is solicited by another to be entrusted with the expenditure of his money, but that it is done for the sake of gain and emolument.

Hence the ancients entrusted their works to those architects only who were of good family and well brought up; thinking it better to trust the modest, than the bold and arrogant, man. These artists only instructed their own children or relations, having regard to their integrity, so that property might be safely committed to their charge. When, therefore, I see this noble science in the hands of the unlearned and unskilful, of men not only ignorant of architecture, but of every thing relative to buildings, I cannot blame proprietors, who, relying on their own intelligence, are their own architects; since, if the business is to be conducted by the unskilful, there is at least more satisfaction in laying out money at one's own pleasure, rather than at that of another person.

No one thinks of practising at home any art (as that of a shoemaker or fuller, for instance, or others yet easier) except that of an architect; and that because many who profess the art are not really skilled in it, but are falsely called architects. These things have induced me to compose a treatise on architecture and its principles, under an idea that it would be acceptable to all persons. As in the fifth book I treated on the construction of public works, I shall in this explain the arrangement and symmetry of private buildings.

CHAPTER I.

OF THE SITUATION OF BUILDINGS ACCORDING TO THE NATURE OF DIFFERENT PLACES

These are properly designed, when due regard is had to the country and climate in which they are erected. For the method of building which is suited to Egypt would be very improper in Spain, and that in use in Pontus would be absurd at Rome: so in other parts of the world a style suitable to one climate, would be very unsuitable to another; for one part of the world is under the sun's course, another is distant from it, and another, between the two, is temperate. Since, therefore, from the position of the heaven in respect of the earth, from the inclination of the zodiac and from the sun's course, the earth varies in temperature in different parts, so the form of buildings must be varied according to the temperature of the place, and the various aspects of the heavens.
In the north, buildings should be arched, enclosed as much as possible, and not exposed, and it seems proper that they should face the warmer aspects. Those under the sun's course in southern countries where the heat is oppressive, should be exposed and turned towards the north and east. Thus the injury which nature would effect, is evaded by means of art. So, in other parts, due allowance is to be made, having regard to their position, in respect of the heavens.
This, however, is determined by consideration of the nature of the place and observations made on the limbs and bodies of the inhabitants. For where the sun acts with moderate heat, it keeps the body at a temperate warmth, where it is hot from the proximity of the sun, all moisture is dried up: lastly, in cold countries which are distant from the south, the moisture is not drawn out by the heat, but the dewy air, insinuating its dampness into the system, increases the size of

the body, and makes the voice more grave. This is the reason why the people of the north are so large in stature, so light in complexion, and have straight red hair, blue eyes, and are full of blood, for they are thus formed by the abundance of the moisture, and the coldness of their country.

Those who live near the equator, and are exactly under the sun's course, are, owing to its power, low in stature, of dark complexion, with curling hair, black eyes, weak legs, deficient in quantity of blood. And this deficiency of blood makes them timid when opposed in battle, but they bear excessive heat and fevers without fear, because their limbs are nourished by heat. Those, however, born in northern countries are timid and weak when attacked by fever, but from their sanguineous habit of body more courageous in battle.

The pitch of the voice is various, and of different qualities in different nations. For the eastern and western boundaries round the level of the earth, where the upper is divided from the under part of the world, and the earth appears to be balanced by nature, are designated by a circle which mathematicians call the horizon; keeping this circumstance in mind, from the edge on the northern extremity, let a line be drawn to that above the southern axis, and therefrom another in an oblique direction up to the pole near the northern stars, and we shall immediately perceive the principle of the triangular instrument called by the Greeks σαμβύκη.

Thus the people who live in the region near the lower point, that is in the southern part towards the equator, from the small elevation of the pole have shrill and high toned voices similar to those on the instrument near the angle; next come those whose tone of voice is of lower pitch, such as the people in the central parts of Greece. Thus, proceeding by degrees from the middle to the northern extremity, the voice of the inhabitants gradually becomes of lower pitch. Herein we may perceive how the system of the world is harmonically arranged, by the obliquity of the zodiac from the appropriate temperature of the sun.

Hence those who are in the middle, between the equator and the pole, are gifted with a middle pitch of voice, similar to the tones in the central part of the musical diagram. Advancing to the northern nations, where the pole is more elevated, the people, from an increased quantity of moisture, naturally possess lower toned voices, similar to the hypatè and the proslambanomenos. And finally, those nations extending from the middle regions to the south have shrill and acute voices similar to the tones of paranetè and netè.

That the tone of the voice is rendered deeper by the damp nature of a place, and higher by its being of a hot nature, may be proved by the following experiment. Let two vases be selected, both equally baked in a furnace, of equal weight, and yielding the same tone, and one of them be immersed in water and then taken out: let both of them be then struck, and a great difference will be perceived in the tones they yield, as well as an inequality in their weight. Thus it is with the human body; for although all men are born of the same form, and under the same heaven, yet some from the warmth of the climate are shrill in voice, and others from a superabundance of moisture have a low tone of voice.

So moreover, from the clearness of the atmosphere, aided also by the intense heat, the southern nations are more ready and quick in expedients: but the northern nations, oppressed by a gross atmosphere, and cooled by the moisture of the air, are of duller intellect. That this is so, may be proved from the nature of serpents, which in the hot season, when the cold is dispelled by the heat, move with great activity, but in the rainy and winter seasons, from the coldness of the air, they become torpid. Hence it is not surprising that man's intellect should be sharpened by heat and blunted by a cold atmosphere.

Though, however, the southern nations are quick in understanding, and sagacious in council, yet in point of valour they are inferior, for the sun absorbs their animal spirits. Those, on the contrary, who are natives of cold climates are more courageous in war, and fearlessly attack their enemies, though, rushing on without consideration or judgment, their attacks are repulsed and their designs frustrated. Since, then, nature herself has provided throughout the world, that all nations should differ according to the variation of the climate, she has also been pleased that in the middle of the earth, and of all nations, the Roman people should be seated; on this account the people of Italy excel in both qualities, strength of body and vigour of mind. For as the planet Jupiter moves through a temperate region between the fiery Mars and icy Saturn, so Italy enjoys a temperate and unequalled climate between the north on one side, and the south on the other. Hence it is, that by stratagem she is enabled to repress the attacks of the barbarians, and by her strength to overcome the subtilty of southern nations. Divine providence has so ordered it that the metropolis of the Roman people is placed in an excellent and temperate climate, whereby they have become the masters of the world.

Since, then, it is climate which causes the variety in different countries, and the dispositions of the inhabitants, their stature and qualities are naturally dissimilar, there can be no doubt that the arrangement of buildings should be suitable to the qualities of the nations and people, as nature herself wisely and clearly indicates. To the best of my power I have made general observations on the properties of places as dependent upon nature, and I have given explanations for adapting buildings to the wants of different nations according to the sun's course and the inclination of the pole. I shall now, therefore, briefly explain the symmetry, as well of the whole, as of the detail of private dwellings.

CHAPTER II.

OF THE PROPORTIONS OF PRIVATE BUILDINGS TO SUIT THE NATURE OF THEIR SITES

Nothing requires the architect's care more than the due proportions of buildings. When the proportions are adjusted, and the dimensions found by calculation, then it is the part of a skilful man to consider the nature of the place, the purpose of the building, and the beauty of it; and either by diminutions or additions to find expedients, by means of which the appearance may not be injured by the additions to, or diminutions of, the established proportions that may be necessary.

For an object under the eye will appear very different from the same object placed above it; in an inclosed space, very different from the same in an open space. In all these matters it requires great judgment to adopt the proper means, since the eye does not always form to itself the true image of an object, and the mind is often deceived by the false impression. Thus in painted scenery, though the surface is a perfect plane, the columns seem to advance forward, the projections of the mutuli are represented, and figures seem to stand out. The oars of ships, also, though the parts immersed in the water are really straight, have the appearance of being broken; those parts only appearing straight which are above the level of the water. This arises from the part immersed in the water reflecting its image in an undulating state up to the surface of the water, through a transparent medium, which, being there agitated, gives the oar a broken appearance.

But whether the sight arises from the impression which images make on the eye, or by an effusion of visual rays from the eye, as naturalists contend, it is certain that, in some way or other, the eye is often deceived.

Since, then, some images are falsely conveyed, and others appear different from what they really are, I think it beyond doubt, that, according to nature and the circumstances of the place, diminutions or additions should be made, so that no defect may be apparent. To do this, however, is the result of genius, not the result of learning.

The proportion of the symmetries is, therefore, to be first settled, so that thereon the necessary changes may be made with certainty. Then the length and breadth of the plan of the work is to be set out, and the parts thereof; after which, the proportions are adjusted as propriety requires, so that the pleasing arrangement may not be disturbed. The method of effecting this I am now about to describe, and shall begin with the court (cavædium).

CHAPTER III.

OF COURTS (CAVÆDIA)

There are five species of courts; which receive their names from their forms. The Tuscan, Corinthian, the Tetrastylôn (with four columns), the Displuviatum (open at top), and the Testudinatum (roofed). The Tuscan cavædia are those in which the beams across the breadth of the court have trimmers (interpensivæ) to them, and valleys (colliquiæ) from the internal angles of the walls to the angles formed by the junctions of the beams and trimmers. Thus the rain falls into the middle of the court from the eaves of the rafters. In the Corinthian cavædium, the beams and uncovered middle of the court (compluvium) are as in the foregoing; but the beams around are detached from the walls, and rest on columns. The tetrastyle are those wherein columns are placed under the beams at the angles, which give strength and support to the beams; for thus they are not so liable to sag with their own weight, nor are they loaded by the trimmers.

The displuviatum is that in which the water is carried off above the gutter plates (deliquiæ), which support the body of the roof. These are useful for winter apartments, because the compluvium being upright, the light of the triclinia is not obstructed. But they are constantly in want of repair; for the pipes which receive the water from the eaves being against the walls, and not capable of taking, at once, the water which should be carried off, it overflows from the check it meets, and injures the wood-work and walls in this sort of buildings. The roofed court is used when the span is not great, and large dwelling-rooms are made in the floor over it.

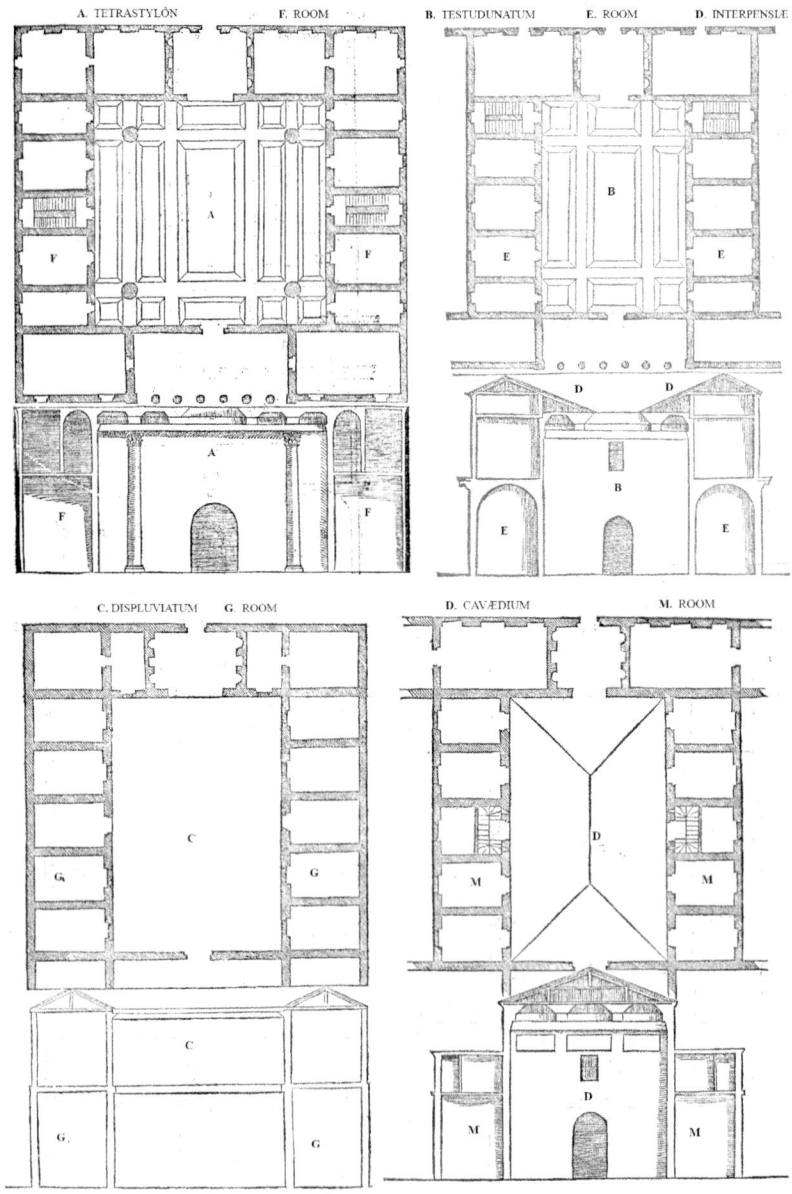

CHAPTER IV.

OF COURTS (ATRIA), WINGS OR AISLES (ALÆ), THE TABLINUM AND THE PERISTYLIUM

The length and breadth of courts (atria) are regulated in three ways. The first is, when the length is divided into five parts, and three of them are given to the width. The second, when it is divided into three parts, and two are given to the width. The third is, when a square being described whose side is equal to the width, a diagonal line is drawn therein, the length of which is to be equal to the length of the atrium.
Their height, to the underside of the beams, is to be one-fourth less than the length; the remaining fourth is assigned for the proportion of the lacunaria and roof above the beams. The width of the alæ, on the right and left, when the atrium is from thirty to forty feet long, is to be one third part thereof. From forty to fifty feet, the length must be divided into three parts and a half; of these, one is given to the alæ: but when the length is from fifty to sixty feet, a fourth part thereof is given to the alæ. From sixty to eighty feet, the length is divided into four parts and a half, of which one part is the width of the alæ. From eighty feet to one hundred, the length is divided into five parts, and one of them is the true width of the alæ. The lintel beams (trabes liminares) are placed at a height which will make the breadths and heights equal.
The muniment-room (tablinum), if the width of the atrium be twenty feet, is to be two thirds thereof. If from thirty to forty feet wide, one half is assigned to the tablinum. From forty to sixty feet, the width is divided into five parts, and two given to the tablinum. The proportions of small atria cannot be the same as those of large ones; for if the propor-

tions of the smaller be used in the greater, the tablinum, as well as the alæ, would be inconvenient: and if those of the larger be used in the smaller, their parts would be large and clumsy. I therefore thought it right to describe, with preci-

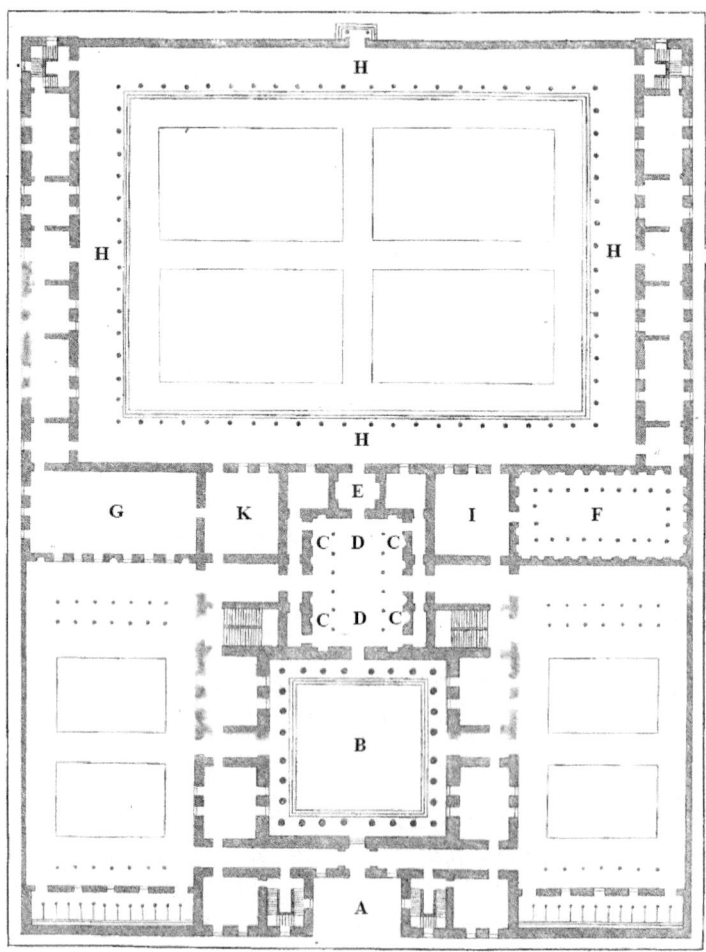

A. PROTHYRUM B. CAVÆDIUM CDC. ATRIUM C. AISLES D. OPEN AREA
E. CABINET F. EGYPTIAN ROOM G. GREEK DINING ROOM
H. PERISTYLIUM I. CŒCI K. EXEDRÆ

sion, their respective proportions, so that they might be both commodious and beautiful.

The height of the tablinum to the beam is one eighth part more than the breadth. The lacunaria are carried up one-third of the width higher. The passages (fauces) towards courts which are on a smaller scale, are to be one-third less than the width of the tablinum; but if larger, they are to be one half. The statues, with their ornaments, are to be placed at a height equal to the width of the alæ. The proportions of the height and width of doors, if Doric, are to be formed in that method: if Ionic, according to the Ionic mode, agreeably to the rules given for doors in the fourth book. The width of the uncovered part of the atrium (impluvii lumen) is not to be less than a fourth nor more than one-third of the width of the same; its length will be in proportion to that of the atrium.

The cloister (peristylium) is transversely one third part longer than across. The columns are to be as high as the width of the portico; and the intercolumniations of the peristylia are not to be less than three nor more than four diameters of the columns. But if the columns of a peristylium are of the Doric order, modules are taken, and the triglyphs arranged thereby, as described in the fourth book.

CHAPTER V.

OF TRICLINIA, ŒCI, EXEDRÆ, PINACOTHECÆ AND THEIR DIMENSIONS

The length of a triclinium is to be double its breadth. The height of all oblong rooms is thus regulated: add their length and breadth together, of which take one half, and it will give the dimension of the height. If, however, exedræ or oeci are square, their height is equal to once and a half their width. Pinacothecæ (picture rooms), as well as exedræ, should be of large dimensions. The Corinthian tetrastyle and Egyptian oeci (halls) are to be proportioned similarly to the triclinia, as above described; but inasmuch as columns are used in them, they are built of larger dimensions.

There is this difference between the Corinthian and Egyptian oecus. The former has a single order of columns, standing either on a podium or on the ground, and over it architraves and cornices, either of wood or plaster, and a semicircular ceiling above the cornice. In the Egyptian oecus, over the lower columns is an architrave, from which to the surrounding wall is a boarded and paved floor, so as to form a passage round it in the open air. Then perpendicularly over the architrave of the lower columns, columns one fourth smaller are placed. Above their architraves and cornices they are decorated with ceilings, and windows are placed between the upper columns. Thus they have the appearance of basilicæ, rather than of Corinthian triclinia.

CHAPTER X.

OF THE ARRANGEMENT AND PARTS OF GRECIAN HOUSES

The Greeks using no atrium, and not building as we do, make a passage, of no great breadth, from the entrance gate, on one side whereof the stable is placed, and on the other the porter's rooms, which immediately adjoin the inner gates. The space between the two gates, is, by the Greeks, called θυρωρεῖον. From this you enter into the peristylium, which has a portico on three sides. On that side facing the south are two antæ, at a considerable distance apart, which carry beams, and the recess behind them is equal to one-third less than their distance from each other. This part is called προστὰς (prostas) by some, and by others παραστὰς (parastas).

Interior to this the great oecus is placed, in which the mistress of the family sits with the spinsters. On the right and left of the prostas are the bed-chambers, of which one is called the thalamus, the other the antithalamus. Round the porticos are the triclinia for common use, the bed chambers, and other apartments for the family. This part of the building receives the name of Gynæconitis.

Adjoining this is a larger house, with a more spacious peristylium, in which there are four porticos equal in height, though that towards the south may have higher columns. If a peristylium have one portico higher than the rest, it is called a Rhodian portico. These houses have magnificent vestibules, elegant gates, and the porticos of the peristylia are decorated with stucco and plastering, and with inlaid ceilings. In the porticos to the north the cyziceni, triclinia, and pinacothecæ, are situated. The libraries are on the east side, the exedræ on the west, and to the south are square oeci, of such ample dimensions that there is room therein for four triclinia and the attendants on them, as well as for the games.

These oeci are used only for entertainments given to men; for it is not the practice with women to recline on a couch at dinner. The peristylium, and this part of the house, is called Andronitis, because the men employ themselves therein without interruption from the women. On the right and left, moreover, are small sets of apartments, each having its own door, triclinium, and bed-chamber, so that on the arrival of guests they need not enter the peristylium, but are received in rooms (hospitalia) appropriated to their occupation. For when the Greeks were more refined, and possessed greater wealth, they provided a separate table with triclinia and bed-chambers for their guests. On the day of their arrival they were invited to dinner, and were afterwards supplied with poultry, eggs, herbs, fruits, and other produce of the country. Hence the painters gave the name of Xenia to those pictures which represent the presents made to guests. Masters of families therefore, living in these apartments, were quite, as it were, at home, being at liberty to do as they pleased therein.

Between the peristylium and the lodging rooms are passages, which are called Mesaulæ, from their situation between two aulæ (halls). By us these are called Andrones. But it is remarkable that this appellation seems to suit neither the Greek nor Latin terms. For the Greeks call the oeci, in which male guests are entertained, ἀνδρῶνες, because the women do not enter them. There are other discrepancies similar to this, as the xystus, prothyrum, telamones, and others of that sort: ξυστός, in Greek means a portico of large dimensions, in which athletæ exercise in the winter season: we, on the contrary, call by the name of xysti those open walks which the Greeks call περιδρόμιδες. The vestibule in front of a house, by the gates, is called prothyrum by the

Greeks; we, however, give the name of prothyrum to that which the Greeks call διάθυρον (diathyrum).

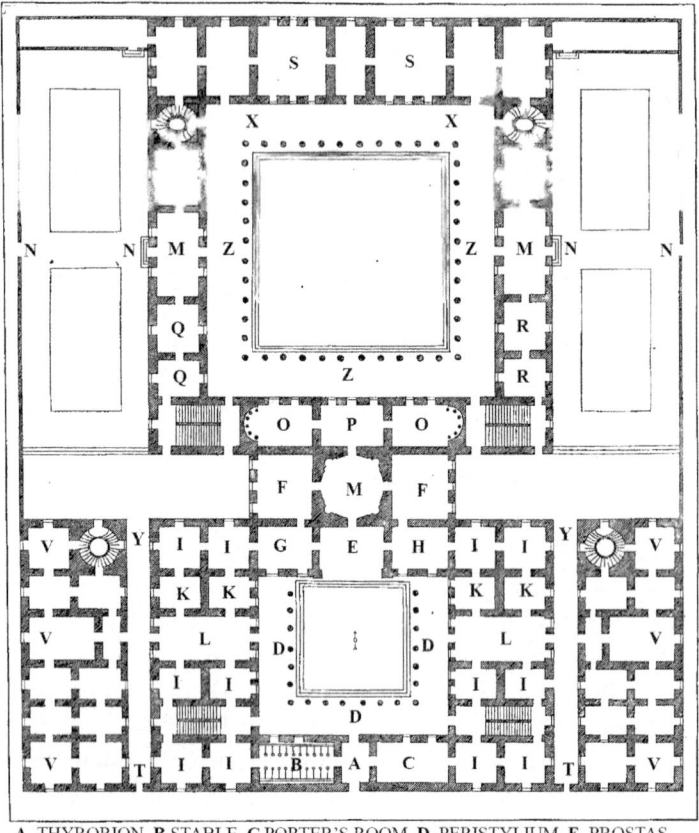

A. THYRORION B. STABLE C. PORTER'S ROOM D. PERISTYLIUM E. PROSTAS
F. FAMILY'S ROOM G. THALAMUS H. ANTITHALAMUS I. BED CHAMBER
K. DRESSINGS L. DINING ROOM M. MEN'S APARTMENT N. DOOR
O. CYZICENI P. PAINTING Q. LIBRARY R. TALKING ROOM S. DINING ROOM
T.V. MESAULÆ V. APARTMENT X. RHODIAN PORTICO Z. PORTICO

We call telamones those figures placed for the support of mutuli or cornices, but on what account is not found in history. The Greeks, however, call them ἄτλαντες (atlantes).

Atlas, according to history, is represented in the act of sustaining the universe, because he is said to have been the first person who explained to mankind the sun's course, that of the moon, the rising and setting of the stars, and the celestial motions, by the power of his mind and the acuteness of his understanding. Hence it is, that, by painters and sculptors, he is, for his exertions, represented as bearing the world: and his daughters, the Atlantides, whom we call Vergiliæ, and the Greeks, Πλειάδες, were honoured by being placed among the constellations.

I mention these things, not to induce persons to change the names at this period, but that they may be known to philologists. I have explained the different arrangement of buildings after the practice of the Italians, as well as that of the Greeks, by giving the proportions and divisions of each; and, as we have already laid down the principles of beauty and propriety, we shall now consider the subject of strength, by which a building may be without defects, and durable.

CHAPTER XI.

OF THE STRENGTH OF BUILDINGS

In those buildings which are raised from the level of the ground, if the foundations are laid according to the rules given in the preceding books for the construction of walls and theatres, they will be very durable; but if under-ground apartments (hypogea) and vaults are to be built, their foundations must be thicker than the walls of the upper part of the edifice, which, as well as the pilasters and columns, must stand vertically over the middle of the foundations below, so that they may be on the solid part. For if the weight of the walls or the columns have a false bearing, they cannot last long.

It is, moreover, a good practice to place posts under the lintels, between the piers and pilasters; for when lintels and beams are loaded, they sag in the middle, and cause fractures in the work above: but when posts are introduced and wedged up under them, the beams are prevented from sagging and being injured.

Care also should be taken to discharge the weight of walls by arches consisting of wedges concentrically arranged; for if these are turned over beams or lintels, the beam, being relieved from the weight, will not sag; and when afterwards it is decayed through age, it may be easily replaced, without the necessity of shores.

So in buildings, which are constructed on piers and arches, consisting of wedges whose joints are concentric, the outer piers should be wider than the others, that they may have more power to resist the action of the wedges, which, loaded with the weight of the superincumbent wall, press towards the centre, and have a tendency to thrust out the abutments.

But if the outer piers be of large dimensions, by restraining the power of the wedges they will give stability to the work.

Having paid due attention to these points, care must next be taken, and particularly is it to be observed, that the work be carried up perpendicularly and without inclination in any part. The greatest attention must be bestowed on the lower parts of the walls, which are often damaged by the earth lying against them. This is not always of the same weight as in summer; for in the winter season, imbibing a great quantity of water from the rain, it increases in weight and bulk, and breaks and extrudes the walls.

To remedy this evil, the thickness of the wall must be proportioned to the weight of earth against it, and, in front, counterforts (anterides) or buttresses (erismæ) are carried up with the wall, at a distance from each other equal to the height of the foundations, and of the same width as the foundations. Their projection at bottom is equal in thickness to the wall, and diminishing as they rise, their projection at top is equal to the thickness of the work: adjoining the inside of the wall, towards the mass of ground, teeth similar to those of a saw are constructed, each of which projects from the wall a distance equal to the height of the foundations, and their thickness is to be equal to that of the foundation wall. An extent equal to the height of the foundations is taken at the outer angles, and marked by points on each side; and through these a diagonal is drawn, on which a wall is carried up, and from the middle of this another is attached to the angle of the wall. The teeth and diagonal walls being thus constructed, will discharge the weight of earth from the wall, by distributing its pressure over a large surface.

Thus I have described the precautions to be taken at the beginning of a building, to prevent defects. The same importance does not attach to the roof, with its beams and rafters, because if these at any time are found defective, they may be easily changed. I have also explained how those parts which are not built solid are to be strengthened.

The quality of the materials it is not in the power of the architect to control: for the same species of materials are not found in every place; and it depends on the employer whether the building shall be of brick, of rough stone, or of squared stone. The merit of every work is considered under three heads; the excellence of the workmanship, and the magnificence and design thereof. When a work is conducted as magnificently as possible, its cost is admired; when well built, the skill of the workman is praised; when beautifully, the merit belongs to the architect, on account of the proportion and symmetry which enter into the design.

These will ever be apparent when he submits to listen to the opinions even of workmen, and ignorant persons. For other men, as well as architects, can distinguish the good from the bad; but between the ignorant man and the architect there is this difference, that the first can form no judgment till he sees the thing itself; whereas the architect, having a perfect idea in his mind, can perceive the beauty, convenience, and propriety of his design, before it is begun. I have laid down as clearly as I could the rules necessary for the construction of private buildings: in the following book I shall treat of the method of finishing them, so that they may be elegant and durable.

CHAPTER VI.

OF THE GRECIAN ŒCI

Œci are sometimes constructed differently from those of Italy; the Greeks call them κυζίκηνοι. They face the north, with a prospect towards the gardens, and have doors in the middle. They are of such length and breadth that two tables (triclinia) with their accessories may stand in them opposite to each other. The windows, as well on the right as on the left, are to open like doors, so that the verdure may be seen through them whilst the guests recline on the couches. The height of them is equal to once and a half the width.

In these apartments, convenience must regulate the proportions. If the windows are not obscured by high walls adjoining, they may be easily contrived. But if any impediment occur, either through nearness of adjoining buildings or other obstruction, some ingenuity and skill will be requisite to diminish or increase their established proportions, so as to produce a pleasing effect not apparently different therefrom.

CHAPTER VII.

OF THE PROPER ASPECTS OF DIFFERENT SORTS OF BUILDINGS

I shall now describe how the different sorts of buildings are placed as regards their aspects. Winter triclinia and baths are to face the winter west, because the afternoon light is wanted in them; and not less so because the setting sun casts its rays upon them, and by its heat warms the aspect towards the evening hours. Bed chambers and libraries should be towards the east, for their purposes require the morning light: in libraries the books are in this aspect preserved from decay; those that are towards the south and west are injured by the worm and by the damp, which the moist winds generate and nourish, and spreading the damp, make the books mouldy.

Spring and autumn triclinia should be towards the east, for then, if the windows be closed till the sun has passed the meridian, they are cool at the time they are wanted for use. Summer triclinia should be towards the north, because that aspect, unlike others, is not heated during the summer solstice, but, on account of being turned away from the course of the sun, is always cool, and affords health and refreshment. Pinacothecæ should have the same aspect, as well as rooms for embroidering and painting, that the colours used therein, by the equability of the light, may preserve their brilliancy.

CHAPTER VIII.

OF THE FORMS OF HOUSES SUITED TO DIFFERENT RANKS OF PERSONS

The aspects proper for each part being appropriated, we must determine the situation of the private rooms for the master of the house, and those which are for general use, and for the guests. Into those which are private no one enters, except invited; such are bed chambers, triclinia, baths, and others of a similar nature. The common rooms, on the contrary, are those entered by any one, even unasked. Such are the vestibule, the cavædium, the peristylia, and those which are for similar uses. Hence, for a person of middling condition in life, magnificent vestibules are not necessary, nor tablina, nor atria, because persons of that description are those who seek favours which are granted by the higher ranks.

Those, however, who have to lay up stores that are the produce of the country, should have stalls and shops in their vestibules: under their houses they should have vaults (cryptæ), granaries (horrea), store rooms (apothecæ), and other apartments, suited rather to preserve such produce, than to exhibit a magnificent appearance. The houses of bankers and receivers of the revenue may be more commodious and elegant, and well secured from the attacks of thieves. For advocates, and men of literature, houses ought to be still handsomer and more spacious, to allow the reception of persons on consultations. But for nobles, who in bearing honours, and discharging the duties of the magistracy, must have much intercourse with the citizens, princely vestibules must be provided, lofty atria, and spacious peristylia, groves, and extensive walks, finished in a magnificent style. In addition to these, libraries, pinacothecæ, and basilicæ, of similar form to those which are made for the public use, are to be provided; for in the houses of the noble, the affairs of the public, and the decision and judgment of private causes are often determined.

If, therefore, houses are erected, thus adapted to the different classes of society, as directed in the first book under the head of propriety, there will be nothing to reprehend, for they will be suitable to their destination. These rules are no less applicable to country than to town dwellings, except that in town the atria must be close to the gates, whereas, in the country villa, the peristylium is near the entrance, then the atrium, with paved porticos round it looking towards the palæstra and walk. I have thus briefly described the proportions of town residences as I promised. I shall now proceed to those of houses in the country, so that they may afford the requisite accommodation.

CHAPTER IX.

OF THE PROPORTIONS OF HOUSES IN THE COUNTRY

First of all the salubrity of the situation must be examined, according to the rules given in the first book for the position of a city, and the site may be then determined. Their size should be dependent on the extent of the land attached to them, and its produce. The courts and their dimensions will be determined by the number of cattle, and the yokes of oxen employed. The kitchen is to be placed in the warmest part of the court; adjoining to this are placed the stalls for oxen, with the mangers at the same time towards the fire and towards the east, for oxen with their faces to the light and fire do not become rough-coated. Hence it is that husbandmen, who are altogether ignorant of the nature of aspects, think that oxen should look towards no other region than that of the east.

The width of the stalls should not be less than ten feet, nor more than fifteen; lengthwise, each yoke is to be at least seven feet. The baths should be contiguous to the kitchen, for they will be then serviceable also for agricultural purposes. The press-room should also be near the kitchen, for the convenience of expressing the oil from the olive; and near that the cellar, lighted from the north, for if it have any opening through which the heat of the sun can penetrate, the wine affected by the heat becomes vapid.

The oil room is to be lighted from the southern and warmer parts of the heaven, that the oil may not be congealed, but be preserved liquid by means of a gentle heat. Its size must be proportioned to the quantity of fruit yielded on the estate, and the number of vessels, which, if of twenty amphoræ (cullearia), are about four feet diameter. The press, if worked by levers instead of screws, should occupy an apartment not less than forty feet long, so as to allow room for the revolution of the levers. Its width must not be less than sixteen feet, which will give ample room to turn and expedite the work. If two presses are employed, the width must be twenty-four feet.

The sheep and goat houses are to be constructed so that not less than an area of four feet and a half, nor more than six feet, be allotted to each animal. The granaries are raised, and must be towards the north or east, so that the grain may not heat, but be preserved by the coolness of air; if towards other aspects, the weevil, and other insects injurious to corn, will be generated. The stable, especially in the villa, should be in the warmest place, and not with an aspect towards the fire, for if horses are stalled near a fire, their coats soon become rough.

Hence those stalls are excellent which are away from the kitchen in the open space towards the east; for when the weather is clear in the winter season, the cattle brought thither in the morning to feed, may be then rubbed down. The barn, hay-room, meal-room, and mill, may be without the boundaries of the villa, which will be thereby rendered more secure from fire. If villas are required to be erected of more magnificence than ordinary, they must be formed according to the proportions laid down for town houses above described, but with the precautions necessary to prevent the purposes of a country house being interfered with.

Care should be taken that all buildings are well lighted: in those of the country this point is easily accomplished, because the wall of a neighbour is not likely to interfere with the light. But in the city the height of party walls, or the narrowness of the situation may obscure the light. In this case we should proceed as follows. In that direction from which the light is to be received, let a line be drawn from the top of the obstructing wall, to that part where the light is to be introduced, and if, looking upwards along that line, a large space of open sky be seen, the light may be obtained from that quarter without fear of obstruction thereof; but if there be any impediment from beams, lintels, or floors, upper lights must be opened, and the light thus introduced. In short, it may be taken as a general rule, that where the sky is seen, in such part apertures are to be left for windows, so that the building may be light. Necessary as light may be in triclinia and other apartments, not less is it so in passages, ascents, and staircases, in which persons carrying loads frequently meet each other. I have explained to the best of my ability the arrangement used in our buildings, so that it may be clearly known by builders, and in order that the Greek arrangement may be also understood, I shall now briefly explain it.

DE ARCHITECTURA

BOOK VII
Pavements and decorative plasterwork

INTRODUCTION

The ancients by means of writing established the wise and useful practice of handing down to posterity their sentiments on different subjects, so that not only those might not be lost, but that by their works continually increasing, a gradual advancement might be made to the highest point of learning. Our obligations to them therefore are great and many, from their not having sullenly kept their knowledge to themselves, but on the contrary, having recorded their opinions on every subject.

Had they omitted to do this, we should not have known what happened in Troy, nor the sentiments of Thales, Democritus, Anaxagoras, Xenophanes, and other physiologists respecting the nature of things; nor the system of ethics laid down by Socrates, Plato, Aristotle, Zeno, Epicurus, and other philosophers. Of the actions of Croesus, Alexander, Darius, and other kings, and the principles on which they acted, we should have been uninformed, unless the antients had handed them down to posterity in their writings.

As we are indebted to these, so we are on the contrary bound to censure those, who, borrowing from others, publish as their own that of which they are not the authors; not less are they censurable, who, distorting the meaning of an author, glory in their perversion of it; indeed they deserve punishment for their dishonest conduct. It is said that this practice was strictly punished by the antients; I do not therefore think it foreign to the purpose to relate from history the result of some examples made by them.

The Attalic kings, stimulated by their great love for philology, having established an excellent public library at Pergamus, Ptolemy, actuated by zeal and great desire for the furtherance of learning, collected with no less care, a similar one for the same purpose at Alexandria, about the same period. When by dint of great labour he had completed it, he was not satisfied, unless, like the seed of the earth, it was to go on increasing. He therefore instituted games to the Muses and Apollo, and in imitation of those in which wrestlers contended, he decreed rewards and honors to the victorious in literature.

These being established, when the time of the games arrived, learned judges were to be selected for the decisions. The king having chosen six, and not readily finding a seventh, applied to those persons who had the care of the library, to ascertain whether they knew any one fit for the purpose. They told him that there was a certain man named Aristophanes, who with great labour and application was day after day reading through the books in the library. At the celebration of the games, Aristophanes was summoned and took his seat among those allotted for the judges.

The first that contended were the poets, who recited their compositions, and the people unanimously signified to the judges the piece which they preferred. When the judges were required to decide, six of them agreed to award the first prize to him who had most pleased the multitude, and the second prize to some other candidate. The opinion of Aristophanes being required, he observed that the best poet had pleased the people the least.

The king and the whole multitude expressed their great indignation at this opinion, but he rose and besought that they would allow him to speak. Silence being obtained, he told them that one only of the competitors was a poet, that the others had recited other men's compositions, and that the judges ought not to decide upon thefts but upon compositions. The people were astonished, and the king in doubt; but Aristophanes relying on his memory, quoted a vast number of books on certain shelves in the library, and comparing them with what had been recited, made the writers confess that they had stolen from them. The king then ordered them to be proceeded against for the theft, and after their condemnation dismissed them with ignominy. Aristophanes, however, was honoured with great rewards, and appointed librarian.

Some time afterwards Zoilus of Macedonia, who assumed the cognomen of Homeromastix, came to Alexandria, and recited before the king his compositions in derogation of the Iliad and Odyssey. When Ptolemy perceived that the father of poetry and all philology, whose works are in esteem throughout all nations, was, because out of the reach of reply, abused by this man, he was enraged and did not deign to answer him. Zoilus, however, remaining some time longer in the country, oppressed with poverty, besought the king to bestow something on him.

The king is said to have answered, that Homer, who had been dead more than a thousand years, had been the means during that period of affording a livelihood to thousands; that he, therefore, who boasted that he possessed greater talent, ought to be able to support, not only himself, but many other persons. Having been condemned as a parricide, his death is variously related. Some have written that he was crucified by Philadelphus, some that he was stoned at Chios, others that he was burnt alive at Smyrna. Whichever of these circumstances occurred he richly deserved it, for that person does not seem to have merited a better fate, who reflects on those that are beyond the reach of hearing and explaining what is said of their writings.

I, therefore, O Cæsar, do not publish this work, merely prefixing my name to a treatise which of right belongs to others, nor think of acquiring reputation by finding fault with the works of any one. On the contrary, I own myself under the highest obligations to all those authors, who by their great ingenuity have at various times on different subjects, furnished us with copious materials; from which, as from a fountain, converting them to our own use, we are enabled to write more fully and expediently, and, trusting to whom we are prepared to strike out something new.

Thus adhering to the principles which I found in those of their works adapted to my purpose, I have endeavoured to advance further. Agatharcus, at the time when Æschylus taught at Athens the rules of tragic poetry, was the first who contrived scenery, upon which subject he left a treatise. This led Democritus and Anaxagoras, who wrote thereon, to explain how the points of sight and distance ought to guide the lines, as in nature, to a centre; so that by means of pictorial deception, the real appearances of buildings appear on the scene, which, painted on a flat vertical surface, seem, nevertheless, to advance and recede.

Silenus afterwards produced a treatise on the symmetry of Doric buildings; Theodorus, on the Doric temple of Jupiter in Samos; Ctesiphon and Metagenes, on that of the Ionic order in the temple of Diana at Ephesus. Phileos wrote a volume on the Ionic temple of Minerva at Priene, and Ictinus and Carpion on the Doric temple of Minerva at Athens, on the Acropolis; Theodorus Phoceus on the vaulted temple at Delphi; Philo on the symmetry of temples, and on the arsenal at the Piræus; Hermogenes on the Ionic pseudodipteral temple at Magnesia, and the monopteral one of Father Bacchus at Teos. Argelius wrote on the proportions of buildings of the Corinthian order, and on the Ionic temple of Æsculapius at Tralles, which he is said to have built; Satyrus and Phyteus, who were extremely fortunate, on the Mausoleum, to which some contributed their exertions whose talents have been admired in all ages, and who have gained lasting reputation. Each front was assigned to a separate artist, to ornament and try his skill thereon. Those employed were Leochares, Bryaxes, Scopas, and Praxiteles; some say that Timotheus was employed. The great art displayed by these men, caused this work to be ranked among the seven wonders.

Besides these, many of less celebrity have written precepts on proportions, as Nexaris, Theocydes, Demophilos, Pollis, Leonides, Silanion, Melampus, Sarnacus, and Euphranor. Many on mechanics, as Cliades, Archytas, Archimedes, Ctesibius, Nymphodorus, Philo Byzantius, Diphilus, Democles, Charidas, Polyidus, Phyros, Agesistratus. From the commentaries of these, what I thought useful I have thrown together, and that the more especially because I observe that on this branch the Greeks have published much, and our own countrymen very little. Fussitius, however, and he was the first, produced an excellent work on the subject. Terentius Varro, in his work on the nine sciences, includes one on architecture. Publius Septimius wrote two.

Besides these, I do not recollect any one that up to this time has written, though we have formerly produced great architects, and such as were well qualified to have written with elegance. In fact the foundations of the temple of Jupiter Olympius at Athens were prepared by Antistates, Callæschrus, Antimachides and Porinus, architects employed by Pisistratus, after whose death, on account of the troubles which affected the republic, the work was abandoned. About two hundred years afterwards, king Antiochus, having agreed to supply the money for the work, a Roman citizen, named Cossutius, designed with great skill and taste the cell, the dipteral arrangement of the columns, the cornices, and other ornaments. This work is not only universally esteemed, but is accounted one of the rarest specimens of magnificence.

For in four places only are the temples embellished with work in marble, and from that circumstance the places are very celebrated, and their excellence and admirable contrivance is pleasing to the gods themselves. The first is the temple of Diana at Ephesus, of the Ionic order, built by Ctesiphon of Gnosus, and his son Metagenes, afterwards completed by Demetrius, a priest of Diana, and Pæonius, the Ephesian. The second is the temple of Apollo, at Miletus, also of the Ionic order, built by the above-named Pæonius, and Daphnis, the Milesian. The third is the Doric temple of Ceres and Proserpine, at Eleusis, the cell of which was built by Ictinus, of extraordinary dimensions, for the greater convenience of the sacrifices, and without an exterior colonnade. This structure, when Demetrius Phalereus governed Athens, was turned by Philus into a prostyle temple, with columns in front, and by thus enlarging the vestibule, he not only provided accommodation for the noviciates, but gave great dignity to its appearance. Lastly, in Athens it is said that Cossutius was the architect of the temple of Jupiter Olympius, which was of large dimensions, and of the Corinthian order and proportions, as above mentioned. From the pen of this man no treatise is extant; nor is it from him alone that such would have been less desirable, than from Caius Mutius, who with great science, and according to the just rules of art, completed the cell, columns, and entablature of the temples of Honour and Virtue, near the trophy of Marius, a work, which, had it been of marble, and thereby endowed with the splendour and richness which the material must have added, would have been reckoned among the first and most excellent examples.

It therefore appears that our country can boast of as great architects as Greece herself, many of them even within our own times, but since few have left behind them any treatises, I thought it improper to omit any thing, and to treat of the different branches in different books. In the sixth book I have given rules for building private houses; in this, the seventh, I shall describe their finishing, and how that is to be rendered both beautiful and durable.

CHAPTER I.

OF PAVEMENTS

I shall begin with pavements, which are the principal of the finishings, and should be executed with the greatest care and attention to their solidity. If the pavement be made on the ground itself, the soil must be examined, to ascertain that it is solid throughout, then over it is to be spread and levelled a layer of rubbish. But if the whole or any part of the earth be loose, it is to be made solid with a rammer. In timber floors care must be taken that no wall be built under them, so as to touch the under side of the floors; but that a space be rather left between them and the floors. For if they be made solid, the timber of the floors drying and settling, whilst the wall remains in its place, will cause fissures in the pavement to the right and left.

Care must also be taken that holm timber be not used with oak; for as soon as oak becomes damp, it warps, and causes cracks in the pavement. If, however, holm is not to be had, and on that account it be absolutely necessary to use oak, it should be cut very thin, by which means its power will be diminished, and it will be more easily fastened with the nails. Then through the edges of the boards two nails are to be driven into every joist, so that no part of the edges may warp. I do not mention the chestnut, beech, or the farnus, because neither of them are durable. The floor being prepared, fern, if at hand, and if not, straw, is to be spread over it, so that the timber may not be injured by the lime.

On this is placed a layer of stones, each of which is not to be less than will fill a man's hand. These being spread, the pavement is laid thereon. If the rubbish be new, let three parts of it be mixed with one of lime; but if from old materials, the proportion is five parts to two of lime. It is then laid on, and brought to a solid consistence with wooden beaters and the repeated blows of a number of men, till its thickness is about three quarters of a foot. Over this is spread the upper layer, composed of three parts of potsherds to one of lime, of a thickness not less than six inches. Over the upper layer the pavement is laid to rule and level, whether composed of slabs or of tesseræ.

When laid with their proper inclination, they are to be rubbed off, so that, if in slabs, there may be no rising edges of the ovals, triangles, squares, or hexagons, but that the union of the different joints may be perfectly smooth. If the pavement be composed of tesseræ, the edges of them should be completely smoothed off, or the work cannot be said to be well finished. So, also, the Tiburtine tiles, peaked at the points, should be laid with care, that there may be neither hollows on them, nor ridges, but that they be flat, and rubbed to a regular surface. After the rubbing and polishing, marble dust is strewed over it, and over that a coat of lime and sand.

Pavements are, however, more fit to be used in the open air, inasmuch as timbers expanding in a moist atmosphere, and contracting in a dry one, or sagging in the middle, cause defects in the pavement by their settlements. Moreover, frosts and ice soon ruin them. But as they are sometimes required, they must be made as follows. Over the first flooring, boards, others crossing them, must be laid, fastened with nails; thus giving a double covering to the beams. The pavement is composed of two parts of fresh rubbish, one of potsherds, and two of lime.

After the first layer of rubbish on the floor, this composition is spread over it, and pounded into a mass not less than a foot thick. The upper layer being then spread, as above directed, the pavement, consisting of tesseræ, each about two inches thick, is laid, with an inclination of two inches to ten feet: if thus executed, and afterwards properly rubbed, it will not be liable to defects. In order that the mortar at the joints may not suffer by the frost, at the approach of winter every year it should be saturated with the dregs of oil, which will prevent the frost affecting it.

If extraordinary care be required, the pavement is covered with tiles two feet square, properly jointed, having small channels, of the size of an inch, cut on each edge. These are filled with lime tempered with oil, the edges being rubbed and pressed together. Thus the lime in the channels growing hard, suffers neither water nor any thing else to penetrate. After this preparation the upper layer is spread and beaten with sticks. Over this either large tesseræ or angle tiles are laid at the inclination above directed, and work so executed will not be easily injured.

CHAPTER II.

OF TEMPERING LIME FOR STUCCO

Having given the necessary directions in respect of pavement, we shall explain the method of stuccoing. This requires that the lime should be of the best quality, and tempered a long time before it is wanted for use; so that if any of it be not burnt enough, the length of time employed in slaking it may bring the whole mass to the same consistence. If the lime be not thoroughly slaked, but used fresh, it will when spread throw out blisters, from the crude particles it contains, which, in execution, break and destroy the smoothness of the stucco.

When the slaking is properly conducted, and care taken in the preparation of the materials, a hatchet is used, similar to that with which timber is hewn, and the lime is to be chopped with it, as it lies in the heap. If the hatchet strikes upon lumps, the lime is not sufficiently slaked, and when the iron of the instrument is drawn out dry and clean, it shews that the lime is poor and weak; but if, when extracted, the iron exhibits a glutinous substance adhering to it, that not only indicates the richness and thorough slaking of the lime, but also shews that it has been well tempered. The scaffolding being then prepared, the compartments of the rooms are executed, except the ceilings be straight.

CHAPTER III.

OF STUCCO WORK

When arched ceilings are introduced, they must be executed as follows. Parallel ribs are set up, not more than two feet apart: those of cypress are preferable, because fir is soon injured by the rot and age. These ribs being got out to the shape of the curve, they are fixed to the ties of the flooring or roof, as the case may require, with iron nails. The ties should be of wood not liable to injury from rot, nor age nor damp, such as box, juniper, olive, heart of oak, cypress, and the like, common oak always excepted, which, from its liability to warp, causes cracks in the work whereon it is employed.

The ribs having been fixed, Greek reeds, previously bruised, are tied to them, in the required form, with cords made of the Spanish broom. On the upper side of the arch a composition of lime and sand is to be laid, so that if any water fall from the floor above or from the roof, it may not penetrate. If there be no supply of Greek reeds, the common slender marsh-reeds may be substituted, tied together with string in bundles of appropriate length, but of equal thickness, taking care that the distance from one ligature to another be not more than two feet. These are bound with cord to the ribs, as above directed, and made fast with wooden pins. All the remaining work is to be performed as above described.

The arches being prepared and interwoven with the reeds, a coat is to be laid on the underside. The sand is afterwards introduced on it, and it is then polished with chalk or marble. After polishing, the cornices are to be run along the springing: they are to be as slender and light as possible; for, when large, they settle by their own weight, and are incapable of sustaining themselves. But little plaster should be used in them, and the stuff should be of uniform quality, such as marble-dust; for the former, by setting quickly, does not allow the work to dry of one consistence. The practice of the antients, in arched ceilings, is also to be avoided; for their cornices are dangerous, from their great projection and consequent weight.

Some cornices are of plain, others of carved, work. In small private rooms, or where fire or many lights are used, they should be plain, to allow of being more easily cleaned; in summer rooms, and exedræ, where the smoke is in such small quantity that it can do no injury, carved cornices may be used; for white works, from the delicacy of their colour, are always soiled, not only with the smoke of the house itself, but also with that of the neighbouring buildings.

The cornices being completed, the first coat of the walls is to be laid on as roughly as possible, and, while drying, the sand coat thereon; setting it out, in the direction of the length, by the rule and square; in that of the height, perpendicularly; and in respect of the angles perfectly square; inasmuch as plastering, thus finished, will be proper for the reception of paintings. When the work has dried, a second and afterwards a third coat is laid on. The sounder the sand coat is, the more durable will the work be.

When, besides the first coat, three sand coats at least have been laid, the coat of marble-dust follows; and this is to be so prepared, that when used, it does not stick to the trowel, but easily comes away from the iron. Whilst the stucco is drying, another thin coat is to be laid on: this is to be well worked and rubbed, and then still another, finer than the last. Thus, with three sand coats, and the same number of marble-dust coats, the walls will be rendered solid, and not liable to cracks or other defects.

When the work is well beaten, and the under coats made solid, and afterwards well smoothed by the hardness and whiteness of the marble-powder, it throws out the colours mixed therein with great brilliancy. Colours, when used with care on damp stucco, do not fade, but are very durable; because the lime being deprived of its moisture in the kiln, and having become porous and dry, readily imbibes whatever is placed on it. From their different natures the various particles unite in the mixture, and, wherever applied, grow solid; and when dry, the whole seems composed of one body of the same quality.

Stucco, therefore, when well executed, does not either become dirty, or lose its colour when washed, unless it has been carelessly done, or the colour laid on after the work was dry: if however executed as above directed, it will be strong, brilliant, and of great durability. When only one coat of sand and one of marble-dust are used, it is easily broken, from its thinness; and is not, on that account, capable of acquiring a brilliant appearance.

As a silver mirror, made from a thin plate, reflects the image confusedly and weakly, whilst from a thick solid plate it takes a high polish, and reflects the image brilliantly and strongly; so plastering, when thin in substance, not only cracks, but soon decays. On the contrary, that which is well covered with plaster and stucco, and closely laid on, when well polished, not only shines, but reflects to the spectators the images falling on it.

The plasterers of the Greeks thus not only make their work hard, by adhering to the above directions, but, when the plaster is mixed, cause it to be beaten with wooden staves by a great number of men, and use it after this preparation. Hence, some persons, cutting slabs of plaster from the antient walls, use them for tables; and the pieces of plaster so cut out for tables and mirrors, are, of themselves, very beautiful in appearance.

If stucco be used on timber partitions, which are necessarily constructed with spaces between the upright and cross pieces, and thence, when smeared with clay, liable to swell with the damp, and when dry to shrink, and cause cracks, the following expedient should be used. After the partition has been covered with the clay, reeds, by the side of each other, are to be nailed thereon with bossed nails; and clay having been laid over these, and another layer of reeds nailed on the former, but crossed in their direction, so that one set is nailed upright, and the other horizontally; then, as above described, the sand and marble coats and finishing are to be followed up. The double row of reeds thus crossed on walls prevents all cracks and fissures.

CHAPTER IV.

OF STUCCO WORK IN DAMP PLACES

I have explained how plastering is executed in dry situations; now I shall give directions for it, that it may be durable in those that are damp. First, in apartments on the ground-floor; a height of three feet from the pavement is to have its first coat of potsherds, instead of sand, so that this part of the plastering may not be injured by the damp. But if a wall is liable to continual moisture, another thin wall should be carried up inside it, as far within as the case will admit; and between the two walls a cavity is to be left lower than the level of the floor of the apartment, with openings for air. At the upper part, also, openings must be left; for if the damp do not evaporate through these holes above and below, it will extend to the new work. The wall is then to be plastered with the potsherd mortar, made smooth, and then polished with the last coat.

If, however, there be not space for another wall, channels should nevertheless be made, and holes therefrom to the open air. Then tiles of the size of two feet are placed on one side, over the side of the channel, and, on the other side, piers are built, of eight-inch bricks, on which the angles of two tiles may lie, that they may not be more distant than one palm from each other. Over them other tiles, with returning edges, are fixed upright, from the bottom to the top of the wall; and the inner surfaces of these are to be carefully pitched over, that they may resist the moisture; they are, moreover, to have air-holes at bottom, and at top above the vault.

They are then to be whited over with lime and water, that the first coat may adhere to them; for, from the dryness they acquire in burning, they would neither take that coat nor sustain it, but for the lime thus interposed, which joins and unites them. The first coat being laid on, the coat of pounded potsherds is spread, and the remainder is finished according to the rules above given.

The ornaments for polished stuccos ought to be used with a regard to propriety, suitable to the nature of the place, and should be varied in their composition. In winter triclinia, neither large pictures nor delicate ornaments in the cornice, under the vault, are to be introduced, because they are soon injured by the smoke of the fire, and of the quantity of lights used therein. In these, above the podium, polished pannels of a black colour are introduced, with yellow or red margins round them. The method of finishing plain as well as enriched ceilings having been described, it will not be amiss, in case any one should wish to know it, to explain the construction of the pavements used in the Grecian winter rooms; which is not only economical but useful.

The floor of the triclinium is excavated to the depth of about two feet; and after the bottom is well rammed, a pavement of rubbish or potsherds is spread over it, with a declivity towards the holes of the drain. A composition of pounded coals, lime, sand, and ashes, is mixed up and spread thereover, half a foot in thickness, perfectly smooth and level. The surface being then rubbed with stone, it has the appearance of a black pavement. Thus, at their banquets, the liquor that is spilt, and the expectoration which falls on it, immediately dry up; and the persons who wait on the guests, though barefooted, do not suffer from cold on this sort of pavement.

CHAPTER V.

OF THE USE OF PAINTING IN BUILDINGS

In the other rooms, namely, those for vernal, autumnal and summer use: in atria also, and peristylia, certain kinds of pictures were used by the ancients. Painting represents subjects which exist or may exist, such as men, houses, ships, and other things, the forms and precise figures of which are transferred to their representations. Hence those of the ancients who first used polished coats of plastering, originally imitated the variety and arrangement of inlaid marbles. Afterwards the variety was extended to the cornices, and the yellow and red frames of pannels, from which they proceeded to the representations of buildings, columns, and the projections of roofs. In spacious apartments, such as exedræ, on account of their extent, they decorated the walls with scenery, after the tragic, comic or satyric mode; and galleries from their extended length, they decorated with varied landscapes, the representations of particular spots. In these they also painted ports, promontories, the coasts of the sea, rivers, fountains, straits, groves, mountains, cattle, shepherds, and sometimes figures representing gods, and stories, such as the Trojan battles, or the wanderings of Ulysses over different countries, and other subjects, founded on real history.

But those which were used by the ancients are now tastelessly laid aside: inasmuch as monsters are painted in the present day rather than objects whose prototype are to be observed in nature. For columns reeds are substituted; for pediments the stalks, leaves, and tendrils of plants; candelabra are made to support the representations of small buildings, from whose summits many stalks appear to spring with absurd figures thereon. Not less so are those stalks with figures rising from them, some with human heads, and others with the heads of beasts; because similar forms never did, do, nor can exist in nature. These new fashions have so much prevailed, that for want of competent judges, true art is little esteemed. How is it possible for a reed to support a roof, or a candelabrum to bear a house with the ornaments on its roof, or a small and pliant stalk to carry a sitting figure; or, that half figures and flowers at the same time should spring out of roots and stalks? And yet the public, so far from discouraging these falsehoods, are delighted with them, not for a moment considering whether such things could exist. Hence the minds of the multitude, misled by improper judges, do not discern that which is founded on reason and the rules of propriety. No pictures should be tolerated but those established on the basis of truth; and although admirably painted, they should be immediately discarded, if they transgress the rules of propriety and perspicuity as respects the subject.

At Tralles, a town of Lydia, when Apaturius of Alabanda had painted an elegant scene for the little theatre which they call ἐκκλησιαστήριον, in which, instead of columns, he introduced statues and centaurs to support the epistylium, the circular end of the dome, and angles of the pediments, and ornamented the cornice with lions' heads, all which are appropriate as ornaments of the roofing and eaves of edifices; he painted above them, in the episcenium, a repetition of the domes, porticos, half pediments, and other parts of roofs and their ornaments. Upon the exhibition of this scene, which on account of its richness gave great satisfaction, everyone was ready to applaud, when Licinius, the mathematician, advanced, and thus addressed them:

"The Alabandines are sufficiently informed in civil matters, but are without judgment on subjects of less moment; for the statues in their Gymnasium are all in the attitude of pleading causes, whilst those in the forum are holding the discus, or in the attitude of running, or playing with balls, so that the impropriety of the attitudes of the figures in such places disgraces the city. Let us therefore, be careful by our treatment of the scene of Apaturius, not to deserve the appellation of Alabandines or Abderites; for who among you would place columns or pediments on the tiles which cover the roofs of your houses? These things stand on the floors, not on the tiles. If, then, approbation is conferred on representations in painting which cannot exist in fact, we of this city shall be like those who for a similar error are accounted illiterate."

Apaturius dared not reply, but took down and altered the scene, so as to make it consistent with truth, and then it was approved. O that the gods would restore Licinius to life, that he might correct the folly, and fashionable inconsistency in our stucco work. It is not foreign to my purpose to show how inconsistency overcomes truth. The ancients laboured to accomplish and render pleasing by dint of art, that which in the present day is obtained by means of strong and gaudy colouring, and for the effect which was formerly obtained only by the skill of the artist, a prodigal expense is now substituted, who in former times used minium otherwise than as a medicine? In the present age, however, walls are every where covered with it To this may be added the use of chrysocolla, purple, and azure decorations, which, without the aid of real art, produce a splendid effect. These are so costly, that unless otherwise stated in agreements, they are to be, by law, charged to the account of the employer. To my utmost I have described the means for avoiding defective plastering, and as lime has previously been sufficiently treated of, it now remains to treat of marble.

CHAPTER VI.

OF THE PREPARATION OF MARBLE FOR PLASTERING

Marble is not alike in all countries. In some places it contains pellucid particles, similar to those of salt, which, when bruised and ground, impart great solidity to plastering and cornices. When these are not to be obtained, the chips (assulæ), as they are denominated, which the workers in marble throw off in working, may be substituted after being pounded and sifted. They are to be separated into three sorts, of which that which contains the larger particles, is, as we have above directed, to be laid on with the sand and lime: then follows the second coat, and afterwards, the third which is finer in texture. After this preparation, and a careful polishing of the work, the colours which it is to receive are to be considered, so that they may be brilliant. Their variety and the method of preparing them will be found in the following pages.

CHAPTER VII.

OF NATURAL COLOR

Some are found in certain places in a native state, and thence dug up, whilst others are composed of different substances, ground and mixed together, so as to answer the same purpose. First we shall explain the nature of that which is found native, called by the Greeks ὤχρα. This, as in Italy, is discovered in many places, but the best is the Attic sort, which cannot now be procured, for in working the silver mines at Athens, if by chance they fell upon a vein of ochre, they followed it up just as they would one of silver. Hence the ancients used abundance of ochre in their finishings.

Red ochre is also found in many places, but the best only in a few, as at Sinope, in Pontus; in Egypt; in the Balearic Islands, near the coast of Spain; also in Lemnos, the revenue of which island the senate and people of Rome granted to the Athenians. The Parætonion takes its name from the place where it is dug up. The Melinon on a similar account is so called, from its abundance in Melos, one of the Cyclades. Green chalk is also found in many places; but the best comes from Smyrna, and is called by the Greeks θεοδότιον, because Theodotus was the owner of the land in which it was first discovered. Orpiment, which is called ἀρσένικον in Greek, is obtained from Pontus. Red lead is also obtained from many places, but the best comes from Pontus, near the river Hypanis. In other spots as in the country between the borders of Magnesia and Ephesus, it is procured from the earth in such a state as to want neither grinding nor sifting, but quite as fine as that which is ground and pounded by hand.

CHAPTER VIII.

OF VERMILION AND QUICKSILVER

I shall now speak of vermilion. This is said to have been first found in the Cilbian fields of the Ephesians, and the manner of procuring and preparing it is very curious. A clod of earth is selected, which, before it is manufactured into vermilion, is called Anthrax, wherein are veins resembling iron, but of a red colour, and having a red dust round them. When dug up, it is beaten with iron bars till a great number of drops of quicksilver exude from it; these are immediately collected by the excavators.

The clods, when collected in the laboratory, on account of their great dampness, are thrown into a furnace to dry; and the fumes that rise from them through the action of the fire fall condensed on the floor of the furnace, and are found to be quicksilver. But as, from the smallness of the drops which thus remain, they cannot be gathered up, they are swept into a vessel of water, in which they run together and re-unite. These, when they fill a vessel of the capacity of four sextarii, weigh one hundred pounds.

If quicksilver be placed in a vessel, and a stone of a hundred pounds weight be placed on it, it will swim at the top, and will, notwithstanding its weight, be incapable of pressing the liquid so as to break or separate it. If this be taken out, and only a single scruple of gold be put in, that will not swim, but immediately descend to the bottom. This is a proof that the gravity of a body does not depend on its weight, but on its nature.

Quicksilver is used for many purposes; without it, neither silver nor brass can be properly gilt. When gold is embroidered on a garment which is worn out and no longer fit for use, the cloth is burnt over the fire in earthen pots; the ashes are thrown into water, and quicksilver added to them: this collects all the particles of gold, and unites with them. The water is then poured off, and the residuum placed in a cloth: which, when squeezed with the hands, suffers the liquid quicksilver to pass through the pores of the cloth, but retains the gold in a mass within it.

CHAPTER IX.

OF THE PREPARATION OF VERMILION

I now return to the preparation of vermilion. When the clods are dry, they are pounded and reduced to powder with iron beaters, and then, by means of repeated washings and dryings, the colour is produced. When this is effected, the vermilion, deprived of the quicksilver, loses its natural tenacity, and becomes soft and disconnected; and used in the last coat of the plastering of rooms, keeps its colour without fading.

But in open places, such as peristylia or exedræ, and similar situations whereto the rays of the sun and moon penetrate, the brilliancy of the colour is destroyed by contact with them, and it becomes black. Thus, as it has happened to many others, Faberius, the scribe, wishing to have his house on the Aventine elegantly finished, coloured the walls of the peristylia with vermilion. In the course of thirty days they turned to a disagreeable uneven colour; on which account he was obliged to agree with the contractors to lay on other colours.

Those who are particular in this respect, and are desirous that the vermilion should retain its colour, should, when the wall is coloured and dry, rub it with a hard brush charged with Punic wax melted and tempered with oil: then, with live coals in an iron pan, the wall should be thoroughly heated, so as to melt the wax and make it lie even, and then rubbed with a candle and clean cloth, as they do marble statues. This practice is called καῦσις by the Greeks.

The coat of Punic wax prevents the effect of the moon's as well as that of the sun's rays thereon which injure and destroy the colours in work of this nature. The laboratories which were formerly carried on at the mines in Ephesus are now transferred to Rome, on account of mines of the same sort having been discovered in some parts of Spain, whence the clods are brought and worked by manufacturers at Rome. These laboratories are situated between the temples of Flora and Quirinus.

Vermilion is occasionally adulterated with lime. The following is a method by which its goodness may be proved. Let the vermilion be placed on an iron plate over the fire, and remain till the plate is red hot: when the heat has changed the colour, and it appears black, let the plate be removed from the fire. If, when cooled, it returns to its original colour, it may be considered pure. but if it remain of a black colour, it is quite clear that it has been adulterated.

I have written all that I remember respecting vermilion. Chrysocolla comes from Macedonia, and is found in the vicinity of copper mines. Minium and indigo, by their names, indicate the places from whence they are obtained.

CHAPTER X.

OF ARTIFICIAL COLOURS. OF BLACK

I have now to speak of those bodies which, from particular treatment, change their qualities, and acquire the properties of colours; and first, of black, which is much employed in different works, in order that it may be known how it is prepared for use.

An apartment is built similar to a laconicum, plastered with marble stucco, and polished. In front of it is built a furnace, which communicates with the laconicum; the mouth of this is to be very carefully closed, for the purpose of preventing the escape of the flame. Resin is then placed in the furnace, whose smoke, when the material is set on fire, passes by means of communications into the laconicum, and therein adheres to the walls and the arched ceiling. It is then collected, and some part of it is tempered with gum, to make ink for transcribers; the remainder is used by stuccoers in colouring walls, being previously mixed with size.

But if this cannot be procured, in order to prevent delay, the following expedient may be adopted. Pine branches or chips must be burnt, and, when thoroughly charred, pounded in a mortar with size. Thus the plasterer will procure an agreeable black colour.

A black colour, not less pleasing, is made by drying and burning lees of wine in a furnace, and grinding the result with size. Indeed, this makes a very agreeable black. The better the wine whose lees are used, the better will be the black colour; which will, in such case, approach the colour of indigo.

CHAPTER XI.

OF BLUE, AND BURNT OF YELLOW

Blue was first manufactured at Alexandria, and afterwards by Vestorius at Puzzuoli. The method of making it, and the nature of the ingredients, merit our attention. Sand is ground with flowers of sulphur, till the mixture is as fine as flour, to which coarse filings of Cyprian copper are added, so as to make a paste when moistened with water; this is rolled into balls with the hand, and dried. The balls are then put into an earthen vessel, and that is placed in a furnace. Thus the copper and sand heating together by the intensity of the fire, impart to each other their different qualities, and thereby acquire their blue colour.

Burnt yellow, which is much used in stuccos, is thus made. A lump of good yellow earth is heated red hot; it is then quenched in vinegar, by which it acquires a purple colour.

CHAPTER XII.

OF WHITE LEAD, VERDIGREASE AND RED LEAD

It will be proper to explain in what manner white lead is made, and also verdigrease, which we call æruca. The Rhodians place, in the bottoms of large vessels, a layer of twigs, over which they pour vinegar, and on the twigs they lay masses of lead. The vessels are covered, to prevent evaporation; and when, after a certain time, they are opened, the masses are found changed into white lead. In the same way they make verdigrease, which is called æruca, by means of plates of copper.

The white lead is roasted in a furnace, and, by the action of the fire, becomes red lead. This invention was the result of observation in the case of an accidental fire; and, by the process, a much better material is obtained than that which is procured from mines.

CHAPTER XIII.

OF PURPLE

I shall now speak of purple, which, above all other colours, has a delightful effect, not less from its rarity than from its excellence. It is procured from the marine shell which yields the scarlet dye, and possesses qualities not less extraordinary than those of any other body whatever. It does not in all places where it is found possess the same quality of colour; but varies in that respect according to the sun's course.

Thus, that which is obtained in Pontus and in Galatia, from the nearness of those countries to the north, is brown; in those between the south and the west, it is pale; that which is found in the equinoctial regions, east and west, is of a violet hue; lastly, that which comes from southern countries possesses a red quality: the red sort is also found in the island of Rhodes, and other places near the equator.

After the shells are gathered they are broken into small pieces with iron bars; from the blows of which, the purple dye oozes out like tears, and is drained into mortars and ground. It is called ostrum, because extracted from marine shells. Inasmuch as this colour, from its saltness, soon dries, it is prepared for use with honey.

CHAPTER XIV.

OF FACTITIOUS COLOURS

Purple colours are also made by tinging chalk with madder-root and hysginum. Divers colours are also made from flowers. Thus, when dyers are desirous of imitating the Attic ochre, they put dry violets into a vessel, and boil them. When so prepared, they pour the contents of the vessel on to a cloth, and, squeezing it with their hands, receive in a mortar the water thus coloured by the violet, and then, mixing Eretrian earth with it, and grinding it, the colour of Attic ochre is produced.

In the same way an excellent purple is obtained by preparing vaccinium, and mixing it with milk. So also, those who cannot afford the use of chrysocolla, mix blue with the herb weld, and thus obtain a brilliant green. These are called factitious colours. On account of the dearness of indigo, Selinusian chalk, or that used for making rings, is mixed with glass, which the Greeks call ὑαλος; and thus they imitate indigo.

In this book I have explained, as they have occurred to me, the methods of making colours for painting, so that they may be durable and appropriate. Thus, in seven books, are methodically laid down all the rules that relate to the perfection and convenience of buildings. In the following book I shall treat of water, how it is to be found and conveyed to any place; as also how to ascertain its salubrity, and fitness for the purposes to which it is to be applied.

DE ARCHITECTURA

BOOK VIII

Water supplies and aqueducts

INTRODUCTION

Thales, the Milesian, one of the seven wise men, taught that water was the original cause of all things. Heraclitus maintained the same of fire: the priests of the magi, of water and fire. Euripides, a disciple of Anaxagoras, called by the Athenians the dramatic philosopher, attributed it to air and earth; and contended that the latter, impregnated by the seed contained in the rain falling from the heavens, had generated mankind and all the animals on the earth; and that all these, when destroyed by time, returned to their origin. Thus, such as spring from the air, also return into air, and not being capable of decay, are only changed by their dissolution, returning to that element whereof they first consisted. But Pythagoras, Empedocles, Epicharmus, and other physiologists, and philosophers, maintained that there were four elements, air, fire, water, and earth; and that their mixture, according to the difference of the species, forms a natural mould of different qualities.

We must recollect, that not only from these elements, are all things generated, but that they can neither be nourished, nor grow without their assistance. Thus bodies cannot live without abundance of air; that is, without its being furnished for inspiration and respiration in considerable quantity. So, also, if a body do not possess a due proportion of heat, it can neither be endued with animal spirits nor a strong constitution, nor will the hardness of its food be duly attenuated: and if the members of the body are not nourished by the fruits of the earth, they will waste, because deprived of the mixture of that element with them.

Lastly, animals deprived of moisture, from want of water dry up, and are bloodless and parched. Divine Providence has made those things neither scarce nor dear which are necessary for mankind, as are pearls, gold, silver, and the like, which are neither necessary for the body nor nature; but has diffused abundantly, throughout the world, those things, without which the life of mortals would be uncertain. Thus, if a body be deficient in spirit, the deficiency is supplied by the air. The power of the sun, and the discovery of fire, are always ready to assist us, and render life more certain. The fruits of the earth also, furnishing nourishment even to excess, feed and support animals continually. Water is of infinite utility to us, not only as affording drink, but for a great number of purposes in life; and it is furnished to us gratuitously.

Hence the priests of the Egyptian worship teach, that all things are composed of water; and when they cover the vase of water, which is borne to the temple with the most solemn reverence, kneeling on the earth, with their hands raised to heaven, they return thanks to divine goodness for its creation.

CHAPTER I.

OF THE METHOD OF FINDING WATER

As it is the opinion of physiologists, philosophers and priests that all things proceed from water, I thought it necessary, as in the preceding seven books rules are laid down for buildings, to describe in this the method of finding water, its different properties, according to the varied nature of places, how it ought to be conducted, and in what manner it should be judged of; inasmuch as it is of infinite importance, for the purposes of life, for pleasure, and for our daily use. This will be easily accomplished if the springs are open and flowing above ground. If that be not the case, their sources under ground are to be traced and examined. In order to discover these, before sunrise one must lie down prostrate in the spot where he seeks to find it, and with his chin placed on the ground and fixed, look around the place; for the chin being fixed, the eye cannot range upwards farther than it ought, and is confined to the level of the place. Then, where the vapours are seen curling together and rising into the air, there dig, because these appearances are not discovered in dry places.

We should also consider the nature of the place when we search for water. In clay, the vein of water is small, the supply little, and not of the best flavour; and if in low places, it will be muddy and ill tasted. In black earth, only tricklings and small drops are found, which, collected from the winter rain, subside in compact hard places, and are of very excellent flavour. In gravel, the veins are small and variable, but they are exceeding well flavoured. In the strong, common and red sands, the supply is to be depended on with more certainty, and is of good taste. In red stone, abundance and that of good quality may be obtained, if it do not filter away and escape through the pores. At the feet of mountains, and about flinty rocks the supply is copious and abundant; it is there cold and more wholesome. In champaign countries, the springs are salt, gross, tepid, and unpleasant, except those, which percolating from the mountains beneath the surface, issue forth in the plains, where, especially when shadowed by trees, they are as delicious as those of the mountains themselves.

Besides the above signs for ascertaining in what places water may be found, are the following: when a place abounds with the slender bulrush, the wild willow, the alder, the withy, reeds, ivy, and other plants of a similar sort, which neither spring up nor flourish without moisture. For these plants usually grow about lakes, which, being lower than the other parts of a country, receive both the rain water and that of the district, through the winter, and, from their size, preserve the moisture for a longer period. On these, however, we must not rely. But in those districts and lands, no lakes being near, where the plants in question grow spontaneously, there we may search.

In places where these signs do not appear, the following plan must be adopted. Dig a hole three feet square, and at least five feet deep, and in it, about sunset, place a brazen or leaden basin, or larger vessel, if one be at hand. It must be rubbed over with oil inside and inverted, and the upper part of the excavation is to be covered with reeds or leaves; on these the earth is to be thrown. On the following day let it be opened, and if the inside of the vase be covered with damp and drops of water, water will be there found.

If the vase placed in the pit be of unburnt clay, having been covered as above directed, when uncovered it will be damp, and perhaps destroyed by the moisture. A fleece of wool being placed in the same pit, if, on the following day, water can be expressed from it, the existence of water in the place is indicated, and that in abundance. Also, if a trimmed lamp full of oil be lighted, and placed in the covered pit, and on the following day it be not exhausted, but still retain unconsumed some of the wick and oil, and present a humid appearance, it shows that water will be found there, inasmuch as heat invariably draws the moisture towards it. Moreover, if in such place a fire be made on the ground, and the ground, when heated, throw out cloudy vapours, water will be found in it.

These experiments having been made, and the requisite indications being manifest, a well is to be sunk on the spot; and if the head of the spring be found, many other wells are to be dug round about it, and, by means of under-cuttings, connected with it so as to concentrate them. The spring-heads, however, are chiefly to be sought in mountains and northern districts, because, in those situations, they are generally sweeter, more wholesome, and more copious, on account of their being sheltered from the rays of the sun, of the trees and shrubs in those places being in greater abundance, and of the sun's rays coming obliquely on them, so that the moisture is not carried off.

Valleys in the midst of mountains receive a very large proportion of rain, and from the closeness of their woods, as well from the shade which the trees afford, added to the snow, which so long remains on them, allow it to percolate through their strata, and thus arrive at the foot of the mountain, when, issuing forth, it becomes the source of a river. On the contrary, in a champaign country, much water will not probably be found; or if it should, it will not be wholesome, because the great power of the sun, unobstructed by shade, attracts and carries off all humidity from the plains; and were even the water to appear, the air would attract and dissipate the lightest, subtlest, and wholesomest parts, and leave the heaviest, most unpleasant, and most unwholesome in the spring.

CHAPTER II.

OF RAIN WATER

Water collected from showers possesses wholesome qualities, because it consists of the lightest and most subtle particles of all springs, which, cleansed by the action of the air, and loosened by the tempests, descend upon the earth: and the reason why showers do not fall so often upon plains as they do on mountains or their vicinity is, because the vapours ascending from the earth at sunrise, to whatever part of the heavens they incline, drive the air before them, and, being in motion, receive an impetus from the air which rushes after them.

The air rushing on, and driving in every direction the vapour before it, creates gales, and blasts, and eddies of wind. Hence the winds, wherever they travel, extract from springs, rivers, marshes, and from the sea, when heated by the sun, condensed vapours, which rise and form clouds. These, borne up by the winds when they come against the sides of mountains, from the shock they sustain, as well as from storms, swell, and, becoming heavy, break and disperse themselves on the earth.

The vapours, clouds, and exhalations which rise from the earth, seem to depend on its retention of intense heat, great winds, cold moisture, and its large proportion of water. Thus when, from the coolness of the night, assisted by the darkness, winds arise, and clouds are formed from damp places, the sun, at its rising, striking on the earth with great power, and thereby heating the air, raises the vapours and the dew at the same time.

A corroboration of this may be seen in a hot bath; for it is absurd to suppose that there can be a spring above its ceiling; and yet that, when warmed by the heated air from the furnace, attracts the moisture from the pavement, whence it is carried up to the vaulting of the ceiling, where it hangs. For hot vapours always ascend, and at first, from their lightness, do not fall down, but as soon as condensed, their gravity prevents buoyancy, and they drop on the heads of the bathers. In the same manner the atmospheric air, when warmed by the sun, raises the moisture from all places, and gathers it to the clouds: for the earth acted upon by heat, drives out its moisture, as heat drives out perspiration from the human body.

This is manifest from the winds, among which, those that blow from the coldest quarters, as the north, and the northeast, bring dry and pure air, but the south and other winds, which blow from the direction of the sun's course, are very damp, and always bring showers with them, because they reach us heated by the torrid regions, and imbibing vapours from the countries they pass over, transport them to the northern quarters.

That this is the case, is evident from an inspection of the sources of rivers, as marked in geographical charts; as also from the descriptions of them, wherein we find that the largest, and greatest number are from the north. First, in India, the Ganges and Indus spring from Mount Caucasus: in Syria, the Tigris and Euphrates: in Asia, and especially in Pontus, the Borysthenes, Hypanis and Tanaïs: in Colchis, the Phasis: in France, the Rhône: in Belgium, the Rhine: southward of the Alps, the Timavus and Po: in Italy, the Tiber: in Maurusia, which we call Mauritania, the river Dyris, from Mount Atlas, which, rising in a northern region, proceeds westward to the lake Heptabolus, where, changing its name, it is called the Niger, and thence from the lake Heptabolus, flowing under barren mountains, it passes in a southern direction, and falls into the marsh Coloe, which encircles Meroe, a kingdom of the southern Ethiopians. From this marsh turning round near the rivers Astasoba, Astabora, and many others, it passes through mountains to the Cataract, and falling down towards the north it passes between Elephantis and Syene and the Thebaic Fields in Egypt, where it receives the appellation of the Nile.

That the source of the Nile is in Mauritania, is certain, because on the other side of the Mount Atlas are other springs whose course is towards the western ocean, in which are found the ichneumon, the crocodile, and other animals and fishes of a similar nature, the hippopotamus excepted.

Since, therefore, all the large known rivers in the world seem to flow from the north, and towards the land of Africa, because those are in the southern regions under the sun's course, where there is little moisture, and but few springs and rivers, it follows that those sources which are in the north and north-east, are much better than others, unless they run over a sulphureous, aluminous, or bituminous soil, for their quality is thereby changed, and whether hot or cold, their water is then of bad smell and taste. It is not that water, by its nature, is hot, but when cold, it is heated by running over a hot soil, and issues warm from the earth through the different pores: it does not, however, long remain in that state, but soon becomes cold; whereas, if it were naturally hot, it would not so soon grow cool; for it does not lose its taste, smell, and colour, which, from the purity of its nature, remain unchanged and discoloured.

CHAPTER III.

OF THE NATURE OF VARIOUS WATERS

There are some hot springs from which water of an excellent flavour is procured, so pleasant to the taste, that it is inferior neither to that of the fountains of the Camænæ nor of the Martian aqueduct. These are naturally so, on the following account. When fire is generated under ground, and the soil is heated all round, either from abundance of alum, bitumen, or sulphur, the hot vapour ascends to the upper parts, and, if there are therein springs of sweet water affected by its spreading through the pores, they grow hot, without injury to the flavour.

There are also cold springs whose smell and taste are bad. These arise in the lower subterranean places, then pass through hot districts, and afterwards continuing their course for a considerable distance, are cold when they rise to the surface, and of a vitiated taste, smell, and colour. Such is the river Albula, in the Tiburtine way: such are the cold fountains in the lands of Ardea, both of a similar smell, which is like sulphur: such, also, are found in other places. But these, though cold, seem, nevertheless, to boil: for, falling from a high place on to a heated soil, and acted on by the meeting of the water and fire, they rush together with great violence and noise; and, apparently inflated by the violence of the compressed air, they issue boiling from the spring. Among them, however, those whose course is not open, but obstructed by stones or other impediments, are, by the force of the air through the narrow pores driven up to the tops of hills.

Hence, those who think they have found springs at such a height as the tops of hills, are mistaken when they dig their wells. For as a brazen vase, not filled to the brim, but about two-thirds full of water, with a cover thereon, when subjected to the great heat of a fire communicates that heat to the water, this, from its natural porosity, receiving the heat and swelling out, not only fills the vase, but, raising the cover by the force of the steam, increases and boils over. If the cover be taken away, the steam passes off to the open air, and the water subsides. In the same manner, when springs are forced through narrow channels, the pressure of the air drives the bubbles of the water to the top; but as soon as they come into wide open channels, the pores of the liquid having vent, it subsides and returns to its natural level.

All hot springs are, therefore, medicinal; because boiling in the soils through which they pass, they acquire many virtues. Thus sulphureous waters restore, by their heat, those suffering under nervous complaints, by warming and extracting the vitious humours of the body. If any member of the body, either from paralysis or other malady, become useless, aluminous waters warm it, and introducing, through the open pores, the opposing power of heat, restore it, and thus it immediately regains its former strength. Bituminous waters, taken inwardly, act as purgatives, and are excellent for the cure of inward complaints.

There is a species of cold nitrous spring like that at Pinna a city of the Vestini, at Cutilium, and other similar places, which, when taken, purges, and, in its passage through the bowels, diminishes schrophulous tumours. In those places where gold, silver, iron, brass, lead, and other similar substances, are excavated, very copious springs are found. These, however, are very pernicious. Indeed they produce effects contrary to those of the hot springs which emit sulphur, alum, and bitumen: for when taken inwardly, passing through the intestines, they affect the nerves and joints, and produce hard swellings on them. Hence the nerves are contracted by the swelling, in the direction of their length, and thus induce the cramp or the gout, because the vessels become saturated with hard gross cold particles.

But there is a species of water, which, when not clear, has a foam, like a flower, swimming on its surface, of a colour similar to that of purple glass. It is known at Athens more particularly, and, from the places and springs in which it is found, it is conducted to the city and to the Piræus; but, on account of the cause above-mentioned, no one drinks it, though it is in use for washing and other purposes. They, therefore, to avoid its ill effects, drink the well water. The Troezenians are not able to escape this evil; for they have no other sort of water, except that of Cybdelus. Hence, in their city, all or at least the greatest part, of the inhabitants are affected with diseases in the feet. At Tarsus, a city of Cilicia, there is a river whose name is Cydnus, in which, if gouty persons steep their feet, they receive relief from it.

here are, moreover, many other sorts of water, which have particular properties, as the Himera, in Sicily, which, when it departs from its source, is divided into two branches. That branch which flows towards Ætna, passing through a country of sweet humidity, is exceedingly soft; the other, its course being through land where salt is dug, has a salt taste. At Parætonium, also, and on the road to the temple of Ammon, and at Casium in Ægypt, there are marshy lakes containing so much salt, that it congeals on them. In many other places the springs, rivers and lakes, which run near salt-pits, are therefrom rendered salt.

Others, running over veins of fat earth, issue forth impregnated with oil: as at Soloe, a city of Cilicia, a river called Liparis, in which those that swim or wash, are, as it were, anointed by the water. In Ethiopia, also, there is a lake which anoints those that swim therein; and in India there is another, which, when the sky is clear, emits a great quantity of oil. At Carthage there is a spring, on the surface of which swims an oil of the smell of cedar dust, with which they anoint cattle. In the island of Zacynthus, and about

Dyrrachium and Apollonia, are springs which throw up a great quantity of pitch with the water. The vast lake at Babylon, called the Asphaltic pool, contains floating bitumen, with which, and with bricks of baked earth, Semiramis built the wall round Babylon. At Joppa, also, in Syria, and in Numidian Arabia, are lakes of immense size, yielding large masses of bitumen, which are taken away by the inhabitants of the neighbourhood.

This is not, however, surprising; for in that spot there are many quarries of hard bitumen: hence, when the water bursts out from this bituminous earth, it carries it therewith; and having come forth, the bitumen is separated from it and deposited. In Cappadocia, on the road between Mazaca and Tuana, there is a considerable lake, in which, if a piece of reed or any other substance be cast, and taken out on the following day, it will be found to have been turned into stone; but the part out of water will not have changed its quality.

In the same manner, at Hierapolis, in Phrygia, a large head of hot water boils up, and is conducted by ditches round the gardens and vineyards. At the end of a year the ditches become incrusted with stone; and hence, making yearly cuts to the right and left, they carry off the incrustations, and use them for building field walls. This circumstance, as it appears to me, would naturally happen, if, in these spots, and in the land about, there be a juice or moisture whose nature is similar to that of rennet. For then, when this coagulating power issues forth from the earth, through the springs, congelation takes place by the heat of the sun and air, as is seen in salt-pits.

Some springs are exceedingly bitter, from the bitterness of the juices of the earth; as the river Hypanis in Pontus, which, for the first forty miles from its source, is of very sweet flavour; but at a spot one hundred and sixty miles from its mouth, a very small spring falls into it, after which the whole body of the river becomes bitter; and this because the water flows through that sort of earth and veins from whence red lead is procured.

These different flavours are dependent on the quality of the earth, as in the case of fruits. For if the roots of trees, of vines, or of other plants, did not produce fruit according to the quality of the earth and the nature of the moisture, the same sort of fruit would, in all places and countries, possess the same flavour. Whereas we see, that, in the island of Lesbos the Protyran wine is made, in Mæonia the κατακεκαυμενίτη (Catakecaumenitan), in Lydia the Melitan, in Sicily the Mamertine, in Campania the Falernian, at Terracina and Fundi the Cæcuban; and in many other places a vast variety of sorts, of different qualities; which could not be the case, but that the moisture of the earth, penetrating the roots with the particular flavour it possesses, nourishes the tree, and, rising to the top of it, imparts to the fruit the flavour of the place and species.

For if the soil and its moisture did not vary, not only would the reeds and rushes of Syria and Arabia be odoriferous, and the shrubs yield pepper, frankincense, and myrrh; nor would the laser grow only in Cyrene, but in all countries and in all places would the same sort of plants grow. For the varieties that are found in different situations and countries arise from the different climates, and the power of the sun, sometimes at a less and at other times at a greater distance; the effects of which are perceived, not only on the moisture of the earth, but on cattle and flocks. And these circumstances could not occur, if in every country the quality of the land did not depend on the sun's power.

In Boeotia on the rivers Cephisus and Melas, in Lucania on the Crathis, in Troy on the Xanthus, and on the springs and rivers of the Clazomenians, Erythræans, and Laodiceans, the cattle, about the time of bearing, at the proper season of the year, are daily driven to drink; and though themselves of a white colour, in some places they bring forth young of a brown colour, in others of dark brown, and in others of a black colour. Thus the property of a beverage, when it enters the body, communicates thereto its quality, of whatever sort that may be. Hence in the plains of Troy, on the banks of its river, from the flocks and cattle being yellow, the Trojans are said to have called the river Xanthus.

Some sorts of water are mortal in their effects: these receive their quality from the poisonous moisture of the lands through which they flow. Such is said to be the Neptunian spring at Terracina, of which those who thoughtlessly drank, lost their lives; hence the antients are said to have stopped it up: and in the country of the Cychri, in Thrace, there is a lake, of which not only those who drink, but those who bathe therein die. In Thessaly, also, flows a spring which no cattle will drink, nor even approach: near it a shrub grows, which bears a purple flower.

So, in Macedonia, where Euripides is interred, from the right and left of his tomb two streams unite: on one of them travellers usually halt to refresh themselves, on account of the excellence of the water: no one, however, approaches the stream on the other side of the monument, because its effects are said to be mortal. In Arcadia, also, the Nonacrian region contains extremely cold water, which drops from the mountains and rocks. It is called water of the Styx (Στυγὸς ὑδωρ); which neither silver, brass, nor iron vessels will hold, because it bursts and destroys them. Nothing preserves or contains it but the hoof of a mule: indeed it is said to have been conveyed, by Iolaus the son of Antipater, to the province where Alexander was, and to have been the cause of his death.

In the Cottian Alps is a water which those who taste instantly die. In the Faliscan territory, on the Via Campana, and in the Cornetan division is a grove wherein a spring rises, containing bones of snakes, lizards, and other reptiles.

There are other springs whose water is acid, as are those of the Lyncestis, and in Italy, of the Velinus and of the Campana near Theanum, and in many other places, which, when drank, have the effect of dissolving the stone which forms in the bladder.

This seems to arise from an acrid and acid moisture being under the earth, from which the waters acquire their acridity; and when introduced into the system, dissolve that with which they come in contact whether generated by deposition or concretion. That acids will have this effect, is clear, from the experiment on an egg, whose shell, when kept therein for some time, will be softened and dissolve. Lead, also, which is very flexible and heavy, if placed in a vessel and covered with acid, and there left open, will be dissolved, and become white lead.

In the same way brass which is more solid by nature, if treated in the same way, will dissolve, and become verdigrease; and even pearls and flint-stones, which neither iron nor fire can destroy, when submitted to its action, are dissolved and dissipated by an acid. With these facts before our eyes, we may fairly argue, that calculous disorders may be cured by acids, on account of their acridity.

Some springs appear to be mixed with wine; as that in Paphlagonia, which, when taken, inebriate as wine. At Æqui, in Italy, and in the territory of the Medulli on the Alps, there is a species of water, the use of which produces swellings of the neck.

In Arcadia, at the well-known city of Clitorium, is a cave flowing with water, of which those who drink become abstemious. At the spring is an epigram inscribed on stone, in Greek verses, to the following effect: that it is not fit for bathing, and also that it is injurious to the vine, because, near the spot, Melampus cured the daughters of Proteus of their madness, and restored them to reason. The epigram is as follows:

> "Rustic, by Clitor's stream who takest thy way,
> Should thirst oppress thee in the noon of day
> Drink at this fount, and in the holy keep
> Of guardian Naiads place thy goats and sheep.
> But dip not thou thy hand, if wine inflame,
> Lest e'en the vapour chill thy fever'd frame;
> Fly thou my sober spring. Melampus here
> Cleansed the mad Proetides, what time the seer
> Arcadia's rugged hills from Argos sought,
> With purifying power my stream was fraught."

There is also in the island of Chios, a fountain, of which those who imprudently drink become foolish; and thereover is inscribed an epigram to the following purport; that though the water of the fountain might be pleasant to the taste, yet he who drank of it would lose his senses. The lines are thus:

> "Sweet drops of cooling draught the spring supplies,
> But whoso drinks, his reason petrifies."

At Susa, the capital of Persia, there is a fountain, at which those who drink lose their teeth. On this also is written an epigram, stating that the water was excellent for washing, but that if drank it caused the teeth to fall out of their sockets. The verses are as follow:

> "A dreaded spring you see,
> Yet if their hands, good stranger,
> Folks choose to wash, they're free
> To do so without danger;
> But if from your long lip,
> Or only from its tip
> Into your hollow venter,
> This liquor pure should enter,
> Your tools for munching meat

Straight on the ground will tumble,
And leave their empty seat
For toothless jaws to mumble."

CHAPTER IV.

OF THE QUALITIES OF WATERS IN CERTAIN PLACES

The quality of the water, in some places, is such, that it gives the people of the country an excellent voice for singing, as at Tarsus, Magnesia, and other countries. In Africa there is a city called Zama, which king Juba surrounded with double walls, and built a palace there; about twenty miles from which, is the town of Ismuc, whose territory is of vast extent. Though Africa is the nursing mother of wild animals, and especially of serpents, in that territory none breed, and if any are brought there they immediately die; and if earth from this place be removed to another, it has the same effect. This sort of earth is also found in the Balearic Isles, where, as I have heard, it has even a more extraordinary quality.
C. Julius, the son of Masinissa, to whom the town and territory belonged, fought under Cæsar the elder. Lodging in my house, our daily intercourse led us to discuss subjects of philology. On an occasion, talking on the power of water and its virtues, he assured me that in the above territory there were springs of the same sort, and that persons born there had excellent voices for singing; and that on this account persons went to the transmarine market to buy male and female slaves, whom they coupled for the purpose of procuring progeny, not only of excellent voice, but of great beauty.
Thus has nature exhibited variety in every thing, except the human body, which in every instance consists of earth; but therein are many sorts of fluids, as blood, milk, perspiration, urine, and tears. Wherefore, if in so small a portion of earth such variety exists, it is not surprising, that in the whole world an infinite variety of liquids are found, through the veins of which a spring of water passing, becomes impregnated with their quality before arriving at its head. Hence so

many fountains of different sorts, arising, as well from the diversity of their situations, as from the quality of the countries, and the properties of the soils.

Of some of these things I have been an eye-witness; of others I have read in Greek books, whose authors are Theophrastus, Timæus, Posidonius, Hegesias, Herodotus, Aristides, and Metrodorus, who, with the greatest care and accuracy have described how the properties of places and the virtues of different waters, depend on the various climates of the earth. From these I have borrowed and copied into this book all that I thought necessary respecting the varieties of water, whereby, from the directions given, persons can more readily choose springs from which they may conduct water to cities and states, inasmuch as nothing is more necessary than water.

For such is the nature of all animals, that if they do not receive a supply of grain, they can subsist on fruits, flesh, or fish, or something of those sorts; but without water, neither the body of an animal, nor even food itself can be raised, preserved, nor provided. The utmost diligence and labour, therefore, should be used in choosing springs, on which the health of mankind depends.

CHAPTER V.

OF THE MEANS OF JUDGING OF WATER

The trial and proof of water are made as follows. If it be of an open and running stream, before we lay it on, the shape of the limbs of the inhabitants of the neighbourhood should be looked to and considered. If they are strongly formed, of fresh colour, with sound legs, and without blear eyes, the supply is of good quality. Also, if digging to a fresh spring, a drop of it be thrown into a Corinthian vessel made of good brass, and leave no stain thereon, it will be found excellent. Equally good that water will be, which, after boiling in a cauldron, leaves no sediment of sand or clay on the bottom.

So if vegetables are quickly cooked over the fire in a vessel full of this water, it shews that the water is good and wholesome. Moreover, if the water itself, when in the spring is limpid and transparent, and the places over which it runs do not generate moss, nor reeds, nor other filth be near it, every thing about it having a clean appearance, it will be manifest by these signs, that such water is light and exceedingly wholesome.

CHAPTER VI.

OF LEVELLING, AND THE INSTRUMENTS USED FOR THAT PURPOSE

I shall now describe how water is to be conveyed to houses and cities, for which purpose levelling is necessary. This is performed either with the dioptra, the level (libra aquaria), or the chorobates. The latter instrument is however the best, inasmuch as the dioptra and level are often found to be incorrect. The chorobates is a rod about twenty feet in length, having two legs at its extremities of equal length and dimensions, and fastened to the ends of the rod at right angles with it; between the rod and the legs are cross pieces fastened with tenons, whereon vertical lines are correctly marked, through which correspondent plumb lines hang down from the rod. When the rod is set, these will coincide with the lines marked, and shew that the instrument stands level.

But if the wind obstructs the operation, and the lines are put in motion, so that one cannot judge by them, let a channel be cut on the top of the rod five feet long, one inch wide, and half an inch high, and let water be poured into it; if the water touch each extremity of the channel equally, it is known to be level. When the chorobates is thus adjusted level, the declivity may be ascertained.

Perhaps some one who may have read the works of Archimedes will say that a true level cannot be obtained by means of water, because that author says, that water is not level, but takes the form of a spheroid, whose centre is the same as that of the earth. Whether the water have a plane or spheroidal surface, the two ends of the channel on the rod right and left, when the rod is level, will nevertheless sustain an equal height of water. If it be inclined towards one side, that end which is highest will not suffer the water to reach to the edge of the channel on the rule. Hence it follows, that though water poured in may have a swelling and curve in the middle, yet its extremities to the right and left will be level. The figure of the chorobates will be given at the end of the book. If there be much fall, the water will be easily conducted, but if there be intervals of uneven ground, use must be made of substructions.

CHAPTER VI.

OF CONDUCTING WATER

Water is conducted in three ways, either in streams by means of channels built to convey it, in leaden pipes or in earthen tubes, according to the following rules. If in channels, the structure must be as solid as possible, and the bed of the channel must have a fall of not less than half a foot to a length of one hundred. These channels are arched over at top, that the sun may strike on the water as little as possible. When they are brought home to the walls of the city a reservoir (castellum) is built, with a triple cistern attached to it to receive the water. In the reservoir are three pipes of equal sizes, and so connected that when the water overflows at the extremities, it is discharged into the middle one, in which are placed pipes for the supply of the pools and fountains, in the second those for the supply of the baths, thus affording a yearly revenue to the people; in the third, those for the supply of private houses. This is to be so managed that the water for public use may never be deficient, for that cannot be diverted if the mains from the heads are rightly constructed. I have made this division in order that the rent which is collected from private individuals who are supplied with water, may be applied by the collectors to the maintenance of the aqueduct.

If hills intervene between the city walls and the spring head, tunnels under ground must be made preserving the fall above assigned; if the ground cut through be sandstone or stone, the channel may be cut therein, but if the soil be earth or gravel, side walls must be built, and an arch turned over, and through this the water may be conducted. The distance between the shafts over the tunnelled part is to be one hundred and twenty feet.

If the water is to be brought in leaden pipes, a reservoir is first made near the spring, from whence to the reservoir in the city, pipes are laid proportioned to the quantity of water. The pipes must be made in lengths of not less than ten feet: hence if they be one hundred inches wide (centenariæ), each length will weigh twelve hundred pounds; if eighty inches (octogenariæ), nine hundred and sixty pounds; if fifty inches (quinquagenariæ), six hundred pounds; if forty inches (quadragenariæ), four hundred and eighty pounds; if thirty inches (tricenariæ), three hundred and sixty pounds; if twenty inches (vicenariæ), two hundred and forty pounds; if fifteen inches (quinumdenum), one hundred and eighty pounds; if ten inches (denum), one hundred and twenty pounds; if eight inches (octonum), ninety-six pounds; if five inches (quinariæ), sixty pounds. It is to be observed that the pipes take the names of their sizes from the quantity of inches in width of the sheets, before they are bent round: thus, if the sheet be fifty inches wide, before bending into a pipe, it is called a fifty-inch pipe; and so of the rest.

An aqueduct which is made of lead, should be thus constructed; if there be a proper fall from the spring head to the city, and hills high enough to cause an impediment do not intervene, the low intervals must be brought to a level by means of substructions preserving the fall directed for channel aqueducts, or by means of a circuitous course, provided it be not too much about; but if there be long valleys, let it be laid according to the slope of the hill, and when it arrives at the bottom, let it be carried level by means of a low substruction as great a distance as possible; this is the part called the venter, by the Greeks κοιλία; when it arrives at the opposite acclivity, the water therein being but slightly swelled on account of the length of the venter, it may be directed upwards.

If the venter were not made use of in valleys, nor the level substruction, but instead of that the aqueduct were brought to an elbow, the water would burst and destroy the joints of the pipes. Over the venter long stand pipes should be placed, by means of which, the violence of the air may escape. Thus, those who have to conduct water through leaden pipes, may by these rules, excellently regulate its descent, its circuit, the venter, and the compression of the air.

It will moreover be expedient, when the level of the fall from the spring is obtained, to build reservoirs at distances of twenty thousand feet from each other, because if damage be done to any part, it will not then be necessary to take the whole work to pieces, and the defective places will be more easily found. These reservoirs, however, are not to be made on a descent, nor on the venter, nor on a rise, nor, generally speaking, in valleys, but only on plains.

But if the water must be conveyed more economically, the following means may be adopted. Thick earthen tubes are to be provided, not less than two inches in thickness, and tongued at one end, so that they may fit into one another. The joints are then to be coated with a mixture of quick lime and oil, and in the elbows made by the level part of the venter, instead of the pipe, must be placed a block of red stone, which is to be perforated, so that the last length of inclined pipe, as well as the first length of the level part may be received into it. Then, on the opposite side, where the acclivity begins, the block of red stone receives the last length of the venter, and the first length of the rising pipe.

Thus adjusting the direction of the tubes, both in the descents and acclivities, the work will never be dislodged. For a great rush of air is generated in an aqueduct, strong enough to break even stones, unless the water is softly and sparingly let down from the head, and unless in elbows or bending joints it be restrained by means of ligatures, or a weight of ballast. In other respects it is similar to one with leaden pipes. When the water is first let down from the head, ashes are put in which will stop those joints not sufficiently coated. Earthen pipes have these advantages, first as to the work; next, that if damaged any one can repair it.

Water conducted through earthen pipes is more wholesome than that through lead; indeed that conveyed in lead must be injurious, because from it white lead is obtained, and this is said to be injurious to the human system. Hence, if what is generated from it is pernicious, there can be no doubt that itself cannot be a wholesome body.

This may be verified by observing the workers in lead, who are of a pallid colour; for in casting lead, the fumes from it fixing on the different members, and daily burning them, destroy the vigour of the blood; water should therefore on no account be conducted in leaden pipes if we are desirous that it should be wholesome. That the flavour of that conveyed in earthen pipes is better, is shewn at our daily meals, for all those whose tables are furnished with silver vessels, nevertheless use those made of earth, from the purity of the flavour being preserved in them.

If there be no springs from which water can be obtained, it is necessary to dig wells, on which every care is to be bestowed, and the utmost ingenuity and discretion used in the examination of the natural indications of the circumstances thereabout, inasmuch as the different sorts of soil which are met with, are many and various. That, like every other body, is composed of four elements; first of earth itself; water, whence are the springs; heat, whence sulphur, alum, and bitumen are generated; and air, whence arise great vapours, which, piercing through the pores to the opening of wells, strike upon the excavators and suffocate them by their natural influence, so that those who do not immediately escape lose their lives.

To avoid this the following method may be adopted; a lighted lamp must be lowered; if it continue to burn, a man may safely descend, but if the strength of the vapour extinguish it, then to the right and left of the well let air holes be dug, so that as it were through nostrils, the vapour may pass off. When this is done and we come to water, the well must be lined with a wall, but in such a manner as not to shut out the springs.

If the soil be hard, and there be no veins of water found at the bottom, we must then have recourse to cisterns made of cement, in which water is collected from roofs and other high places. The cement is thus compounded; in the first place, the purest and roughest sand that can be had is to be procured; then work must be of broken flint whereon no single piece is to weigh more than a pound, the lime must be very strong, and in making it into mortar, five parts of sand are to be added to two of lime, the flint work is combined with the mortar, and of it the walls in the excavation are brought up from the bottom, and shaped by wooden bars covered with iron.

The walls being shaped, the earth in the middle is to be thrown out as low as the foot of the walls, and when levelled, the bottom is to be covered with the same materials to the requisite thickness. If these receptacles are made in two or three divisions, so that the water may be passed from one to another, it will be more wholesome for use; for the mud in it will be thus allowed to subside, and the water will be clearer, preserve its flavor, and be free from smell; otherwise it will be necessary to use salt for purifying it. In this book I have explained to my utmost ability the virtues and varieties of waters, their use and conveyance, and how their goodness may be ascertained; in the following book I intend to describe the principles of gnomonics and the rules of dialling.

DE ARCHITECTURA

BOOK IX
Sciences influencing architecture

INTRODUCTION.

The ancestors of the Greeks held the celebrated wrestlers who were victors in the Olympic, Pythian, Isthmian and Nemean games in such esteem, that, decorated with the palm and crown, they were not only publicly thanked, but were also, in their triumphant return to their respective homes, borne to their cities and countries in four horse chariots, and were allowed pensions for life from the public revenue. When I consider these circumstances, I cannot help thinking it strange that similar honours, or even greater, are not decreed to those authors who are of lasting service to mankind. Such certainly ought to be the case; for the wrestler, by training, merely hardens his own body for the conflict; a writer, however, not only cultivates his own mind, but affords every one else the same opportunity, by laying down precepts for acquiring knowledge, and exciting the talents of his reader.

What does it signify to mankind, that Milo of Crotona, and others of this class, should have been invincible, except that whilst living they were ennobled by their fellow countrymen? On the other hand the doctrines of Pythagoras, Democritus, Plato, Aristotle, and other sages, the result of their daily application, and undeviating industry, still continue to yield, not only to their own country, but to all nations, fresh and luscious fruit, and they, who from an early age are satiated therewith, acquire the knowledge of true science, civilize mankind, and introduce laws and justice, without which no state can long exist.

Since, therefore, individuals as well as the public are so indebted to these writers for the benefits they enjoy, I think them not only entitled to the honour of palms and crowns, but even to be numbered among the gods. I shall produce in illustration, some of their discoveries as examples, out of many, which are of utility to mankind, on the exhibition whereof it must be granted without hesitation that we are bound to render them our homage. The first I shall produce will be one of Plato, which will be found of the greatest importance, as demonstrated by him.

CHAPTER I.

OF THE METHOD OF DOUBLING THE AREA OF A SQUARE

If there be an area or field, whose form is a square, and it is required to set out another field whose form is also to be a square, but double in area, as this cannot be accomplished by any numbers or multiplication, it may be found exactly by drawing lines for the purpose, and the demonstration is as follows. A square plot of ground ten feet long by ten feet wide, contains an hundred feet; if we have to double this, that is, to set out a plot also square, which shall contain two hundred feet, we must find the length of a side of this square, so that its area may be double, that is two hundred feet. By numbers this cannot be done; for if the sides are made fourteen feet, these multiplied into each other give one hundred and ninety-six feet; if fifteen feet, they give a product of two hundred and twenty-five.

Since, therefore, we cannot find them by the aid of numbers, in the square of ten feet a diagonal is to be drawn from angle to angle, so that the square may thereby be divided into two equal triangles of fifty feet area each. On this diagonal another square being described, it will be found, that whereas in the first square there were two triangles, each containing fifty feet, so in the larger square formed on the diagonal there will be four triangles of equal size and number of feet to those in the larger square. In this way Plato shewed and demonstrated the method of doubling the square, as the figure appended explains.

CHAPTER II.

OF THE METHOD OF CONSTRUCTING A RIGHT ANGLED TRIANGLE

Pythagoras demonstrated the method of forming a right angle without the aid of the instruments of artificers: and that which they scarcely, even with great trouble, exactly obtain, may be performed by his rules with great facility. Let three rods be procured, one three feet, one four feet, and the other five feet long; and let them be so joined as to touch each other at their extremities; they will then form a triangle, one of whose angles will be a right angle. For if, on the length of each of the rods, squares be described, that whose length is three feet will have an area of nine feet; that of four, of sixteen feet; and that of five, of twenty-five feet: so that the number of feet contained in the two areas of the square of three and four feet added together, are equal to those contained in the square, whose side is five feet. When Pythagoras discovered this property, convinced that the Muses had assisted him in the discovery, he evinced his gratitude to them by sacrifice. This proposition is serviceable on many occasions, particularly in measuring, no less than in setting out the staircases of buildings, so that each step may have its proper height.

For if the height from the pavement to the floor above be divided into three parts, five of those parts will be the exact length of the inclined line which regulates the blocks of which the steps are formed. Four parts, each equal to one of the three into which the height from the pavement to the floor was divided, are set off from the perpendicular, for the position of the first or lower step. Thus the arrangement and ease of the flight of stairs will be obtained, as the figure will shew.

CHAPTER III.

OF THE METHOD OF DETECTING SILVER WHEN MIWED WITH GOLD

Though Archimedes discovered many curious matters which evince great intelligence, that which I am about to mention is the most extraordinary. Hiero, when he obtained the regal power in Syracuse, having, on the fortunate turn of his affairs, decreed a votive crown of gold to be placed in a certain temple to the immortal gods, commanded it to be made of great value, and assigned an appropriate weight of gold to the manufacturer. He, in due time, presented the work to the king, beautifully wrought, and the weight appeared to correspond with that of the gold which had been assigned for it.

But a report having been circulated, that some of the gold had been abstracted, and that the deficiency thus caused had been supplied with silver, Hiero was indignant at the fraud, and, unacquainted with the method by which the theft might be detected, requested Archimedes would undertake to give it his attention. Charged with this commission, he by chance went to a bath, and being in the vessel, perceived that, as his body became immersed, the water ran out of the vessel. Whence, catching at the method to be adopted for the solution of the proposition, he immediately followed it up, leapt out of the vessel in joy, and, returning home naked, cried out with a loud voice that he had found that of which he was in search, for he continued exclaiming, in Greek, εὑρηκα, (I have found it out).

After this, he is said to have taken two masses, each of a weight equal to that of the crown, one of them of gold and the other of silver. Having prepared them, he filled a large vase with water up to the brim, wherein he placed the mass of silver, which caused as much water to run out as was equal to the bulk thereof. The mass being then taken out, he poured in by measure as much water as was required to fill the vase once more to the brim. By these means he found what quantity of water was equal to a certain weight of silver.

He then placed the mass of gold in the vessel, and, on taking it out, found that the water which ran over was lessened, because, as the magnitude of the gold mass was smaller than that containing the same weight of silver. After again filling the vase by measure, he put the crown itself in, and discovered that more water ran over then than with the mass of gold that was equal to it in weight; and thus, from the superfluous quantity of water carried over the brim by the immersion of the crown, more than that displaced by the mass, he found, by calculation, the quantity of silver mixed with the gold, and made manifest the fraud of the manufacturer.

Let us now consider the discoveries of Archytas the Tarentine, and Eratosthenes of Cyrene, who, by the aid of mathematics, invented many things useful to mankind; and though for other inventions they are remembered with respect, yet they are chiefly celebrated for their solution of the following problem. Each of these, by a different method, endeavoured to discover the way of satisfying the response of Apollo of Delos, which required an altar to be made similar to his, but to contain double the number of cube feet, on the accomplishment of which, the island was to be freed from the anger of the gods.

Archytas obtained a solution of the problem by the semicylinder, and Eratosthenes by means of a proportional instrument. The pleasures derivable from scientific investigations, and the delight which inventions afford when we consider their effects, are such that I cannot help admiring the works of Democritus, on the nature of things, and his commentary, entitled Χειροτόνητον, wherein he sealed with a ring, on red wax, the account of those experiments he had tried.

The discoveries, therefore, of these men are always at hand, not only to correct the morals of mankind, but also to be of perpetual advantage to them. But the glory of the wrestler and his body soon decay, so that neither whilst in vigour, nor afterwards by his instructions, is he of that service to society which the learned are by publication of their sentiments.

Since honours are not awarded for propriety of conduct, nor for the excellent precepts delivered by authors, their minds soaring higher, are raised to heaven in the estimation of posterity, they derive immortality from their works, and even leave their portraits to succeeding ages. For, those who are fond of literature, cannot help figuring to themselves the likeness of the poet Ennius, as they do that of any of the gods. So also those who are pleased with the verses of Accius, think they have himself, not less than the force of his expressions, always before them.

Many even in after ages will fancy themselves contending with Lucretius on the nature of things, as with Cicero on the art of rhetoric. Many of our posterity will think that they are in discourse with Varro when they read his work on the Latin language: nor will there be wanting a number of philologers, who, consulting in various cases the Greek philosophers, will imagine that they are actually talking with them. In short, the opinions of learned men who have flourished in all periods, though absent in body, have greater weight in our councils and discussions than were they even present.

Hence, O Cæsar, relying on these authorities, and using their judgment and opinions, I have written these books; the first seven related to buildings, the eighth to the conduct of water, and in this I propose treating on the rules of dialling, as deducible from the shadow produced by the rays of the sun from a gnomon, and I shall explain in what proportions it is lengthened and shortened.

CHAPTER IV.

OF THE UNIVERSE AND THE PLANETS

It is clearly by a divine and surprising arrangement, that the equinoctial gnomons are of different lengths in Athens, Alexandria, Rome, Piacenza, and in other parts of the earth. Hence the construction of dials varies according to the places in which they are to be erected; for from the size of the equinoctial shadow, are formed analemmata, by means of which the shadows of gnomons are adjusted to the situation of the place and the lines which mark the hours. By an analemma is meant a rule deduced from the sun's course, and founded on observation of the increase of the shadow from the winter solstice, by means of which, with mechanical operations and the use of compasses, we arrive at an accurate knowledge of the true shape of the world.

By the world is meant the whole system of nature together with the firmament and its stars. This continually turns round the earth and sea on the extreme points of its axis, for in those points the natural power is so contrived that they must be considered as centres, one above the earth and sea at the extremity of the heavens by the north stars, the other opposite and below the earth towards the south; moreover in these central points as round the centres of wheels, which the Greeks call πόλοι, the heavens perpetually revolve. Thus the earth and sea occupy the central space.

Hence from the construction, the polar centre is raised above the earth in the northern part, whilst that in the southern part, which is underneath, is hidden from our view by the earth, and through the middle obliquely and inclined to the south, is a large band comprising the twelve signs, which, by the varied combination of the stars being divided into twelve equal parts, contains that number of representations of figures. These are luminous, and with the firmament and the other stars and constellations, make their circuit round the earth and sea; all these, visible as well as invisible, have their fixed seasons, six of the signs turning above the earth, the remaining six below it; which latter are hidden by the earth. Six of them, however, are always above the earth; for the portion of the last sign, which by the revolution is depressed below the earth and hidden by it, is on the opposite side equal to that of a fresh sign emerging from darkness by the force of the moving power; since it is the same power and motion which cause the rising and setting at the same moment.

As these signs are twelve in number, each occupies a twelfth part of the heaven, and they move continually from east to west: and through them in a contrary course, the moon, Mercury, Venus, the sun itself, Mars, Jupiter and Saturn, as if ascending, pass through the heavens from west to east in different orbits. The moon making her circuit in twenty-eight days and about one hour, and thus returning to the sign from which she departed, completes the lunar month.

The sun, in the course of a month, passes through the space of one sign which is a twelfth part of the heavens; hence in twelve months going through the twelve signs, when he has returned to that sign from which he set out, the period of a year is completed: but that circle which the moon passes through thirteen times in twelve months, the sun passes through only once in the same time. The planets Mercury and Venus nearest the rays of the sun, move round the sun as a centre, and appear sometimes retrograde and sometimes progressive, seeming occasionally, from the nature of their circuit, stationary in the signs.

This may be observed in the planet Venus, which when it follows the sun, and appears in the heavens with great lustre after his setting, is called the evening star; at other times preceding him in the morning before sunrise, it is called the morning star. Wherefore these planets at times appear as if they remained many days in one sign, whilst at other times they pass rapidly from one to another; but though they do not remain an equal number of days in each sign, the longer they are delayed in one the quicker they pass through the succeeding one, and thus perform their appointed course: in this manner it happens that being delayed in some of the signs, when they escape from the retention, they quickly pass through the rest of their orbit.

Mercury revolves in the heavens in such a manner, that passing through the several signs in three hundred and sixty days, he returns to that sign from which he set out, remaining about thirty days in each sign.

The planet Venus, as soon as she escapes from the influence of the sun's rays, runs through the space of one sign in forty days; and what she loses by stopping a long time in one sign, she makes up by her quick passage through others. She completes her circuit through the heavens in four hundred and eighty-five days; by which time she has returned to the sign from whence she set out.

Mars, on about the six hundred and eighty-third day, completes the circuit of the signs, and returns to his place; and if, in any sign, he move with a greater velocity, his stationary state in others equalizes the motion, so as to bring him round in the proper number of days. Jupiter moving also in contrary rotation, but with less velocity, takes three hundred and sixty days to pass through one sign; thus lengthening the duration of his circuit to eleven years and three hundred and twenty-three days before he returns to the sign in which he was seen twelve years before his setting out. Lastly, Saturn, remaining thirty-one months and some days in each sign, returns to his point of departure at the end of twenty-nine years, and about one hundred and sixty days, or nearly thirty years. Hence, the nearer he is to the extremity of the universe, the larger does his circuit appear, as well as the slower his motion.

All those which make their circuit above that of the sun, especially when they are in trine aspect, do not advance, but, on the contrary, are retrograde, and seem to stop till the sun passes from the trinal sign into another. Some are of opinion, that this happens on account of their great distance from the sun, on which account their paths not being sufficiently lighted, they are retarded by the darkness. But I am not of that opinion, since the brightness of the sun is perceptible, evident and unobscured throughout the system, just as it appears to us, as well when the planets are retrograde as when they are stationary. If, then, our vision extends to such a distance, how can we imagine it possible to obscure the glorious splendour of the planets?

It appears more probable, that it is the heat which draws and attracts all things towards itself: we, in fact, see the heat raise the fruits of the earth to a considerable height, and the spray of waters from fountains ascend to the clouds by the rainbow: in the same manner the excessive power of the sun spreading his rays in a triangular form, attracts the planets which follow him, and, as it were, stops and restrains those which precede him, preventing them from leaving him, and, indeed, forcing them to return to him, and to remain in the other trinal sign.

One may perhaps ask, whence it happens that the sun, by its heat, causes a detention in the fifth sign from itself, rather than in the second or third, which are nearer. This may be thus explained. Its rays diverge through the heavens in lines which form a triangle whose sides are equal. Those sides fall exactly in the fifth sign. For if the rays fell circularly throughout the system, and were not bounded by a triangular figure, the nearer places would be absolutely burnt. This seems to have struck the Greek poet, Euripides; for he observes, that those places more distant from the sun are more intensely heated than those temperate ones that are nearer to him: hence, in the tragedy of Phaëthon, he says, Καίει τὰ πόρρω, τὰ δ' ἐγγὺς εὔκατ' ἔχει. (The distant places burn, those that are near are temperate.)

If, therefore, experience, reason, and the testimony of an antient poet, prove it, I do not see how it can be otherwise than I have above shewn. Jupiter performs his circuit between those of Mars and Saturn: thus it is greater than that of Mars, but less than that of Saturn. In short, all the planets, the more distant they are from the extremity of the heaven, and the nearer their orbit is to the earth, seem to move swifter; for those which have a smaller orbit, often pass those above them.

Thus, on a wheel similar to those in use among potters, if seven ants be placed in as many channels round the centre, which are necessarily greater in proportion to their distance therefrom, and the ants are forced to make their circuits in these channels, whilst the wheel moves round in an opposite direction, they will assuredly complete their circuit, notwithstanding the contrary motion of the wheel; and, moreover, that nearest the centre will perform his journey sooner than he who is travelling in the outer channel of the wheel, who, though he move with equal velocity, yet, from the greater extent of his circuit, will require a longer time for its completion. It is even so with the planets, which, each in its particular orbit, revolve in a direction contrary to the motion of the heavens, although, in their diurnal motion, they are carried backwards by its rotation.

The reason why some planets are temperate, some hot, and others cold, appears to be this; that all fire has a flame, whose tendency is upward. Hence the sun warms, by his rays, the air above him, wherein Mars moves, and that planet is therefore heated thereby. Saturn, on the contrary, who is near the extremity of the universe, and comes in contact with the frozen regions of the heavens, is exceedingly cold. Jupiter, however, whose orbit lies between those of the two just mentioned, is tempered by the cold and heat, and has an agreeable and moderate temperature. Of the band comprising the twelve signs, of the seven planets, and their contrary motions and orbits, also of the manner and time in which they pass from one sign into another, and complete their circuits, I have set forth all that I have learnt from authors. I will now speak of the moon's increase and wane, as taught by the antients.

Berosus, who travelled into Asia from the state or country of the Chaldeans, teaching his doctrines, maintained that the moon was a ball, half whereof was luminous, and the remaining half of a blue colour; and that when, in its course, it approached the sun; attracted by the rays and the force of the heat, it turned its bright side in that direction, from the sympathy existing between light and light; whence, when the sun is above it, the lower part, which is not luminous, is not visible, from the similarity of its colour to the air. When thus perpendicular to the sun's rays, all the light is confined to its upper surface, and it is then called the new moon.

When it passes towards the east, the sun begins to have less effect upon it, and a thin line on the edge of its bright side emits its splendour towards the earth. This is on the second day: and thus, from day to day, advancing in its circuit, the third and fourth days are numbered: but, on the seventh day, when the sun is in the west, the moon is in the middle, between the east and the west; and being distant from the sun half the space of the heavens, the luminous half side will be towards the earth. Lastly; when the sun and the moon are the whole distance of the heavens from each other, and the former, passing towards the west, shines full on the moon behind it in the east, being the fourteenth day, it is then at the greatest distance from its rays, and the complete circle of the whole orb emits its light. In the remaining days it gradually decreases till the completion of the lunar month, and then returns to re-pass under the sun; its monthly rays being determined by the number of days.

I shall now subjoin what Aristarchus, the Samian mathematician, learnedly wrote on this subject, though of a different nature. He asserted, that the moon possesses no light of its own, but is similar to a speculum, which receives its splendour from the sun's rays. Of the planets, the moon makes the smallest circuit, and is nearest to the earth; whence, on the first day of its monthly course, hiding itself under the sun, it is invisible; and when thus in conjunction with the sun, it is called the new moon. The following day, which is called the second, removing a little from the sun, it receives a small portion of light on its disc. When it is three days distant from him, it has increased, and become more illuminated; thus daily elongating from him, on the seventh day, being half the heavens distant from the western sun, one half of it shines, namely, that half which is lighted by the sun.

On the fourteenth day, being diametrically opposite to the sun, and the whole of the heavens distant from him, it becomes full, and rises as the sun sets; and its distance being the whole extent of the heavens, it is exactly opposite to, and its whole orb receives, the light of the sun. On the seventeenth day, when the sun rises, it inclines towards the west; on the twenty-first day, when the sun rises, the moon is about mid-heaven, and the side next the sun is enlightened, whilst the other is in shadow. Thus advancing every day, about the twenty-eighth day it again returns under the rays of the sun, and completes its monthly rotation. I will now explain how the sun, in his passage through a sign every month, causes the days and hours to increase and diminish.

CHAPTER V.

OF THE SUN'S COURSE THROUGH THE TWELVE SIGNS

When the sun has entered the sign of Aries, and run through about an eighth part of it, it is the vernal equinox. When he has arrived at the tail of Taurus and the Pleiades, for which the fore part of the Bull is conspicuous, he has advanced in the heavens more than half his course towards the north. From Taurus, he enters into Gemini, at the time when the Pleiades rise, and being more over the earth increases the length of the days. From Gemini entering into Cancer, which occupies the smallest space in the heavens, and coming to the eighth division of it he determines the solstice, and moving forward arrives at the head and breast of Leo, which are parts properly within the division assigned to Cancer.

From the breast of Leo and the boundaries of Cancer, the sun moving through the other parts of Leo, has by that time diminished the length of the day, as well as of his circuit, and resumes the equal motion he had when in Gemini. Hence from Leo passing to Virgo and proceeding to the indented part of her garment, he contracts his circuit, which is now equal to that which it had in Taurus. Proceeding then from Virgo through the indentation which includes the beginning of Libra, in the eighth part of that sign, the autumnal equinox is completed; the circuit being then equal to that in the sign Aries.

When the sun enters into Scorpio at the setting of the Pleiades, he diminishes, in passing to the southern parts, the length of the days; and from Scorpio passing to a point near the thighs of Sagittarius, he makes a shorter diurnal circuit. Then beginning from the thighs of Sagittarius, which are in Capricornus, at the eighth part of the latter he makes the shortest course in the heavens. This time from the shortness of the days, is called Bruma (winter) and the days Brumales. From Capricornus passing into Aquarius, the length of the days is increased to that of those when he was in Sagittarius. From Aquarius he passes into Pisces at the time that the west wind blows; and his course is equal to that he made in Scorpio. Thus the sun travelling through these signs at stated times, increases and diminishes the duration of the days and hours. I shall now treat of the other constellations on the right and left of the zodiac, as well those on the south as on the north side of the heavens.

CHAPTER VI.

OF THE NORTHERN CONSTELLATIONS

The Great Bear, which the Greeks call ἄρκτος, and also ἑλίκη, has his keeper behind him. Not far distant is the constellation of the Virgin, on whose right shoulder is a very brilliant star, called by us Provindemia Major, and by the Greeks προτρύγετος, which shines with extraordinary lustre and colour. Opposite to it is another star, between the knees of the Keeper of the Bear, which bears the name of Arcturus.

Opposite the head of the Bear, across the feet of the Twins, is Auriga (the charioteer) standing on the point of the horns of the Bull, and one side, above the left horn towards the feet of Auriga, there is a star called the hand of Auriga; on the other side the Goat's Kids and the Goat over the left shoulder. Above both the Bull and the Ram stands Perseus, which on the right extends under the bottom of the Pleiades, on the left towards the head of the Ram; his right hand rests on the head of Cassiopeia, the left holding the Gorgon's head by its top over the Bull, and laying it at the feet of Andromeda.

Above Andromeda are the Fishes, one under her belly, and the other above the back of the Horse; the brilliant star in the belly of the Horse is also in the head of Andromeda. The right hand of Andromeda is placed on the figure of Cassiopeia, the left upon the north eastern fish. Aquarius stands on the head of the horse; the ears of the horse turn towards the knees of Aquarius, and the middle star of Aquarius is also common to Capricornus. Above on high is the Eagle and the Dolphin, and near them Sagitta. On the side is the Swan, the right wing of which is turned towards the hand

and sceptre of Cepheus, the left leans on Cassiopeia, and under the tail of Avis the feet of the horse are hidden.

Above Sagittarius, Scorpio, and Libra, comes the Serpent, the point of whose snout touches the Crown; in the middle of the Serpent is Ophiuchus, who holds the Serpent in his hands, and with his left foot treads on the head of the Scorpion. Near the middle of the head of Ophiuchus is the head of the Kneeler; their heads are easily distinguished from being marked with luminous stars.

The foot of the Kneeler is placed on the temple of the Serpent, which is entwined between the two northern bears, called Septentriones. The Dolphin is a short distance from them. Opposite the bill of the Swan is the Lyre. The Crown lies between the shoulders of the Keeper and the Kneeler. In the northern circle are two Bears, with their shoulders and breasts in opposite directions; of these the Less is called κυνοσούρα, and the Larger ἑλίκη by the Greeks. Their heads are turned downwards, and each of their tails is towards the other's head, for both their tails are raised, and that which is called the pole-star, is that near the tail of the Little Bear. Between these tails, as we have before stated, extends the Serpent, who turns round the head of that nearest to him, whence he takes a folding direction round the head of the smaller bear, and then spreading under his feet, and rising up, returns and folds from the head of the Less to the Greater Bear, with his snout opposite and shewing the right temple of his head. The feet of Cepheus are also on the tail of the Small Bear; towards which part more above our heads, are the stars which form the equilateral triangle above Aries. There are many stars common to the Lesser Bear and Cepheus. I have enumerated the constellations which are in the heavens to the right of the east between the zodiac and the north. I shall now describe those which are distributed on the southern side to the left of the east.

CHAPTER VII.

OF THE SOUTHERN CONSTELLATIONS

First, under Capricornus is the southern Fish looking towards the tail of the whale. Between it and Sagittarius is a vacant space. The Altar is under the sting of Scorpio. The fore parts of the Centaur are near Libra and Scorpio, and he holds in his hand that constellation which astronomers call the Beast. Near Virgo, Leo, and Cancer, the Snake stretches through a range of stars, and with its foldings encircles the region of Cancer, raising its snout towards Leo and on the middle of its body supporting the cup; its tail extends towards the hand of Virgo, and upon that is the Crow; the stars on its back are all equally luminous.
Under its belly, at the tail, is the Centaur. Near the cup and Leo is the ship Argo, whose prow is hidden, but the mast and parts about the steerage are clearly seen. The Ship and its poop touch the tip of the Dog's tail. The smaller Dog is behind the Twins at the head of the Snake, and the larger follows the smaller Dog. Orion lies transversely under, pressed on by the hoof of the Bull, holding a shield in his left hand and with the club in his right hand raised towards Gemini; near his feet is the Dog at a short distance following the Hare. Below Aries and Pisces is the Whale, from whose top to the two Fishes a small train of stars, which the Greeks call Ἑρμηδόνη, regularly extends, and this ligature of the Fishes twisting considerably inwards, at one part touches the top of the Whale. A river of stars, in the shape of the river Po, begins from the left foot of Orion. The water that runs from Aquarius takes its course between the head of the southern Fish and the tail of the Whale.
I have explained the constellations displayed and formed in the heavens by nature with a divine intelligence, according to the system of the philosopher Democritus, confining my-

self to those whose rising and setting are visible. Some, however, such as the two Bears turning round the pole, never set nor pass under the earth. So also, the constellations about the south pole, which from the obliquity of the heavens is under the earth, are always hidden, and their revolution never brings them above the horizon. Whence the interposition of the earth prevents a knowledge of their forms. The constellation Canopus proves this, which is unknown in these countries, though well known to merchants who have travelled to the extremity of Egypt and other boundaries of the earth.

I have described the true circuit of the heavens about the earth, the arrangement of the twelve signs, also that of the northern and southern constellations, because therefrom, from the opposite course of the sun through the signs, and from the shadows of gnomons at the equinoxes, are formed the diagrams of analemmata.

2. The rest which relates to astrology, and the effects produced upon human life by the twelve signs, the five planets, the sun and the moon, must be left to the discussions of the Chaldeans, whose profession it is to cast nativities, and by means of the configurations of the stars to explain the past and the future. The talent, the ingenuity, and reputation of those who come from the country of the Chaldeans, is manifest from the discoveries they have left us in writing. Berosus was the first of them. He settled in the island and state of Cos, and there established a school. Afterwards came Antipater and Achinapolus, which latter not only gave rules for predicting a man's fate by a knowledge of the time of his birth, but even by that of the moment wherein he was conceived.

In respect of natural philosophy Thales the Milesian, Anaxagoras of Clazomenæ, Pythagoras the Samian, Xenophanes of Colophon Democritus the Abderite, have published systems which explain the mode in which Nature is regulated, and how every effect is produced. Eudoxus, Endæmon, Callippus, Melo, Philip, Hipparchus, Aratus, and others, following in the steps of the preceding, found, by the use of instruments, the rising and setting of the stars and the changes of the seasons, and left treatises thereon for the use of posterity. Their learning will be admired by mankind, because, added to the above, they appear as if by divine inspiration to have foretold the weather at particular seasons of the year. For a knowledge of these matters reference must therefore be made to their labours and investigation.

CHAPTER VIII.

OF THE CONSTRUCTION OF DIALS BY THE ANALEMMA

From the doctrines of the philosophers above mentioned, are extracted the principles of dialling, and the explanation of the increase and decrease of the days in the different months. The sun at the times of the equinoxes, that is when he is in Aries or Libra, casts a shadow in the latitude of Rome equal to eight ninths of the length of the gnomon. At Athens the length of the shadow is three fourths of that of the gnomon. At Rhodes five sevenths; at Tarentum nine elevenths; at Alexandria three fifths; and thus at all other places the shadow of the gnomon at the equinoxes naturally differs.

Hence in whatever place a dial is to be erected, we must first obtain the equinoctial shadow. If, as at Rome, the shadow be eight ninths of the gnomon, let a line be drawn on a plane surface, in the center whereof is raised a perpendicular thereto; this is called the gnomon, and from the line on the plane in the direction of the gnomon, let nine equal parts be measured. Let the end of the ninth part A, be considered as a centre, and extending the compasses from that centre to the extremity B of the said line, let a circle be described. This is called the meridian.

Then of those nine parts between the plane and the point of the gnomon, let eight be allotted to the line on the plane, whose extremity is marked C. This will be the equinoctial shadow of the gnomon. From the point C through the centre A let a line be drawn, and it will be a ray of the sun at the equinoxes. Then extend the compasses from the centre to the line on the plane, and mark on the left an equidistant point E, and on the right another, lettered I, and join them by a line through the centre, which will divide the circle into two semicircles. This line by mathematicians is called the horizon.

A fifteenth part of the whole circumference is to be then taken, and placing the point of the compasses in that point of the circumference F, where the equinoctial ray is cut, mark with it to the right and left the points G and H. From these, through the centre, draw lines to the plane where the letters T and R are placed, thus one ray of the sun is obtained for the winter, and the other for the summer. Opposite the point E, will be found the point I, in which a line drawn through the centre, cuts the circumference; and opposite to G and H the points K and L, and opposite to C, F, and A, will be the point N.

Diameters are then to be drawn from G to L, and from H to K. The lower one will determine the summer, and the upper the winter portion. These diameters are to be equally divided in the middle at the points M and O, and the points being thus marked, through them and the centre A a line must be drawn to the circumference, where the letters P and Q are placed. This line will be perpendicular to the equinoctial ray, and is called in mathematical disquisitions, the Axon. From the last obtained points as centres (M and O) extending the compasses to the extremity of the diameter, two semicircles are to be described, one of which will be for summer, the other for winter.

In respect of those points where the two parallels cut that line which is called the horizon; on the right hand is placed the letter S, and on the left the letter V, and at the extremity of the semicircle, lettered G, a line parallel to the Axon is drawn to the extremity on the left, lettered H. This parallel line is called Lacotomus. Finally, let the point of the compasses be placed in that point where this line is cut by the equinoctial ray, and letter the point X, and let the other point be extended to that where the summer ray cuts the circumference, and be lettered H. Then with a distance equal to that from the summer interval on the equinoctial point, as a centre, describe the circle of the months, which is called Manacus. Thus will the analemma be completed.

Having proceeded with the diagram and its formation, the hour lines may be projected on the analemma according to the place, either by winter lines, or summer lines, or equinoctial lines, or lines of the months, and as many varieties and species of dials as can be desired, may be constructed by this ingenious method. In all the figures and diagrams the effect will be the same, that is to say, the equinoctial as well as the solstitial days, will always be divided into twelve equal parts. These matters, however, I pass over, not from indolence, but to avoid prolixity. I will merely add, by whom the different species and figures of dials were invented; for I have not been able to invent a new sort, neither will I pass off the inventions of others as my own. I shall therefore mention those of which I have any information, and by whom they were invented.

CHAPTER IX.

OF VARIOUS DIALS, AND THEIR INVENTORS

Berosus the Chaldean, was the inventor of the semicircle, hollowed in a square, and inclined according to the climate. Aristarchus the Samian, of the Scaphe or Hemisphere, as also of the discus on a plane. The Arachne was the invention of Eudoxus the astrologer, though some attribute it to Apollonius. The Plinthium or Lacunar, an example of which is to be seen in the Circus Flaminius, was invented by Scopas the Syracusan. The sort called Πρὸς τὰ ἱστορούμενα, by Parmenio. That called Πρὸς πᾶν κλίμα, by Theodosius and Andrias. The Pelicinon by Patrocles. The Cone by Dionysodorus. The Quiver by Apollonius. The persons above mentioned not only invented other sorts; but the inventions of others have come down to us, such as the Gonarche, the Engonatos, and the Antiboreus. Many also have left instructions for constructing the portable pendulous dial. When any one understands the formation of the analemma, he will be enabled, by reference to their writings, to suit them to any place. By the same writers have been discovered the method of making water dials.

Ctesibius Alexandrinus was the first who found out the properties of the wind, and of pneumatic power, the origin of which inventions is worthy of being known. Ctesibius, whose father was a barber, was born at Alexandria. Endowed with extraordinary talent and industry, he acquired great reputation by his taste for his mechanical contrivances. Wishing to suspend a mirror in his father's shop, in such a way that it might be easily raised and lowered by means of a concealed cord, he used the following expedient.

Fixing a wooden tube under the beam, he attached pulleys to it upon which the cord passed and made an angle in descending into the wood which he had hollowed out: there he placed small tubes, within which a leaden ball attached to the cord was made to descend. It happened that the weight, in passing through the narrow parts of the tube, pressed on the inclosed air, and violently driving out at its mouth the quantity of air compressed in the tubes, produced by obstruction and contact a distinct sound.

Ctesibius having thus observed that by the compression and concussion of the air, sounds might be produced, he made use of the discovery in his application of it to hydraulic machines, to those automata which act by the power of inclosed water, to lever and turning engines, and to many other entertaining devices, but principally to water dials. First he made a perforation in a piece of gold or a smooth gem, because these materials are not liable to be worn by the action of the water, nor to collect filth, by which the passage of the water might be obstructed: the water flowing through the hole equably, raises an inverted bowl, called by the workmen phellos, or the tympanum, with which are connected a rule and revolving drum wheels with perfectly equal teeth, which teeth, acting on one another, produce revolutions and measured motion. There are other rules and other wheels, toothed in a similar manner, which acted upon by the same force in their revolutions, produce different species of motion, by which figures are made to move, cones are turned round, stones or oviform bodies are ejected, trumpets sounded, and similar conceits effected.

On these also, either on columns or pillars, the hours are marked, to which a figure, holding a wand and rising from the lower part, points throughout the day, the increase and decrease whereof is daily and monthly adjusted, by adding or taking away certain wedges. To regulate the flow of the water, stoppers are thus formed. Two cones are prepared, one convex, the other concave, and rounded so as to fit exactly into each other. A rod, by elongating these, or bringing them together, increases or diminishes the flow of water into the vessel. In this manner, and according to the principles of this machine, water-dials for winter are constructed.

If the addition or removal of the wedges should not be attended by a correspondent increase or decrease in the days, for the wedges are frequently imperfect, it is to be thus remedied. Let the hours from the analemma be placed on the column transversely, and let the lines of the months be also marked thereon. The column is to turn round, so that, in its continual revolution, the wand of the figure, as it rises, points to the hours, and, according to the respective months, makes the hours long or short.

Other kinds of winter-dials are made, which are called Anaporica. They are constructed as follows. With the aid of the analemma the hours are marked by brazen rods on their face, beginning from the centre, whereon circles are drawn, shewing the limits of the months. Behind these rods a wheel is placed, on which are measured and painted the heavens and the zodiac with the figures of the twelve celestial signs, by drawing lines from the centre, which mark the greater and smaller spaces of each sign. On the back part of the middle of the wheel is fixed a revolving axis, round which a pliable brass chain is coiled, at one of whose ends a phellos or tympanum hangs, which is raised by the water, and at the other end a counterpoise of sand equal to the weight of the phellos.

Thus as the phellos ascends by the action of the water, the counterpoise of sand descends and turns the axis, as does that the wheel, whose rotation causes at times the greater part of the circle of the zodiac to be in motion, and at other times the smaller; thus adjusting the hours to the seasons. Moreover in the sign of each month are as many holes as there are days in it, and the index which in dials is generally a representation of the sun, shews the spaces of the hours; and whilst passing from one hole to another, it completes the period of the month.

Wherefore, as the sun passing through the signs, lengthens and shortens the days and hours, so the index of the dial, entering by the points opposite the centre round which the wheel turns, by its daily motions, sometimes in greater, at other times in less periods, will pass through the limits of the months and days. The management of the water, and its equable flow, is thus regulated.

Inside, behind the face of the dial, a cistern is placed, into which the water is conveyed by a pipe. In its bottom is a hole, at whose side is fixed a brazen tympanum, with a hole in it, through which the water in the cistern may pass into it. Within this is inclosed a lesser tympanum attached to the greater, with male and female joints rounded, so that the lesser tympanum turning within the greater, similar to a stopple, fits closely, though it moves easily. Moreover, on the lip of the greater tympanum are three hundred and sixty-five points, at equal distances. On the circumference of the smaller tympanum a tongue is fixed, whose tip points to the marks. In this smaller tympanum a proportionable hole is made, through which the water passes into the tympanum, and serves the work.

On the lip of the large tympanum, which is fixed, are the figures of the celestial signs; above, is the figure of Cancer, and opposite to it, below, that of Capricornus. On the right of the spectator is Libra, on his left Aries. All the other signs are arranged in the spaces between these, as they are seen in the heavens.

Thus, when the sun is in the portion of the circle occupied by Capricornus, the tongue stands in that part of the larger tympanum where Capricornus is placed, touching a different point every day: and as it then vertically bears the great weight of the running water, this passes with great velocity through the hole into the vase, which, receiving it, and being soon filled, diminishes and contracts the lengths of the days and hours. When, by the diurnal revolution of the lesser tympanum, the tongue enters Aquarius, all the holes fall perpendicular, and the flow of the water being thus lessened, it runs off more slowly; whence the vase receiving the water with less velocity, the length of the hours is increased.

Thus, going gradually through the points of Aquarius and Pisces, as soon as the hole of the small tympanum touches the eighth part of Aries, the water flows more gently, and produces the equinoctial hours. From Aries, through the spaces of Taurus and Gemini, advancing to the upper points where the Crab is placed, the hole or tympanum touching it at its eighth division, and arriving at the summit, the power is lessened; and hence running more slowly, its stay is lengthened, and the solstitial hours are thereby formed. When it descends from Cancer, and passes through Leo and Virgo, returning to the point of the eighth part of Libra, its stay is shortened by degrees, and the hours diminished, till, arriving at the same point of Libra, it again indicates the equinoctial hours.

The hole being lowered through the space of Scorpio and Sagittarius, in its revolution it returns to the eighth division of Capricornus, and, by the velocity of the water, the winter hours are produced. To the best of my ability I have explained the construction and proportions of dials, so that they may be easily set up. It now remains for me to speak of machines, and the principles which govern them. These will be found in the following book, and will complete this Treatise on Architecture.

DE ARCHITECTURA

BOOK X
Use and construction of machines

INTRODUCTION.

In the magnificent and spacious Grecian city of Ephesus an ancient law was made by the ancestors of the inhabitants, hard indeed in its nature, but nevertheless equitable. When an architect was entrusted with the execution of a public work, an estimate thereof being lodged in the hands of a magistrate, his property was held, as security, until the work was finished. If, when finished, the expense did not exceed the estimate, he was complimented with decrees and honours. So when the excess did not amount to more than a fourth part of the original estimate, it was defrayed by the public, and no punishment was inflicted. But when more than one-fourth of the estimate was exceeded, he was required to pay the excess out of his own pocket.

Would to God that such a law existed among the Roman people, not only in respect of their public, but also of their private buildings, for then the unskilful could not commit their depredations with impunity, and those who were the most skilful in the intricacies of the art would follow the profession. Proprietors would not be led into an extravagant expenditure so as to cause ruin; architects themselves, from the dread of punishment, would be more careful in their calculations, and the proprietor would complete his building for that sum, or a little more, which he could afford to expend. Those who can conveniently expend a given sum on any work, with the pleasing expectation of seeing it completed would cheerfully add one-fourth more; but when they find themselves burdened with the addition of half or even more than half of the expense originally contemplated, losing their spirits, and sacrificing what has already been laid out, they incline to desist from its completion.

Nor is this an evil which occurs in buildings alone, but also in the shows of gladiators in the Forum, and in the scenes of plays exhibited by the magistrates, in which neither delay nor hindrance is admitted, since there is a necessity for their being completed by a certain time. Thus the seats for viewing the shows, the machinery for drawing the Vela, and the contrivances for shifting the scenes, must all be prepared by a given day, that the people may not be disappointed. And in the preparation of all these much readiness and profound thought must be exercised, because they cannot be executed without machinery, and the application of varied and extensive studies.

Since, therefore, this is the case, it does not seem foreign to our purpose, carefully and diligently to explain those principles on which a work should be formed previous to commencing it. But as neither the law nor custom compels the adoption of such a practice, and the prætors and ædiles are bound every year to provide the machinery for the sports, it appeared to me, O Emperor, highly expedient, as in the foregoing books I have treated on buildings, to explain in this which closes the treatise, the principles upon which such machines are constructed.

CHAPTER I.

OF MACHINES AND ENGINES

A machine is a combination of materials capable of moving great weights. It derives its power from that circular application of motion which the Greeks call κυκλικὴ κίνησις. The first species is for scaling (scansoria), which the Greeks call ἀκροβατικὸς. The second, wherein the wind is the moving power, is, by the Greeks, called πνευματικὸς. The third sort of machine is for draft, and they call it βάναυσος. The scaling machine is constructed for the purpose of ascending, without danger, to view works of considerable altitude, and is formed of long pieces of timber connected together by transverse pieces. The pneumatic machine is for the purpose of imitating the sounds of stringed and wind instruments, by means of a rush of air organically introduced.

Machines of draft are constructed for the purpose of removing or raising great weights. The scaling machine is one more of boldness than art, being a combination of longitudinal timbers connected together by cross pieces, the splicings well lashed together, and the whole supported by shores or props. But the machine which, by the action of wind, produces very pleasing effects, requires great ingenuity in its construction. The machines for draft perform much greater and more important operations, in their application to different purposes, and, when skilfully managed, are of great utility.

Of these some act mechanically, others organically. The difference between machines and organs is this, that the former are composed of many subordinate parts, or propelled by a great power, as balistæ for instance, and wine-presses; whereas, the latter, by an ingenious application of the moving power, can be set in motion by a single person, as in turning the axis of the scorpion or anisocycli. Thus organs, as well as machines, are extremely useful and necessary, inasmuch as, without them, no works could be carried into execution.

The laws of mechanics are founded on those of nature, and are illustrated by studying the master-movements of the universe itself. For if we consider the sun, moon and the five planets, we shall perceive, that if they were not duly poised in their orbits, we should neither have light on the earth, nor heat to mature its fruits. Our ancestors reasoned so on these motions, that they adopted nature as their model; and, led to an imitation of the divine institutions, invented machines necessary for the purposes of life. That these might be suitable to their different purposes, some were constructed with wheels, and were called machines; others were denominated organs. Those which were found most useful were gradually improved, by repeated experiments, by art, and by the laws which they instituted.

Let us, for an instant, reflect on an invention, necessarily of an early period, that of clothing; wherein, by the organic arrangement of the loom, the connexion of the warp to the woof not only defends our bodies by the covering it affords, but is likewise an ornament to them. Again; how should we be supplied with food, but for the yokes and ploughs to which oxen and other animals are harnessed? Without the aid of wheels and axles, of presses and levers, we could enjoy neither the comforts of good oil, nor of the fruit of the vine. Without the aid of carts and waggons on land, and ships on the sea, we should be unable to transport any of our commodities. How necessary also, is the use of scales and weights in our dealings, to protect us from fraud. Not less so are innumerable different machines, which it is unnecessary here to discuss, since they are so well known from our daily use of them, such as wheels generally, the blacksmith's bellows, chariots, calêches, lathes, and other things which our habits constantly require. We will, therefore, proceed to explain, in the first place, those which are more rarely wanted.

CHAPTER II.

OF MACHINES OF DRAUGHT

We will begin by describing those engines which are chiefly used in the erection of sacred buildings, and other public works. They are made as follows: three pieces of timber are prepared suitable to the greatness of the weights to be lifted, connected at the top by a pin, but spreading extensively at their feet. These are raised by means of ropes made fast to the top, and when raised, are thereby kept steady. To the top is then made fast a block, by some called rechamus. In this block are two pulleys, turning on axles; over the upper pulley passes the leading rope, which, let fall and drawn through under the lower pulley of the bottom block is returned thence over the lower pulley of the upper block: the rope again descends to the lower block, and its end is made fast to the eye of it. We refer the other end of the rope to the description of the lower part of the machine.

On the back faces of the pieces of timber, where they diverge, are fixed socket-pieces (chelonia), for the gudgeons of the axles to work, so that they may revolve freely. The axles at the ends near the gudgeons, are pierced with two holes, so adjusted as to fit and receive the levers. Iron shears are then made fast to the under part of the lower block, whose teeth are received in holes cut in the piece of stone, for the purpose. The loose end of the rope being now attached to the axle, and that turned round by means of the levers, the rope, in winding round the axle, raises the weight to its height and place in the work.

PULLEY SYSTEM

A. PULLEY B. CAPSTAN C. UPPER PULLEY
D. WINCH E. BEAM F. WEIGHT I. FORCEPS
G. CLAMP H. CLAMP S. MASTHEAD

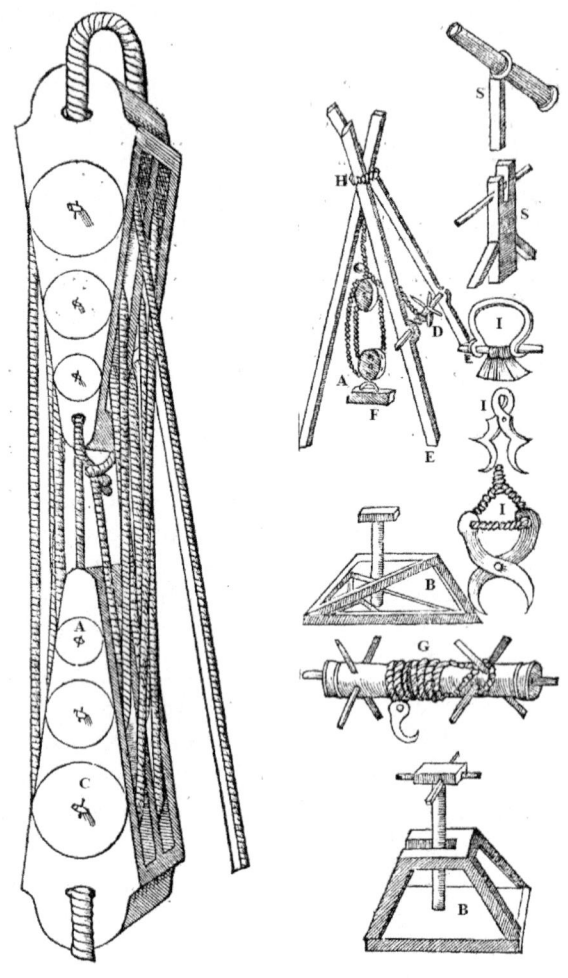

CHAPTER III.

OF ANOTHER SORT OF MACHINE OF DRAUGHT

A block containing three pulleys is denominated Trispastos; when the lower system has two pulleys, and the upper one three, Pentaspastos. A machine for raising heavier weights requires longer and stouter beams, and the pins for joining them at top, as well as the axle below, must be increased in proportion. Having premised this, the raising ropes lying loose, are first distributed; then to the shoulders of the machine are made fast the guys, which, if there be no place to which they can be otherwise firmly fixed, must be attached to sloping piles driven into the ground, and steadied by ramming the ground about them.

A block is to be now slung to the head of the machine, round which ropes must be carried to another block which has been previously fastened to a stake, and, passing over its pulley, must be returned to that on the top of the machine, round which the rope passes and descends to the axle at bottom, to which it is lashed. The axle is now turned round by means of the levers, and the machine is put in motion without danger. Thus the ropes being disposed around, and the guys firmly fastened to the stakes, a machine is stationed for use. The pulleys and leading ropes are applied as described in the foregoing chapter.

CHAPTER IV.

OF A SIMILAR MACHINE, OF GREATER POWER

If exceedingly large weights are to be raised, they must not be trusted to a mere axle; but the axle being retained by the gudgeons, a large drum should be fixed on it, which some call a drum-wheel (tympanum): the Greeks name it ἀμφίρευσις, or περίτροχος.

In these machines the blocks are constructed differently from those already described. Having, at top and bottom, two ranks of pulleys, the rope passes through a hole in the lower block, so that each end of the rope is equal in length when extended. It is there bound and made fast to the lower block, and both parts of the ropes so retained, that neither of them may swerve either to the right or the left. The ends of the rope are then returned to the outside of the upper block, and carried over its lower pulleys; whence they descend to the lower block, and passing round its pulleys on the inner side, are carried up right and left over the tops of the higher pulleys of the upper block; whence descending on the outer sides, they are secured to the axle on the right and left of the drum-wheel, about which another rope is now wound, and carried to the capstan. On the turning of the capstan, the drum-wheel and axle, and consequently the ropes fastened to it, are set in action, and raise the weights gently and without danger. But if a larger drum-wheel be affixed, either in the middle or on one of the sides, of such dimensions that men may walk therein, a more effectual power is obtained than the capstan will afford.

CHAPTER V.

OF ANOTHER MACHINE OF DRAUGHT

There is another species of machine, ingenious in respect of its contrivance, and of ready application in practice; but it should not be used except by experienced persons. A pole or log of timber is raised, and kept in its situation by means of four guy ropes in opposite directions. Under the place where the guy ropes at top are made fast to the pole, two cheeks are fixed, above which the block is tied with ropes. Under the block, a piece of timber about two feet long, six inches wide, and four inches thick, is placed. The blocks have three ranks of pulleys latitudinally, so that it is necessary to conduct three leading ropes from the upper part of the machine; these are brought down to the lower block, and are passed through its upper pulleys from the side next the pole. They then are carried to the upper block, passing from the outer sides of the lower pulleys to the inner sides of the lower pulleys of the upper block.

Descending once more to the inferior block, they pass round the second rank of pulleys from the inner to the outer side, and are then returned to the second rank of pulleys in the higher block, over which they pass and return to the lowest, whence they are again carried upwards, and passing round the uppermost pulley, return to the lower part of the machine. A third block is fixed near the bottom of the pole, whose Greek name is ἐπάγων, but with us it is called Artemo. This block, which is made fast to the pole at a small distance from the ground, has three pulleys through which the ropes are passed, for the men to work them. Thus, three sets of men, working without the intervention of a capstan, quickly raise the weight to its required height.

A. ARTEMO **B.** CHELONIA

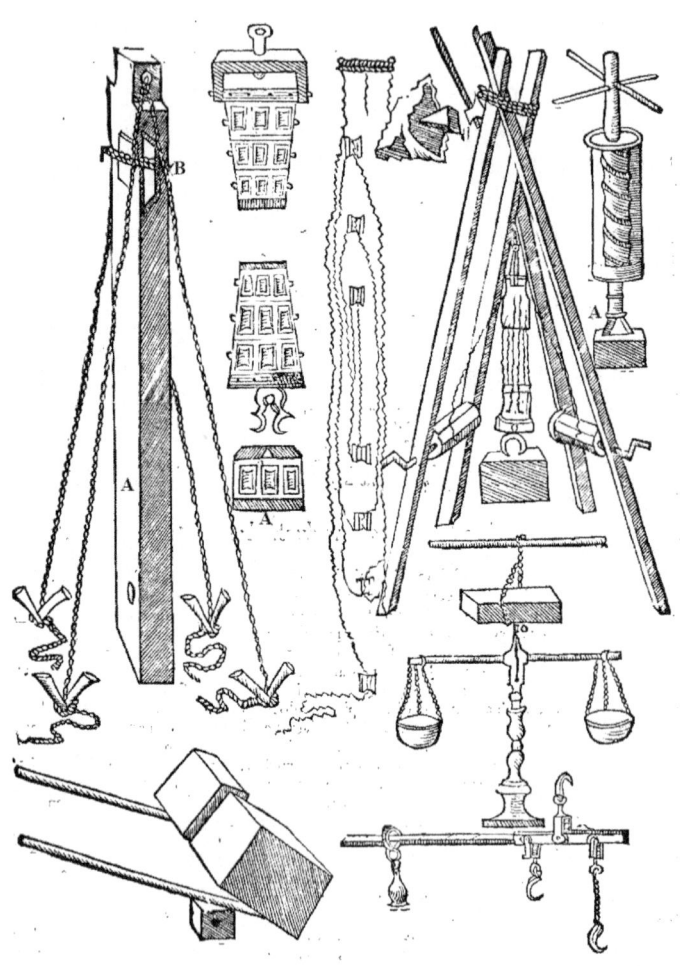

This species of machine is called Polyspaston, because the facility and dispatch in working it, is obtained by means of many pulleys. One convenience in using a single pole is, that the situation of the weight in relation to the pole, whether before it or to the right or left of it, is of no consequence. All the machines above described, are not only adapted to the purposes mentioned, but are also useful in loading and unloading ships, some upright, others horizontal, with a rotatory motion. On the ground, however, without the aid of the poles, ships are drawn on shore by the mere application of blocks and ropes.

CHAPTER VI.

OF CTESIPHON'S CONTRIVANCE FOR REMOVING GREAT WEIGHTS

It will be useful to explain the ingenious contrivance of Ctesiphon. When he removed from the quarry the shafts of the columns which he had prepared for the temple of Diana at Ephesus, not thinking it prudent to trust them on carriages, lest their weight should sink the wheels in the soft roads over which they would have to pass, he devised the following scheme. He made a frame of four pieces of timber, two of which were equal in length to the shafts of the columns, and were held together by the two transverse pieces. In each end of the shaft he inserted iron pivots, whose ends were dovetailed thereinto, and run with lead. The pivots worked in gudgeons fastened to the timber frame, whereto were attached oaken shafts. The pivots having a free revolution in the gudgeons, when the oxen were attached and drew the frame, the shafts rolled round, and might have been conveyed to any distance.

The shafts having been thus transported, the entablatures were to be removed, when Metagenes the son of Ctesiphon, applied the principle upon which the shafts had been conveyed to the removal of those also. He constructed wheels about twelve feet diameter, and fixed the ends of the blocks of stone whereof the entablature was composed into them; pivots and gudgeons were then prepared to receive them in the manner just described, so that when the oxen drew the machine, the pivots turning in the gudgeons, caused the wheels to revolve, and thus the blocks, being enclosed like axles in the wheels, were brought to the work without delay, as were the shafts of the columns. An example of this species of machine may be seen in the rolling stone used for smoothing the walks in palæstræ. But the method would not have been practicable for any considerable distance. From the quarries to the temple is a length of not more than eight thousand feet, and the interval is a plain without any declivity.

Within our own times, when the base of the colossal statue of Apollo in the temple of that god, was decayed through age, to prevent the fall and destruction of it, a contract for a base from the same quarry was made with Pæonius. It was twelve feet long, eight feet wide, and six feet high. Pæonius, driven to an expedient, did not use the same as Metagenes did, but constructed a machine for the purpose, by a different application of the same principle.

He made two wheels about fifteen feet diameter, and fitted the ends of the stone into these wheels. To connect the two wheels he framed into them, round their circumference, small pieces of two inches square not more than one foot apart, each extending from one wheel to the other, and thus enclosing the stone. Round these bars a rope was coiled, to which the traces of the oxen were made fast, and as it was drawn out, the stone rolled on by means of the wheels, but the machine by its constantly swerving from a direct straightforward path, stood in need of constant rectification, so that Pæonius was at last without money for the completion of his contract.

CHAPTER VII.

OF DISCOVERY OF THE QUARRY WHENCE STONE WAS PROCURED FOR THE TEMPLE OF DIANA AT EPHESUS

I must digress a little, and relate how the quarries of Ephesus were discovered. A shepherd, of the name of Pixodarus, dwelt in these parts at the period in which the Ephesians had decreed a temple to Diana, to be built of marble from Paros, Proconnesus, or Thasos. Pixodarus on a certain occasion tending his flock at this place, saw two rams fighting. In their attacks, missing each other, one fell, and glancing against the rock with his horns, broke off a splinter, which appeared to him so delicately white, that he left his flock and instantly ran with it into Ephesus, where marble was then in much demand. The Ephesians forthwith decreed him honours, and changed his name to Evangelus. Even to this day the chief magistrate of the city proceeds every month to the spot, and sacrifices to him; the omission of which ceremony would, on the magistrate's part, be attended with penal consequences to him.

CHAPTER VIII.

OF THE PRINCIPLES OF MECHANICS

I have briefly explained the principles of machines of draught, in which, as the powers and nature of the motion are different, so they generate two effects, one direct, which the Greeks call εὐθεῖα, the other circular, which they call κυκλωτὴ; but it must be confessed, that rectilinear without circular motion, and, on the other hand, circular without rectilinear motion can neither without the other be of much assistance in raising weights.

I will proceed to the explanation of this. The pulleys revolve on axles which go across the blocks, and are acted upon by straight ropes which coil round the axle of the windlass when that is put in motion by the levers, thus causing the weight to ascend. The pivots of the windlass axle are received into, or play in the gudgeons of the cheeks, and the levers being inserted in the holes provided for them in the axle, are moved in a circular direction, and thus cause the ascent of the weight. Thus also, an iron lever being applied to a weight which many hands could not remove; if a fulcrum, which the Greeks call ὑπομόχλιον, be placed under it, and the tongue of the lever be under the weight, one man's strength at the end will raise the weight.

This is accounted for by the fore part of the lever being under the weight, and at a shorter distance from the fulcrum or centre of motion; whilst the longest part, which is from the centre of motion to the head being brought into circular motion, the application of few hands to it will raise a great weight. So if the tongue of the lever be placed under the weight, and instead of the end being pressed downward it be lifted up, the tongue then having the ground for a fulcrum, will act on that as in the first instance it did on the weight, and the tongue will press against the side thereof as it did on the fulcrum: though by this means the weight will not be so easily raised, yet it may be thus moved. If the tongue of the lever lying on the fulcrum be placed too far under the weight, and the end be too near the centre of pressure, it will be without effect; so, as hath been already mentioned, will it be, unless the distance from the fulcrum to the end of the lever be greater than from the fulcrum to the tongue thereof. Any one will perceive the application of this principle in the instruments called steelyards (stateræ); for when the handle of suspension, on which as a centre the beam turns, is placed nearer the end from which the scale hangs, and, on the other side of the centre, the weight be shifted to the different divisions on the beam, the further it is from the centre, the greater will be the load in the scale which it is capable of raising, and that through the equilibration of the beam. Thus, a small weight, which, placed near the centre, would have but a feeble effect, may in a moment acquire power, and raise with ease a very heavy load.

Thus also the steersman of a merchant ship, holding the tiller which the Greeks call οἴαξ with only one hand, by the situation of the centre moves it in a moment as the nature of the case requires, and turns the ship though ever so deeply laden. The sails also, if only half mast high, will cause the vessel to sail slower than when the yards are hoisted up to the top of the mast, because not then being near the foot of the mast, which is as it were the centre, but at a distance therefrom, they are acted on by the wind with greater force.

For as, if the fulcrum be placed under the middle of a lever, it is but with difficulty that the weight is moved, and that only when the power is applied at the extremity of the lever, so when the sails are no higher than the middle of the mast, they have less effect on the motion of the vessel: when, however, raised to the top of the mast, the impulse they receive from an equal wind higher up, causes a quicker motion in the ship. For the same reason the oars, which are made fast with rope to the thowls, when plunged into the water and drawn back by the hand, impel the vessel with great force, and cause the prow thereof to cleave the waves, if their blades are at a considerable distance from the centre, which is the thowl.

Also, when loads of great weight are carried by porters in gangs of four or six, the levers are so adjusted in the middle that each porter may be loaded with a proper proportion of the burden. The middle parts of the levers for four persons over which the tackle passes, are provided with pins to prevent it sliding out of its place, for if it shift from the centre, the weight will press more on the shoulders of him to whom it is nearest, just as in the steelyard the weight is shifted towards the end of the beam.

Thus also oxen have an equal draft when the piece which suspends the pole hangs exactly from the middle of the yoke. But when oxen are not equally strong, the method of apportioning to each his due labour is by shifting the suspending piece so that one side of the yoke shall be longer than the other, and thus relieve the weaker animal. It is the same in the porters' levers as in yokes, when the suspending tackle is not in the centre, and one arm of the lever is longer than the other, namely that towards which the tackle has shifted; for in this case if the lever turn upon the points to which the tackle has slid, which now becomes its centre, the longer arm will describe a portion of a larger circle, and the shorter a smaller circle.

Now as small wheels revolve with more difficulty than larger ones, so levers and yokes press most on the side which is the least distance from the fulcrum, and on the contrary they ease those who bear that arm which is at the greatest distance from the fulcrum. Inasmuch as all these machines regulate either rectilinear or circular motion by means of the centre or fulcrum, so also waggons, chariots, drumwheels,

wheels of carriages, screws, scorpions, balistæ, presses, and other instruments, for the same reasons produce their effects by means of rectilinear and circular motions.

CHAPTER IX.

OF ENGINES FOR RAISING WATER; AND FIRST OF THE TYMPANUM

I shall now explain the machines for raising water, and their various sorts. And first the tympanum, which, though it raise not the water to a great height, yet lifts a large quantity in a small period of time. An axis is prepared in the lathe, or at least made circular by hand, hooped with iron at the ends; round the middle whereof the tympanum, formed of planks fitted together, is adjusted. This axis rests on posts also cased with iron where the axis touches them. In the hollow part of the tympanum are distributed eight diagonal pieces, going from the axis to the circumference of the tympanum, which are equidistant.

The horizontal face of the wheel or tympanum is close boarded, with apertures therein half a foot in size to admit the water. On the axis also channels are cut for each bay. This machine, when moored like a ship, is turned round by men walking in a wheel attached to it, and, by receiving the water in the apertures which are in front of the wheel, brings it up through the channels on the axle into a trough, whence it is conducted in abundance to water gardens, and dilute salt in pits.

If it be necessary to raise the water to a higher level, it must be differently adjusted. The wheel, in that case, applied to the axis must be of such diameter that it shall correspond with the requisite height. Round the circumference of the wheel buckets, made tight with pitch and wax, are fixed; thus when the wheel is made to revolve by means of the persons treading in it, the buckets being carried to the top full of water, as they return downwards, discharge the water they bring up into a conduit. But if water is to be supplied to still higher places, a double chain of iron is made to revolve on the axis of the wheel, long enough to reach to the lower level; this is furnished with brazen buckets, each holding about a gallon. Then by turning the wheel, the chain also turns on the axis, and brings the buckets to the top thereof, on passing which they are inverted, and pour into the conduits the water they have raised.

CHAPTER IX.

OF ANOTHER SORT OF TYMPANUM, AND WATER MILLS

Wheels on rivers are constructed upon the same principles as those just described. Round their circumference are fixed paddles, which, when acted upon by the force of the current, drive the wheel round, receive the water in the buckets, and carry it to the top with the aid of treading; thus by the mere impulse of the stream supplying what is required.

Water mills are turned on the same principle, and are in all respects similar, except that at one end of the axis they are provided with a drum-wheel, toothed and framed fast to the said axis; this being placed vertically on the edge turns round with the wheel. Corresponding with the drum-wheel a larger horizontal toothed wheel is placed, working on an axis whose upper head is in the form of a dovetail, and is inserted into the mill-stone. Thus the teeth of the drum-wheel which is made fast to the axis acting on the teeth of the horizontal wheel, produce the revolution of the mill-stones, and in the engine a suspended hopper supplying them with grain, in the same revolution the flour is produced.

CHAPTER X.

OF THE WATER SCREW

There is a machine, on the principle of the screw, which raises water with considerable power, but not so high as the wheel. It is contrived as follows. A beam is procured whose thickness, in inches, is equal to its length in feet; this is rounded. Its ends, circular, are then divided by compasses, on their circumference, into four or eight parts, by diameters drawn thereon. These lines must be so drawn, that when the beam is placed in an horizontal direction, they may respectively and horizontally correspond with each other. The whole length of the beam must be divided into spaces equal to one eighth part of the circumference thereof. Thus the circular and longitudinal divisions will be equal, and the latter intersecting lines drawn from one end to the other, will be marked by points.

These lines being accurately drawn, a small flexible ruler of willow or withy, smeared with liquid pitch, is attached at the first point of intersection, and made to pass obliquely through the remaining intersections of the longitudinal and circular divisions; whence progressing and winding through each point of intersection it arrives and stops in the same line from which it started, receding from the first to the eighth point, to which it was at first attached. In this manner, as it progresses through the eight points of the circumference, so it proceeds to the eighth point lengthwise. Thus, also, fastening similar rules obliquely through the circumferential and longitudinal intersections, they will form eight channels round the shaft, in the form of a screw.

To these rules or slips others are attached, also smeared with liquid pitch, and to these still others, till the thickness of the whole be equal to one eighth part of the length. On the slips or rules planks are fastened all round, saturated with pitch, and bound with iron hoops, that the water may not injure them. The ends of the shaft are also strengthened with iron nails and hoops, and have iron pivots inserted into them. On the right and left of the screw are beams, with a cross piece at top and bottom, each of which is provided with an iron gudgeon, for the pivots of the shaft to turn in, and then, by the treading of men, the screw is made to revolve.

The inclination at which the screw is to be worked, is equal to that of the right angled triangle of Pythagoras: that is, if the length be divided into five parts, three of these will give the height that the head is to be raised; thus four parts will be the perpendicular to the lower mouth. The method of constructing it may be seen in the diagram at the end of the book. I have now described, as accurately as possible, the engines which are made of wood, for raising water, the manner of constructing them, and the powers that are applied to put them in motion, together with the great advantages to be derived from the use of them.

CHAPTER XI.

OF THE MACHINE OF CTESIBIUS FOR RAISING WATER TO A CONSIDERABLE HEIGHT

It is now necessary to explain the machine of Ctesibius, which raises water to a height. It is made of brass, and at the bottom are two buckets near each other, having pipes annexed in the shape of a fork, which meet at a basin in the middle. In the basin are valves nicely fitted to the apertures of the pipes, which, closing the holes, prevent the return of the liquid which has been forced into the basin by the pressure of the air.

Above the basin is a cover like an inverted funnel, fitted and fastened to it with a rivet, that the force of the water may not blow it off. On this a pipe, called a trumpet, is fixed upright. Below the lower orifices of the pipes the buckets are furnished with valves over the holes in their bottoms.

Pistons made round and smooth, and well oiled, are now fastened to the buckets, and worked from above with bars and levers, which, by their alternate action, frequently repeated, press the air in the pipes, and the water being prevented from returning by the closing of the valves, is forced and conducted into the basin through the mouths of the pipes; whence the force of the air, which presses it against the cover, drives it upwards through the pipe: thus water on a lower level may be raised to a reservoir, for the supply of fountains.

Nor is this the only machine which Ctesibius has invented. There are many others, of different sorts, which prove that liquids, in a state of pressure from the air, produce many natural effects, as those which imitate the voices of singing birds, and the engibita, which move figures that seem to drink, and perform other actions pleasing to the senses of sight and hearing.

From these inventions I have selected those which are most pleasing and necessary, and described them in my treatise on dialling: in this place I confine myself to those which act by the impulse of water. The others, which are more for pleasure than utility, may be seen by the curious in the writings of Ctesibius.

CHAPTER XII.

OF WATER ENGINES

CTESIBIUS MACHINE

I cannot here omit a brief explanation, as clearly as I can give it, of the principles on which hydraulic organs are constructed. A base of framed wood-work is prepared, on which is placed a brazen box. On the base, right and left, uprights are fixed, with cross pieces like those of a ladder, to keep them together; between which are enclosed brass barrels with moveable bottoms, perfectly round, having iron rods fixed in their centres, and covered with leather and woollen, attached by pins to the levers. There are also, on the upper surface, holes about three inches diameter, in which, near the pin-joint, are brazen dolphins with chains hanging from their mouths, which sustain the valves that descend below the holes of the barrels.

Within the box, where the water is deposited, there is a species of inverted funnel, under which two collars, about three inches high, answer the purpose of keeping it level, and preserving the assigned distance between the lips of the wind-chest and the bottom of the box. On the neck a chest, framed together, sustains the head of the instrument, which in Greek is called κανῶν μουσικὸς (canon musicus); upon which, lengthwise, are channels, four in number, if the instrument be tetrachordal, six if hexachordal, and eight if octochordal.

In each channel are fixed stops, that are connected with iron finger-boards; on pressing down which, the communication between the chest and the channels is opened. Along the channels is a range of holes corresponding with others on an upper table, called πίναξ in Greek. Between this table and the canon, rules are interposed, with corresponding holes well oiled, so that they may be easily pushed and return; they are called pleuritides, and are for the purpose of stopping and opening the holes along the channels, which they do by passing backwards and forwards.

These rules have iron jacks attached to them, and being united to the keys, when those are touched they move the rules. Over the table there are holes through which the wind passes into the pipes. Rings are fixed in the rules, for the reception of the feet of the organ-pipes. From the barrels run pipes joined to the neck of the wind-chest, which communicate with the holes in the chest, in which pipes are closely fitted valves; these, when the chest is supplied with wind, serve to close their orifices, and prevent its escape.

Thus, when the levers are raised, the piston-rods are depressed to the bottom of the barrel, and the dolphins turning on their pivots, suffer the valves attached to them to descend, thus filling with air the cavities of the barrels. Lastly; the pistons in the barrels being alternately raised and depressed with a quick motion, cause the valves to stop the upper holes: the air, therefore, which is pent, escapes into the pipes, through which it passes into the wind-chest, and thence, by its neck, to the box.

By the quick motion of the levers still compressing the air, it finds its way through the apertures of the stops, and fills the channels with wind. Hence, when the keys are touched by hand, they propel and repel the rules, alternately stopping and opening the holes, and producing a varied melody founded upon the rules of music. I have done my utmost to give a clear explanation of a complex machine. This has been no easy task, nor, perhaps, shall I be understood, except by those who are experienced in matters of this nature. Such, however, as comprehend but a little of what I have written, would, if they saw the instrument, be compelled to acknowledge the skill exhibited in its contrivance.

CHAPTER XIII.

OF MEASURING A JOURNEY

Let us now consider an invention by no means useless, and delivered to us by the antients as of ingenuity, by means of which, when on a journey by land or sea, one may ascertain the distance travelled. It is as follows. The wheels of the chariot must be four feet diameter; so that, marking a certain point thereon, whence it begins its revolution on the ground, when it has completed that revolution, it will have gone on the road over a space equal to twelve feet and a half. This being adjusted on the inner side of the nave of the wheel, let a drum-wheel be securely fixed, having one small tooth projecting beyond the face of its circumference; and in the body of the chariot let a small box be fastened, with a drum-wheel placed to revolve perpendicularly, and fastened to an axle. The latter wheel is to be equally divided, on its edge, into four hundred teeth, corresponding with the teeth of the lower drum-wheel: besides the above, the upper drum-wheel has on its side one tooth projecting out before the others.

Above, in another enclosure, is a third horizontal wheel toothed similarly, and so that the teeth correspond with that tooth which is fixed to the side of the second wheel. In the third wheel just described are as many holes as are equal to the number of miles in an usual day's journey. It does not, however, signify, if they be more or less. In all the holes let small balls be placed, and in the box or lining let a hole be made, having a channel, through which each ball may fall into the box of the chariot, and the brazen vessel placed under it.

Thus, as the wheel proceeds, it acts on the first drum-wheel, the tooth of which, in every revolution, striking the tooth of the upper wheel, causes it to move on; so that when the lower wheel has revolved four hundred times, the upper wheel has revolved only once, and its tooth, which is on the side, will have acted on only one tooth of the horizontal wheel. Now as in four hundred revolutions of the lower wheel, the upper wheel will only have turned round once, the length of the journey will be five thousand feet, or one thousand paces. Thus, by the dropping of the balls, and the noise they make, we know every mile passed over; and each day one may ascertain, by the number of balls collected in the bottom, the number of miles in the day's journey.

In navigation, with very little change in the machinery, the same thing may be done. An axis is fixed across the vessel, whose ends project beyond the sides, to which are attached wheels four feet diameter, with paddles to them touching the water. That part of the axis within the vessel has a wheel with a single tooth standing out beyond its face; at which place a box is fixed with a wheel inside it having four hundred teeth, equal and correspondent to the tooth of the first wheel fixed on the axis. On the side of this, also, projecting from its face, is another tooth.

Above, in another box, is enclosed another horizontal wheel, also toothed, to correspond with the tooth that is fastened to the side of the vertical wheel, and which, in every revolution, working in the teeth of the horizontal wheel, and striking one each time, causes it to turn round. In this horizontal wheel holes are made, wherein the round balls are placed; and in the box of the wheel is a hole with a channel to it, through which the ball descending without obstruction, falls into the brazen vase, and makes it ring.

Thus, when the vessel is on its way, whether impelled by oars or by the wind, the paddles of the wheels, driving back the water which comes against them with violence, cause the wheels to revolve, whereby the axle is also turned round, and consequently with it the drum-wheel, whose tooth, in every revolution, acts on the tooth in the second wheel, and produces moderate revolutions thereof. Wherefore, when the wheels are carried round by the paddles four hundred times, the horizontal wheel will only have made one revolution, by the striking of that tooth on the side of the vertical wheel, and thus, in the turning caused by the horizontal wheel every time it brings a ball to the hole it falls through the channel. In this way, by sound and number, the number of miles navigated will be ascertained. It appears to me, that I have completed the description in such a manner that it will be easy to comprehend the structure of the machine, which will afford both utility and amusement in times of peace and safety.

CHAPTER XIV.

OF CATAPULTÆA AND SCORPIONS

I shall now proceed to an explanation of those instruments which have been invented for defence from danger, and for the purposes of self-preservation; I mean the construction of scorpions, catapultæ, and balistæ, and their proportions. And first of catapultæ and scorpions. Their proportions depend on the length of the arrow which the instrument is to throw, a ninth part of whose length is assigned for the sizes of the holes in the capitals through which the cords are stretched, that retain the arms of the catapultæ.

The height and width of the holes in the capital are thus fashioned. The plates (tabulæ) which are at the top and bottom of the capital, and which are called parallels (paralleli) are equal in thickness to one hole, in width to one and three quarters, and at their extremities to one hole and a half. The side posts (parastatæ) right and left, exclusive of the tenons four holes high and five thick, the tenons three quarters of a hole. From the hole to the middle post also three quarters of a hole, the width of the middle post one hole and a quarter, its thickness one hole.

The space wherein the arrow is placed in the middle of the post, the fourth part of a hole. The four angle pieces which appear on the sides and front, are strengthened with iron hoops fastened with copper or iron nails. The length of the channel which is called στρὶξ in Greek, is nineteen holes. That of the slips (regulæ) which lie on the right and left of the channel, and which some persons call buckle, is also nineteen holes, their height and width half a hole. Two other slips are fixed for attaching the windlass, three holes long and half a hole wide. The thickness of a slip is called camillum, or according to others the dove-tailed box, and is of the dimension of one hole, its height half a hole. The length of the windlass is eight holes and an eighth. The roller nine holes wide.

The length of the epitoxis is three quarters of a hole, and its thickness one quarter. The chelo or manucla is three holes long, its length and thickness three quarters of a hole. The length of the bottom of the channel sixteen holes, its width and thickness each three quarters of a hole. The small column (columella) with its base near the ground eight holes, the breadth of the plinth in which the small column is fixed three quarters of a hole, its thickness three twelfths. The length of the small column up to the tenon twelve holes; three quarters of a hole wide, and five-sixths of a hole thick. The three braces are nine holes long, half a hole wide, and a sixth of a hole thick; the length of the tenon one hole. The length of the head of the small column is one hole and three quarters. The width of the fore-piece (antefixa) is three eighths of a hole, its thickness one hole.

The smaller back column, which in Greek is called ἀντίβασις, is eight holes long, one hole and a half wide, and three twelfths of a hole thick. The base (subjectio) is twelve holes, and its breadth and thickness the same as that of the smaller column. The chelonium or pillow as it is called, over the smaller column, two holes and a half; also two holes and a half high, and one hole and three quarters wide. The mortices (carchesia) in the axles are two holes and a half; their thickness also two holes and a half, and their width one hole and a half. The length of the transverse pieces with the tenons is ten holes, their width one hole and a half, their thickness ten holes. The length of the arm is seven holes, its thickness at bottom three twelfths, and at top half a hole. The curve part eight holes.

All these proportions are appropriate; some, however, add to them, and some diminish them; for if the capitals are higher than the width, in which case they are called anatona, the arms are shortened: so that the tone being weakened by the height of the capital, the shortness of the arm may make the stroke more powerful. If the height of the capital be less, in which case it is called catatonum, the arms must be longer, that they may be the more easily drawn to, on account of the greater purchase; for as a lever four feet long raises a weight by the assistance of four men, if it be eight feet long, two men will raise the weight; in like manner arms that are longer are more easily drawn to than those that are shorter.

CHAPTER XV.

OF THE CONSTRUCTION OF THE BALISTA

I have explained the structure of catapultæ, their parts and proportions. The constructions of balistæ are various and different, though contrived to produce similar effects. Some of these are worked by windlasses, others by systems of pulleys, others by capstans, and others by wheels: no balista, however, is made without regard to the weight of the stones it is intended to throw. Hence the rules will only be understood by those who are acquainted with arithmetical numbers and their powers.

For instance, holes are made in the capitals, and through them are brought the cords, made either of woman's hair, or of gut, which are proportioned to the weight of the stone that the balista is to throw, as in the catapultæ the proportions are derived from the length of the arrow. But that those who are not masters of geometry and arithmetic, may be prepared against delay on the occasions of war, I shall here state the results of my own experience as well as what I have learnt from masters, and shall explain them, by reducing the Greek measures to their correspondent terms in our own.

CHAPTER XVI.

OF THE PROPORTIONS OF THE BALISTA

A balista capable of throwing a stone of two pounds should have the hole (foramen) in the capital five digits wide; for a stone of four pounds, six digits; for a stone of six pounds, seven digits; for a stone of ten pounds, eight digits; for a stone of twenty pounds, ten digits; for a stone of forty pounds, twelve digits and nine sixteenths; for a stone of sixty pounds, thirteen digits and one eighth; for one of eighty pounds, fifteen digits; for one of one hundred and twenty pounds, one foot and a half and a digit and a half; for one of a hundred and sixty pounds, two feet; for one of a hundred and eighty pounds, two feet and five digits; for one of two hundred pounds, two feet and six digits; for one of two hundred and ten pounds, two feet and seven digits: and lastly, for one of two hundred and fifty pounds, eleven feet and a half.

Having thus determined the size of the hole, which in Greek is called περίτρητος, a sight hole (scutula) is described two holes and a quarter in length, and two holes and one sixth wide. Let the line described be bisected, and when so bisected, let the figure be obliquely turned till its length be equal to one sixth part, and its width on which it turns that of the fourth part of a hole. In the part where the curvature is, at which the points of the angles project, and the holes are turned, the contractions of the breadth return inwardly, a sixth part. The hole must be as much longer as the epizygis is thick. When it has been described, the extremity is to be so divided that it may have a gentle curvature.

Its thickness must be nine sixteenths of a hole. The stocks are made equal to two holes and a quarter, the width to one hole and three quarters, the thickness, exclusive of that part which is inserted into the hole, one hole and a half; the width at the extremity, one hole and a sixteenth; the length of the side posts, five holes and nine sixteenths; the curvature one half of a hole, the thickness four ninths; in the middle the breadth is increased as it was near the hole above described; its breadth and thickness are each five holes; its height one quarter of a hole.

The length of the slip on the table is eight holes, and it is to be half a hole wide and thick. The length of the tenon two holes and a sixth, and its thickness one hole: the curvature of the slip is to be one sixteenth and five quarters of a sixteenth; the breadth and thickness of the exterior slip the same; its length will be found by the turning, and the width of the side post and its curvature one sixteenth: the upper are equal to the lower slips, that is one sixteenth: the transverse pieces of the table two thirds and one sixteenth of a hole: the length of shaft of the small ladder (climacis) thirteen holes, its thickness three sixteenths: the breadth of the middle interval is a quarter of a hole, its thickness five thirty-seconds of a hole: the length of the upper part of the climacis near the arms, where it is joined to the table, is to be divided into five parts; of these, two are given to that part which the Greeks call χηλὸς (the chest), the width one sixteenth, the thickness one quarter, the length three holes and an eighth, the projecting part of the chest half a hole. The pteregoma (or wing), one twelfth of a hole and one sicilicus. The large axis, which is called the cross front, is three holes; the width of the interior slips, one sixteenth of a hole; its thickness five forty-eighths of a hole: the cheek of the chest serves to cover the dove-tail, and is a quarter of a hole: the shaft of the climacis five sixths of a hole and twelve holes and a quarter thick: the thickness of the square piece which reaches to the climacis is five twelfths, at its ends one sixteenth: the diameter of the round axis must be equal to the chêlos, but near its turning points three sixteenths less.

The length of the spur is one twelfth and three quarters; its width at bottom one sixteenth, and its width at top a quarter and one sixteenth. The base, which is called εσχάρα, is a ninth of a hole long; the piece in front of the base (antibasis) four holes and one ninth; the width and thickness of each are to be the ninth of a hole. The half column is a quarter of a hole high, and its width and thickness half a hole; as to its height, that need not be proportioned to the hole, but made, however, of such size as may be fit for the purpose. Of the arm the length will be six holes, its thickness at bottom half a hole; at the bottom one twelfth of a hole. I have now given those proportions of the catapultæ and balistæ, which I consider most useful; I shall not, however, omit to describe, as well as I can by writing, the manner of preparing them with cords twisted of guts and hair.

CHAPTER XVII.

OF THE PREPARATION OF THE BALISTÆ AND CATAPULTÆ

Beams of considerable length must be procured, upon which are fixed cheeks in which the axles are retained; in the middle of those beams holes are made, into which are received the capitals of the catapultæ, well tightened with wedges, so that the strain will not move them. Then brazen stocks are fixed for the reception of the capitals, in which are the small iron pins which the Greeks call ἐπισχίδες.

The ends of the ropes pass through the holes of the capitals, and brought through on the other side, they are then passed round the axle of the windlass, which is turned by the aid of levers, till the ropes, both drawn tight, give the same tone when struck by the hand. Then they are confined at the holes with wedges, to prevent their slipping. Being passed through to the other side, they are in a similar way tightened by the levers and axles till the tones are similar. Thus by the use of the wedges, catapultæ are adjusted, according to the effect of musical tones on the ear.

CHAPTER XVIII.

OF MACHINES FOR ATTACK

I have said as much as I could on these matters; it now remains for me to treat of those things relating to attacks, namely, of those machines with which generals take and defend cities. The first engine for attack was the ram, whose origin is said to have been as follows. The Carthaginians encamped in order to besiege Cadiz, and having first got possession of one of the towers, they endeavoured to demolish it, but having no machines fit for the purpose, they took a beam, and suspending it in their hands, repeatedly battered the top of the wall with the end of it, and having first thrown down the upper courses, by degrees they destroyed the whole fortress.

After that, a certain workman of Tyre, of the name of Pephasmenos, turning his attention to the subject, fixed up a pole and suspended a cross piece therefrom after the method of a steelyard, and thus swinging it backwards and forwards, levelled with heavy blows the walls of Cadiz. Cetras the Chalcedonian, was the first who added a base to it of timber moveable on wheels, and covered it with a roof on upright and cross pieces: on this he suspended the ram, covering it with bulls' hides, so that those who were employed therein in battering the walls might be secure from danger. And inasmuch as the machine moved but slowly, they called it the tortoise of the ram. Such was the origin of this species of machines.

But afterwards, when Philip, the son of Amintas, besieged Byzantium, Polydus the Thessalian used it in many and simple forms, and by him were instructed Diades and Chæreas who fought under Alexander. Diades has shewn in his writings that he was the inventor of ambulatory towers, which he caused to be carried from one place to another by the army, in pieces, as also of the auger and the scaling machine, by which one may step on to a wall; as also the grappling hook, which some call the crane (grus).

He also used a ram on wheels, of which he has left a description in writing. He says that no tower should be built less than sixty cubits high, nor than seventeen wide, and that its diminution at top should be one fifth of the width of the base: that the upright pieces of the tower should be one foot and three quarters at bottom, and half a foot at top: that it should contain ten floors, with windows on each side.

That the greatest tower that is constructed may be one hundred and twenty cubits high, and twenty-three and a half wide, diminishing at the top one fifth of its base; the upright piece one foot at bottom, and half a foot at top. The large tower is made with twenty floors, and to each floor there is a parapet of three cubits, covered with raw hides to protect it from the arrows.

The construction of the tortoise ram is similar: it was thirty cubits wide, and, exclusive of the roof, sixteen high. The height of the roof from the eaves to the ridge, seven cubits. On the top thereof in the centre rose a small tower, not less than twelve cubits wide: it was raised with four stories, on the upper of which the scorpions and catapultæ were placed, and in those below was kept a large store of water, to extinguish the flames in case it should be fired. In it was placed the machine for the ram, which the Greeks call κριοδόκη, wherein was the round smooth roller on which the ram worked backwards and forwards by means of ropes, and produced great effect. This, like the tower, was covered with raw hides.

He describes the auger (terebra) thus: the machine is made like a tortoise, as in those for the reception of the catapultæ and balistæ, and in the middle thereof is a channel on the pilasters fifty cubits long, one high, and across it an axle. In front, on the right and left, are two pulleys, by means of which is moved a beam with an iron point at its end, which works in the channel. Under the channel are rollers, which give it an easier and stronger motion. Above the beam an arch is turned to cover the channel, and receive the raw hides with which the machine is covered.

I do not describe the grappling machine, because I consider it of very little use. I perceive that he only promises to explain, which however he does not do, the construction of the ladder called ἐπιβάθρα by the Greeks, and the other marine machines for boarding ships. Having described the construction of the machines as Diades directs, I shall now explain it in a way that I think will be useful, and as taught me by my masters.

CHAPTER XIX.

OF THE TORTOISE FOR FILLING DITCHES

The tortoise contrived for filling up ditches, which also affords an access to the walls, is thus made. A base, called by the Greeks εσχάρα, is prepared twenty-five feet square, with four cross pieces. These are tied in by two other pieces, one twelfth high, and one half wide, distant from each other about a foot and a half, and under each of their intervals are placed the naves of wheels, called in Greek ἁμαξόποδες, within which the axles of the wheels turn in iron hoops. The naves are so made that they have holes in their heads, in which the handspikes being received, are made to turn them. The naves thus revolving, it may be moved forward or backward, to the right or left, or diagonally, as wanted.

Above the base are placed two beams, projecting six feet on each side; round the projections of which two other beams are fixed in front, seven feet long, and their width and thickness as described for the base. Upon this frame which is to be morticed, posts are placed, nine feet high, exclusive of their tenons, one foot and a palm square, and a foot and a half distant from each other. These are tied in at top by means of morticed beams. Above these beams are braces, with tenons, the end of one being let into the next to the height of nine feet, and over the braces is a square piece of timber, by which they are connected.

They also are kept together by side pieces, and are covered with planks of palm, in preference to other wood: if those are not to be procured, by other wood of a strong nature, pine and ash, however, excepted; for they are weak and easily ignited. About the planking are placed gratings, made of slender twigs recently cut, and closely interwoven; and then the whole machine is covered with raw hides, as fresh as can be procured, doubled and stuffed with seaweed or straw steeped in vinegar, in order that it may resist the strokes of the balistæ and the attacks of fire.

CHAPTER XIX.

OF OTHER SORTS OF TORTOISES

There is another species of tortoise, which is just the same as that above described, except in respect of the braces. This has a parapet and battlements of boarding, and above, an inclined pent-house round it, tied in at top with planks and hides firmly fastened. Over these is a layer of clay with hair, of such thickness as to prevent the machine taking fire. These machines may be made with eight wheels, if need be, and if the nature of the place require it. The tortoises made for undermining, called by the Greeks ὄρυγες, are similar to those already described; but their fronts are formed on a triangular plan, so that the weapons from the wall may not fall direct on the faces, but gliding off from them, the excavators within may be secure from danger.

It does not appear to me foreign to our purpose to explain the proportions and constructions of the tortoise made by Agetor the Byzantine. Its base was sixty feet long, its width eighteen. The upright pieces which rose above the framing, were four in number; they were in two lengths, joined, each thirty-six feet high, one foot and one palm in thickness, and in width one foot and a half. The base had eight wheels, on which it was moved; their height was six feet and three quarters, their thickness three feet, composed of three pieces of wood dove-tailed together, and tied with plates of cold wrought iron.

These turned on naves, or hamaxopodes, as they are called. Above the surface of the cross pieces which were on the base, upright posts were erected, eighteen feet and a quarter high, three quarters wide, and three-twelfths thick, and one and three quarters apart. Above them were beams all round, which tied the machine together, they were one foot and a quarter wide, and three quarters thick. Over these the braces were placed, and were twelve feet high. Above the braces was a beam which united the framing. They had also side pieces fixed transversely, on which a floor, running round them, covered the parts below.

There was also a middle floor above the small beams, where the scorpions and catapultæ were placed. Two upright pieces were also raised, joined together, thirty-five feet long, a foot and a half thick, and two feet wide, united at their heads, dove-tailed into a cross beam, and by another in the middle, morticed between two shafts and tied with iron hooping, above which were alternate beams between the uprights and the cross piece, firmly held in by the cheeks and angle pieces. Into the framing were fixed two round and smooth axles, to which were fastened the ropes that held the ram.

Over the heads of those who worked the ram was a penthouse, formed after the manner of a turret, where two soldiers could stand secure from danger, and give directions for annoying the enemy. The ram was one hundred and six feet long, a foot and a palm wide at the butt, a foot thick, tapering towards the head to a foot in width, and five-eighths in thickness.

It was furnished with a hard iron beak like those fixed on galleys, from which went out four iron prongs about fifteen feet long, to fix it to the beam. Moreover, distributed between the foot and the head of the beam, four stout ropes were stretched eight inches thick, made fast like those which retain the mast of a ship between the poop and the prow. To these were slung others diagonally, which suspended the ram at the distance of a palm and a foot from each other. The whole of the ram was covered with raw hides. At the further end of the ropes, towards the head, were four iron chains, also covered with raw hides, and it had a projection from each floor, framed with much skill, which was kept in its place by means of large stretched ropes, the roughness of which preventing the feet from slipping, made it easy to get thence on to the wall. The machine could be moved in six directions, straight forward, to the right and left, and from its extent it could be used on the ascending and descending slope of a hill. It could, moreover, be so raised as to throw down a wall one hundred feet in height: so, also, when moved to the right and left, it reached not less than one hundred feet. It was worked by one hundred men, and its weight was four thousand talents, or four hundred and eighty thousand pounds.

CHAPTER XX.

OF MACHINES FOR DEFENCE

I have explained what I thought most requisite respecting scorpions, catapultæ, balistæ, no less than tortoises and towers, who invented them, and in what manner they ought to be made. It did not seem necessary to write on ladders, cranes, and other things of simpler construction; these the soldiers of themselves easily make. Neither are they useful in all places, nor of the same proportions, inasmuch as the defences and fortifications of different cities are not similar: for machines constructed to assault the bold and impetuous, should be differently contrived to those for attacking the crafty, and still dissimilar, where the parties are timid.

Whoever, therefore, attends to these precepts, will be able to select from the variety mentioned, and design safely, without further aid, such new schemes as the nature of the places and other circumstances may require. For the defence of a place or army, one cannot give precepts in writing, since the machines which the enemy prepares may not be in consonance with our rules; whence oftentimes their contrivances are foiled by some ready ingenious plan, without the assistance of machines, as was the case with the Rhodians.

Diognetus was a Rhodian architect, who, to his honour, on account of his great skill, had an annual fixed salary. At that period, an architect of Aradus, whose name was Callias, came to Rhodes, obtained an audience, and exhibited a model of a wall, whereon was a revolving crane, by means whereof he could suspend an Helepolis near the spot, and swing it within the walls. The wondering Rhodians, when they saw it, took away the salary from Diognetus, and conferred it on Callias.

Immediately after this, king Demetrius, who, from his resolution, was sirnamed Poliorcetes, prepared to wage war against the Rhodians, and brought in his train Epimachus, a celebrated architect of Athens. This person prepared an helepolis of prodigious expense and of ingenious and laborious construction, whose height was one hundred and twenty-five feet, and its width sixty feet: he secured it, moreover, with hair-cloths and raw hides, so that it might securely withstand the shock of a stone of three hundred and sixty pounds weight, thrown from a balista. The whole machine weighed three hundred and sixty thousand pounds. Callias being now requested by the Rhodians to prepare his machine against the helepolis, and to swing it within the wall, as he had promised, confessed he was unable.

For the same principles do not answer in all cases. In some machines the principles are of equal effect on a large and on a small scale; others cannot be judged of by models. Some there are whose effects in models seem to approach the truth, but vanish when executed on a larger scale, as we have just seen. With an auger, a hole of half an inch, of an inch, or even an inch and a half, may be easily bored; but by the same instrument it would be impossible to bore one of a palm in diameter; and no one would think of attempting in this way to bore one of half a foot, or larger.

Thus that which may be effected on a small or a moderately large scale, cannot be executed beyond certain limits of size. When the Rhodians perceived their error, and how shamefully they had wronged Diognetus; when, also, they perceived the enemy was determined to invest them, and the machine approaching to assault the city, fearing the miseries of slavery and the sacking of the city, they humbled themselves before Diognetus, and requested his aid in behalf of his country.

He at first refused to listen to their entreaties; but when afterwards the comely virgins and youths, accompanied by the priests, came to solicit his aid, he consented, on condition that if he succeeded in taking the machine, it should be his own property. This being agreed to, he ordered a hole to be made in that part of the wall opposite to the machine, and gave general as well as particular notices to the inhabitants, to throw on the other side of the hole, through channels made for the purpose, all the water, filth, and mud, that could be procured. These being, during the night, discharged through the hole in great abundance, on the following day, when the helepolis was advanced towards the wall, it sunk in the quagmire thus created: and Demetrius, finding himself overreached by the sagacity of Diognetus, drew off his army. The Rhodians, freed from war by the ingenuity of Diognetus, gave him thanks publicly, and loaded him with honours and ornaments of distinction. Diognetus afterwards removed the helepolis within the walls, placed it in a public situation, and inscribed it thus: "Diognetus presented this to the people out of the spoils of war." Hence, in defensive operations, ingenuity is of more avail than machines.

A similar circumstance occurred at Chios, where the enemy had got ready sambucæ on board their ships; the Chians, during the night, threw into the sea, at the foot of their wall, earth, sand, and stones; so that when the enemy, on the following day, endeavoured to approach it, the ships got aground on the heaps thus created under water, without being able to approach the wall or to recede; in which situation they were assailed with lighted missiles, and burnt. When, also, the city of Apollonia was besieged, and the enemy was in hopes, by undermining, to penetrate into the fortress unperceived; the spies communicated this intelligence to the Apollonians, who were dismayed, and, through fear, knew not how to act, because they were not aware at what time, nor in what precise spot, the enemy would make his appearance.

Trypho, of Alexandria, who was the architect to the city, made several excavations within the wall, and, digging through, advanced an arrow's flight beyond the walls. In these excavations he suspended brazen vessels. In one of them, near the place where the enemy was forming his mine, the brazen vessels began to ring, from the blows of the mining tools which were working. From this he found the direction in which they were endeavouring to penetrate, and then prepared vessels of boiling water and pitch, human dung, and heated sand, for the purpose of pouring on their heads. In the night he bored a great many holes, through which he suddenly poured the mixture, and destroyed those of the enemy that were engaged in this operation.

Similarly when Marseilles was besieged, and the enemy had made more than thirty mines; the Marseillois suspecting it, lowered the depth of the ditch which encompassed the wall, so that the apertures of all the mines were discovered. In those places, however, where there is not a ditch, they excavate a large space within the walls, of great length and breadth, opposite to the direction of the mine, which they fill with water from wells and from the sea; so that when the mouths of the mine open to the city, the water rushes in with great violence, and throws down the struts, overwhelming all those within it with the quantity of water introduced, and the falling in of the mine.

When a rampart composed of the trunks of trees is raised opposite to a wall, it may be consumed by discharging red hot iron bars against it from the balistæ. When, also, a tortoise is brought up to batter a wall with a ram, a rope with a noose in it may be lowered to lay hold of the ram, which being then raised by means of a wheel and axle above, keeps the head suspended, so that it cannot be worked against the wall: lastly, with burning arrows, and with discharges from the balistæ, the whole machine may be destroyed. Thus all these cities are saved and preserve their freedom, not by machines, but by expedients which are suggested through the ready ingenuity of their architects. I have, in this book, to the best of my ability, described the construction of those machines most useful in peace and war. In the preceding nine I treated of the other branches of Architecture, so that the whole subject is contained in ten books.

Illustrations from:
Sébastien Leclerc – Les Dix Livres D'Architecture de Vitruve (1684)
Andrea Palladio – De Architectura (1567)

Printed in Great Britain
by Amazon